new Simplicity sewing book

You'll be glad you've decided to sew with the New Simplicity Sewing Book. Whether you're an expert or just discovering sewing, this book gives you all the information you need—from choosing patterns and fabrics that flatter you to sewing your fashions the most professional way.

You can stitch up the most super fashions! How? With Simplicity, of course!

Cover photo: Richard Davis

1   *Clothes that flatter you*   2

2   *The right pattern size*   11

3   *Pattern and fabric: the magic mix*   21

4   *Sewing tools*   38

5   *Making your pattern fit*   49

6   *Layout, cutting and marking*   77

7   *Sewing today*   89

8   *Press as you sew*   185

9   *Making your garment fit*   195

10   *Special fabrics*   205

11   *Personal touches*   217

12   *Tailoring*   235

   Index   254

Durell Godfrey

Imaginative illustrations inspire you with bright new sewing and fashion ideas.

Scott Hyde

Close-up photos give a behind-the-scenes look at the way your garment should go together.

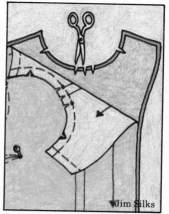

Jim Silks

Detailed drawings focus on important how-to's—cutting, marking, stitching, finishing.

Fashion photos offer a stunning array of beautiful styles for sewing inspiration.

EDITORIAL DIRECTOR
Janet DuBane

MANAGING EDITOR
Irma Fischler

PROJECT EDITOR
Diane Friend

ART DIRECTOR
Ina B. Andersen

PICTURE EDITORS
Patricia Channon
Gretel Courtney

ART ASSISTANTS
Carolyn Mazzello
Lynn E. Yost

EDITORIAL ASSISTANTS
Fran Blanda
Elsa Rohlehr

COPY STAFF
Marion Mylly Bartholomew
Peggy Bendel
Hewitt McGraw Busse
Susan Krall
Alexandra Kuman
Marian O'Connor
Susanna Pfeffer

PRODUCTION MANAGERS
Ralph Fierro, Jr.
Linda Gold

SAMPLE MAKER
Lucy Pesce

ART TRAFFIC
Ellen Wall
Pearl M. Sullivan

tall and heavy

clothes that flatter you

①

Sewing is a great way to have good-looking clothes that make you look terrific. It's not hard to do if you develop a workable fashion strategy.

First, take a look at yourself...do you have a shape that you want to show off? Or would you like to improve on nature's gift by adding a few inches here, losing a few pounds there, or vice versa? Don't wait for a miracle to happen ...create your own! It's a matter of some basic fashion arithmetic. Just determine what styles, fabrics and colors will add up to the most flattering look for you.

The right choices can fool the eye, making you appear shorter, taller, thinner, even curvier! Color alone can make you seem larger or smaller, depending on its hue and intensity. The effects of color, along with silhouette, line, design and texture can give you the most flattering formula for your figure; pages 5–10 tell you how. Here's a sampling of some simple fashion addition that can be used to flatter any figure.

vertical closings
+ cool, medium grey
+ medium weight wool
+ matching jacket and skirt
_____

= slimmer appearance

tall and slender

short and slender

short and heavy

contrasting colors
+ double-breasted jacket
+ crisp gabardine
+ horizontal line at hip
_____
= fuller appearance

shirtdress with vertical details
+ V-neck, breast pockets
+ warm, bright red
+ soft, fluid silk
_____
= taller-looking figure

body-skimming silhouette
+ vertical wrap detail
+ muted dark blue
+ smooth, lightweight jersey
_____
= taller, slimmer appearance

3

dark, smooth fabric above
+ bright-colored pants to draw
the eye downward
+ long, single-breasted jacket
_____
= top and bottom in balance

white blouse to draw
the eye upward
+ dark, full skirt
+ loose-fitting jacket
_____
= bottom and top in balance

top
heavy

bottom
heavy

4

figure-wise strategies

Remember the familiar statement, "If you've got it, flaunt it"? Well, here's a new twist—if you've got something you don't want to flaunt, hide it and flaunt something else! The idea is to choose patterns and fabrics that highlight your best features and play down the worst.

Take the two figures shown here: To appear taller, the short woman made a suit with details that draw your eye upward—narrow shawl collar, center front verticals on skirt and blouse, matching fabric for jacket and skirt.

Her friend has the opposite problem—how to appear shorter? Her suit has features which draw your eye across the body—double-breasted closing, wide lapels, horizontal pockets, contrasting fabric for jacket and skirt.

When you sew, your clothes can be in style and flattering at the same time—no matter how you shape up!

Figure-wise strategies

No "body's" perfect! But everyone can make the most of what they have. How do you shape up—are you tall and thin? Short and plump? Bottom-heavy? Which features deserve emphasis? Which ones would you rather hide?

To find out, wear a leotard or undergarments and take a good look at yourself in a full-length mirror. Since people see you from all sides, study your appearance from the front (A), side and back.

conceal or reveal

All clothes have fool-the-eye qualities—elements, such as silhouette, line, fabric design, color and texture—that can make your shape look different than it really is. By choosing the right eye-fooling styles, you can create your most flattering look.

Silhouettes that are broader at the top (C) can help balance a hip-heavy figure by drawing the eye upward. A style that is broader at the bottom, such as an A-line skirt (D), draws the eye downward and away from a generous bustline or wide shoulders.

In general, a loose-fitting silhouette hides the figure underneath and is a good choice when you want to conceal something. On the other hand, a closely-fitted silhouette emphasizes the body. If this is the style you want to wear, be sure you're willing to reveal your shape!

Ready-made garments can also clue you in. For example, if the hips are always too tight, you might be bottom-heavy—a fact you'll want to *conceal*. But you might have a perfect neck and shoulder line, a point you'll want to *reveal*.

Take a look, too, at the clothes in your closet—you probably have some favorites there, as well as a few mistakes. Decide what makes the favorites sure-fire flatterers. Why are the mistakes all wrong?

Silhouette

The outline shape of a garment is its *silhouette*. Styles that are equally wide at the top and bottom (B) can make you look taller or shorter, depending on how narrow or wide the silhouette rectangle is.

Line

Besides the silhouette or outline you should also think about the inner lines—for example, seams, tucks and pocket edges. The silhouette tends to dominate the appearance of simple styles. But when a garment has lots of design details, they create inner lines—horizontals, verticals, diagonals—that have a more important effect on your appearance.

Horizontal lines, such as waist or yoke seams, hemlines and bateau necklines, add width at the point where they cross your body. They also tend to cut height. Look at the difference when the horizontal line is high (E), at the waist (F), or at the hips (G) on a basic dress. Wherever the line is placed, your body will appear wider. And the lower the line placement, the shorter and broader your body will seem.

Diagonal lines can be slanted seams or edges, closings, darts or V-necklines. A slightly slanted diagonal will have the same effect as a horizontal; the steeper the slant, the more like a vertical it will appear (I).

Curved lines resemble the effect of vertical, horizontal or diagonal straight lines, but are softer.

horizontal stripes. The impression of width they usually give disappears when you add broad stripes, wide spacing or contrasting colors.

The scale and spacing of a print should be related to your size. A small person would be overwhelmed by a very large print or plaid, or a widely-spaced motif.

Color and Texture

Warm colors (red, orange, yellow), as well as light, bright colors, tend to make you look fuller. This

E   F   G   H   I

Vertical lines, such as center front seams, princess seams, front closings, tucks and sharp creases in pants, usually create an illusion of height and slenderness. But sometimes, several widely-spaced vertical rows, like the buttons on a double-breasted closing or rows of tucks (H), make your figure look wider. A single, strong vertical line has the most slimming effect.

Fabric Designs

Scale and spacing play a strong part in the overall impression of size. If the print, check, or plaid you're wearing is big and widely-spaced, you'll look larger than when you're wearing a small-scale, closely-spaced print.

Stripes can work both ways, according to their coloring, width and spacing. People often think a vertical stripe will make them look taller. But wide spacing or wide, contrasting stripes will completely reverse the effect of height. The same thing is true of

doesn't mean that heavy people can never wear brights; they can use these colors as accents or as trimmings. Cool colors (blue, green, violet), or dark and dulled shades, have the opposite effect.

Textures can be used to good advantage also. Smooth-surfaced fabrics are more slimming than bulky, fuzzy or shiny types.

See pages 2-4 and 8-11 for more Figurewise Strategies.

Figure-wise strategies

If You're Short and Slender...

Fashions with vertical lines will seem to add inches to your height. To add softness and curves, choose styles with uncluttered fullness.

Styles that flatter include:
• shirtdresses, narrow tents or tunics with vertical details
• single-breasted jackets with shawl collars or narrow lapels
• narrow, slim or slightly-flared pants and skirts
• neat, small details at the top— stand-up collars, shoulder yoke seaming or tiny pockets

Fabrics that flatter have:
• plain, soft, drapable textures
• light to medium weights
• small to medium-sized prints, plaids and stripes
• light or pale tones with darker, bolder colors for accents
• matching or similar colors for coordinates to add height

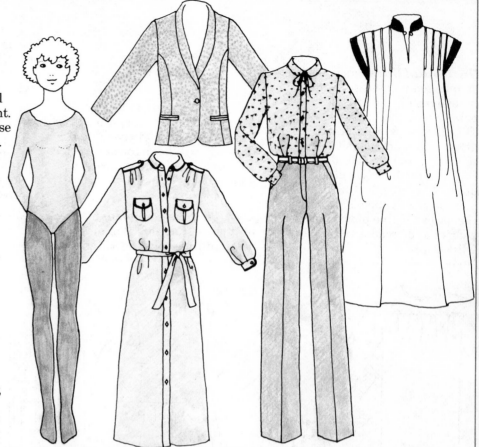

If You're Short and Heavy...

To appear taller, plan on fashions that accent the vertical. And styles that just skim your body will seem to whittle away the inches!

Styles that flatter include:
• dresses with contrasting necklines; narrow, matching belts or no waistline seams
• cardigan jackets that keep your waist size a secret
• pants and skirts that are straight, but not slim

Fabrics that flatter have:
• smooth, plain, crisp textures
• light to medium weights
• prints, plaids and stripes on the small side, in muted colors
• solids in dark or dulled tones
• color-matched schemes for tops and bottoms

If You're Tall and Slender...

Plan to sew fashions that round out your figure and balance your height.

Styles that flatter include:
• pants with hip details and cuffs
• double-breasted, unshaped jackets with wide lapels
• blouses with fullness or tucks at the shoulder seams
• loose, flowing dresses, nipped in at the waist
• skirts with pleats or tucks
• horizontal details, such as flapped pockets or yoke seams

Fabrics that flatter have:
• highly-textured surfaces
• medium to heavy weights, in either soft or crisp styles
• bold prints, checks, plaids, stripes
• bright, light colors
• contrasting colors for separates

If You're Tall and Heavy...

Fashions that softly skim your body will streamline your figure and minimize your weight.

Styles that flatter include:
• uncluttered silhouettes with emphasis on vertical lines
• dresses with softly belted waistlines, wrapped closings
• softly-tailored separates, such as a flared skirt, bow-tied blouse and mid-length, single-breasted jacket
• straight-leg pants
• tunic-length tops

Fabrics that flatter have:
• plain, smooth textures
• medium weights
• soft or crisp styles
• medium-scale plaids, prints or stripes in muted shades
• cool colors in medium to dark tones
• one color family for separates

Figure-wise strategies

If You're Top Heavy...

To balance your proportions, sew contrasting fashions that play up your hips and play down your bust.

Styles that flatter include:
• easy-fitting shirtdresses
• pants and skirts with pockets, pleats, tucks and gathers
• uncluttered, tailored blouses with small collars, softly-gathered shoulders and centered closings
• loose-fitting jackets

Fabrics to wear on top have:
• plain textures, light weights
• dark, muted colors
• solids or small prints

Fabrics to wear below have:
• medium to heavy textures and weights, drapability
• light, bright colors
• bold designs

If You're Bottom Heavy...

You can balance your bottom. Do it with lots of detailing and horizontal lines on top, while you keep the lines below vertical and simple.

Styles that flatter include:
• dresses that skim your hips and have bodice detailing
• simple skirts and pants
• full-blown blouses with unusual design interest
• loose-fitting, long jackets

Fabrics to wear on top have:
• medium to heavy textures and weights, drapability
• light, bright colors
• eye-catching prints and designs

Fabrics to wear below have:
• plain textures, light weights
• dark, muted colors
• solid coloring or subtle designs
• small-scale prints

2 the right pattern size

To start your sewing off smoothly, choose the best pattern size for you. It's the surest way to make fashions that fit and flatter your figure without a lot of adjustments later.

To help you find your size, we've developed a simple 3-Step Plan: Step 1 is taking some key body measurements. This gives you the information needed for Step 2—selecting your figure type, a helpful description of body shape and proportions. Once these two steps are completed, you can go directly to Step 3— pinpointing the best pattern size for you. Before you begin, read the measuring tips below. Then, turn to page 12 for Females, page 16 for Males and page 18 for Children.

measuring tips

● Stand normally and look straight ahead when being measured. Wear the undergarments and shoes you plan to wear with the finished garment; measure men and boys over a T-shirt and shorts or unbelted lightweight slacks.

● Tie a string snugly around the waist to locate the natural waist-line. If the waist is hard to find on men and children, have them bend sideways—the crease formed is at the natural waistline.

● Have a friend hold the tape measure so it's snug and parallel to the floor, but doesn't indent your body.

● Record measurements on the charts on pages 13, 16 or 18. Re-measure from time to time since changes are normal for everyone. We've provided additional charts for this purpose on page 20.

Step 1
Take Body Measurements

Body measurements are what they say—the actual measurements in inches, or centimeters, of your body. Follow the directions on the chart, opposite, to take the body measurements needed for selecting your figure type and pattern size. Fill in on the chart.

no mention of age. Figure types actually have little to do with age, though patterns in the Young Junior/Teen category, which is meant for developing teenagers, do take age into account by emphasizing youthful styles.

Step 3
Select Your Size

Now that you've found your figure type, use the size table for your figure type on the next pages to find the size that most closely matches your bust, waist and hips. These tables also appear in the back of the Simplicity Counter Catalog for quick reference when you're buying a pattern.

Step 2
Find Your Figure Type

There are eight adult female figure types, each representing a differently proportioned figure. You'll find them on pages 14-15, along with capsule descriptions to help you decide where you fit in. Notice that in these descriptions, there's

Use your *height* and *back waist length* measurements to find the figure type that comes closest to yours. If your measurements aren't a perfect match, choose the one with the back waist length closest to yours. Fill in your figure type on the chart.

If your measurements are a bit different, don't worry. Patterns are designed with wearing ease—enough extra room to allow you to move comfortably. Even if your measurements are slightly different, the pattern should fit you without any problems.

f you fall between sizes, buy the maller one; it's easy enough to do simple pattern adjustment later. f there's more of a mis-match, our pattern size will depend on he type of garment you're going o make.

If your bust measures 2″ (5 cm) or more larger than your high bust, use the high bust measurement as if it were the bust measurement to select your pattern size. You may need to add to the pattern bustline later (see Chapter 5).

For maternity patterns, buy your usual size since these patterns allow enough extra fullness for the ninth month. If you've just started sewing and are five months or more along, find your size in the Maternity table on page 15, using your bust and back waist length measurements.

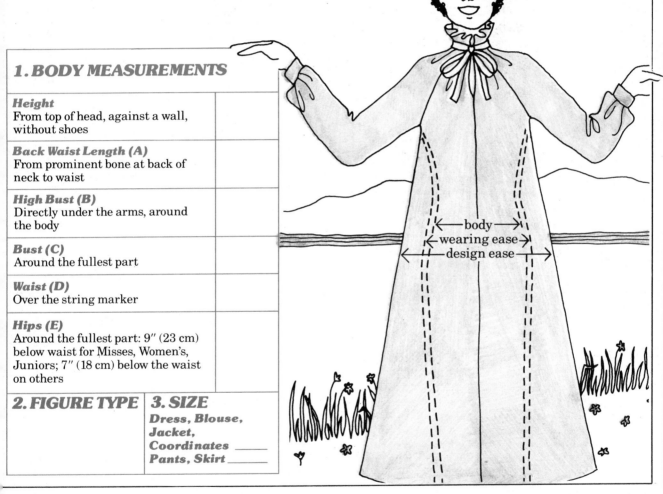

1. BODY MEASUREMENTS

Height From top of head, against a wall, without shoes	
Back Waist Length (A) From prominent bone at back of neck to waist	
High Bust (B) Directly under the arms, around the body	
Bust (C) Around the fullest part	
Waist (D) Over the string marker	
Hips (E) Around the fullest part: 9″ (23 cm) below waist for Misses, Women's, Juniors; 7″ (18 cm) below the waist on others	

2. FIGURE TYPE   3. SIZE

Dress, Blouse, Jacket, Coordinates _____
Pants, Skirt _____

body →
wearing ease →
design ease →

For a dress, blouse, jacket or multi-garment pattern, choose he size with the bust measurement closest to your own. Jacket nd coat patterns include enough wearing ease to be worn over other garments, so don't buy a larger size.

For pants, skirts, shorts or culottes patterns, choose the size which comes closest to matching your waist measurement. It's easier to adjust most patterns later at the hips than it is to adjust the pockets, darts and zipper at the waist.

Note: Design ease is added to many styles purely for fashion effect. Don't buy a smaller size for loose-fitting styles or you'll spoil the fashion appeal. Just use your body measurements as a guide to choosing the right size. Now, complete the chart above by filling in your correct pattern sizes.

Female figure types and sizes

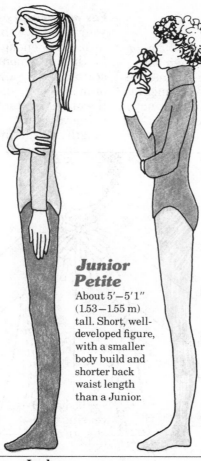

Young Junior/Teen
About 5′1″−5′3″ (1.55−1.60 m) tall. Developing teen and pre-teen figure, with very small, high bust and waistline larger in proportion to bust.

Junior Petite
About 5′−5′1″ (1.53−1.55 m) tall. Short, well-developed figure, with a smaller body build and shorter back waist length than a Junior.

Junior
About 5′4″−5′5″ (1.63−1.65 m) tall. Well-developed figure, slightly shorter in height and back waist than a Miss.

Miss Petite
About 5′2″−5′4″ (1.57-1.60 m) tall. Short, well-developed and well-proportioned figure with a shorter back waist length and slightly larger waist than a Miss.

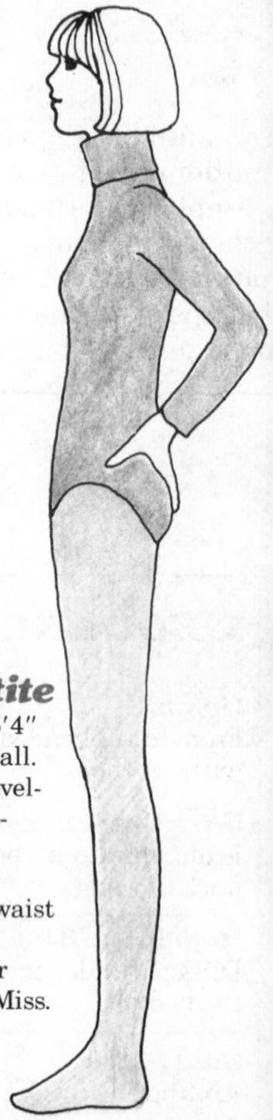

Inches

YOUNG JUNIOR/TEEN:

Size	5/6	7/8	9/10	11/12	13/14	15/16
Bust	28	29	30½	32	33½	35
Waist	22	23	24	25	26	27
Hip	31	32	33½	35	36½	38
Back Waist Length	13½	14	14½	15	15⅜	15¾

JUNIOR PETITE:

Size	3jp	5jp	7jp	9jp	11jp	13jp
Bust	30	31	32	33	34	35
Waist	22	23	24	25	26	27
Hip	31	32	33	34	35	36
Back Waist Length	14	14¼	14½	14¾	15	15¼

JUNIOR:

Size	5	7	9	11	13	15
Bust	30	31	32	33½	35	37
Waist	22½	23½	24½	25½	27	29
Hip	32	33	34	35½	37	39
Back Waist Length	15	15¼	15½	15¾	16	16¼

MISS PETITE:

Size	6mp	8mp	10mp	12mp	14mp	16mp
Bust	30½	31½	32½	34	36	38
Waist	23½	24½	25½	27	28½	30½
Hip	32½	33½	34½	36	38	40
Back Waist Length	14½	14¾	15	15¼	15½	15¾

Centimeters

YOUNG JUNIOR/TEEN:

Size	5/6	7/8	9/10	11/12	13/14	15/16
Bust	71	74	78	81	85	89
Waist	56	58	61	64	66	69
Hip	79	81	85	89	93	97
Back Waist Length	34.5	35.5	37	38	39	40

JUNIOR PETITE:

Size	3jp	5jp	7jp	9jp	11jp	13jp
Bust	76	79	81	84	87	89
Waist	56	58	61	64	66	69
Hip	79	81	84	87	89	92
Back Waist Length	35.5	36	37	37.5	38	39

JUNIOR:

Size	5	7	9	11	13	15
Bust	76	79	81	85	89	94
Waist	57	60	62	65	69	74
Hip	81	84	87	90	94	99
Back Waist Length	38	39	39.5	40	40.5	41.5

MISS PETITE:

Size	6mp	8mp	10mp	12mp	14mp	16mp
Bust	78	80	83	87	92	97
Waist	60	62	65	69	73	78
Hip	83	85	88	92	97	102
Back Waist Length	37	37.5	38	39	39.5	40

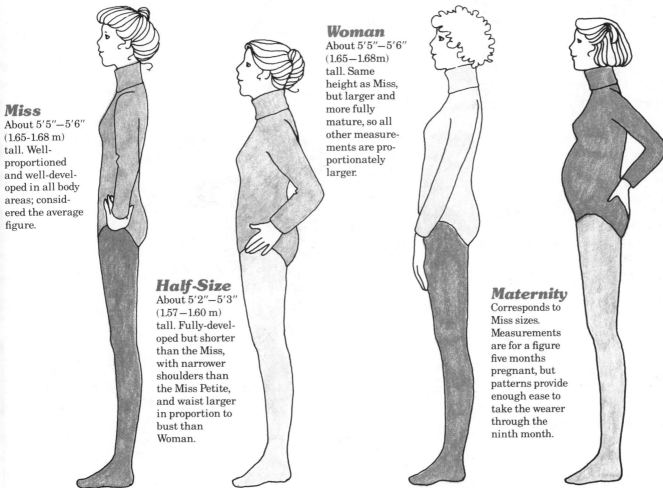

Miss
About 5′5″–5′6″ (1.65-1.68 m) tall. Well-proportioned and well-developed in all body areas; considered the average figure.

Woman
About 5′5″–5′6″ (1.65–1.68m) tall. Same height as Miss, but larger and more fully mature, so all other measurements are proportionately larger.

Half-Size
About 5′2″–5′3″ (1.57–1.60 m) tall. Fully-developed but shorter than the Miss, with narrower shoulders than the Miss Petite, and waist larger in proportion to bust than Woman.

Maternity
Corresponds to Miss sizes. Measurements are for a figure five months pregnant, but patterns provide enough ease to take the wearer through the ninth month.

Inches

MISS:

Size	6	8	10	12	14	16	18	20
Bust	30½	31½	32½	34	36	38	40	42
Waist	23	24	25	26½	28	30	32	34
Hip	32½	33½	34½	36	38	40	42	44
Back Waist Length	15½	15¾	16	16¼	16½	16¾	17	17¼

MATERNITY:

Size	6	8	10	12	14	16
Bust	34	35	36	37½	39½	41½
Waist	28½	29½	30½	32	33½	35½
Hip	35½	36½	37½	39	41	43
Back Waist Length	15½	15¾	16	16¼	16½	16¾

HALF-SIZE:

Size	10½	12½	14½	16½	18½	20½	22½	24½
Bust	33	35	37	39	41	43	45	47
Waist	27	29	31	33	35	37½	40	42½
Hip	35	37	39	41	43	45½	48	50½
Back Waist Length	15	15¼	15½	15¾	15⅞	16	16⅛	16¼

WOMAN:

Size	38	40	42	44	46	48	50	52
Bust	42	44	46	48	50	52	54	56
Waist	35	37	39	41½	44	46½	49	51½
Hip	44	46	48	50	52	54	56	58
Back Waist Length	17¼	17⅜	17½	17⅝	17¾	17⅞	18	18⅛

Centimeters

MISS:

Size	6	8	10	12	14	16	18	20
Bust	78	80	83	87	92	97	102	107
Waist	58	61	64	67	71	76	81	87
Hip	83	85	88	92	97	102	107	112
Back Waist Length	39.5	40	40.5	41.5	42	42.5	43	44

MATERNITY:

Size	6	8	10	12	14	16
Bust	87	89	92	95	100	105
Waist	72	75	77.5	81	85	90
Hip	90	93	95	99	104	109
Back Waist Length	39.5	40	40.5	41.5	42	42.5

HALF-SIZE:

Size	10½	12½	14½	16½	18½	20½	22½	24½
Bust	84	89	94	99	104	109	114	119
Waist	69	74	79	84	89	96	102	108
Hip	89	94	99	104	109	116	122	128
Back Waist Length	38	39	39.5	40	40.5	40.5	41	41.5

WOMAN:

Size	38	40	42	44	46	48	50	52
Bust	107	112	117	122	127	132	137	142
Waist	89	94	99	105	112	118	124	131
Hip	112	117	122	127	132	137	142	147
Back Waist Length	44	44	44.5	45	45	45.5	46	46

Choosing a size...males

Step 1
Take Body Measurements

Begin by reading the Measuring Tips on page 11; then take the six key body measurements in inches or centimeters as directed on the chart below. Use height and body proportions as a guide to finding the right figure type, and the other measurements to zero in on the right size.

Step 2
Find Your Figure Type

There are three male figure types. Each one shown on page 17 represents a certain kind of build, from the just-developing male to the fully adult figure. Use the capsule descriptions next to the illustrations to help you choose the right one.

Enter your figure type in the space provided on the chart.

1. BODY MEASUREMENTS

Height From top of head, against a wall, without shoes	
Neck (A) Around neck at base	
Neckband (garment measurement useful for picking shirt size) Add ½″ (1.3 cm) to Neck measurement	
Chest (B) Around fullest part	
Waist (C) Over string marker	
Hips or Seat (D) Around fullest part: 8″ (20.5 cm) below waist on Men; 7″ (18 cm) below waist for Teen-Boys; 6″ (15 cm) below waist for Boys	

2. FIGURE TYPE	3. SIZE
	Jackets, Suits_____ Pants, Shorts_____ Shirts_____

Step 3
Select Your Size

Now use the size table for your figure type to pick the pattern size that matches most closely your chest, waist and hip measurements. For shirt patterns, use your neckband measurement to select a pattern size, or buy your ready-made shirt size.

If your measurements place you between two sizes, select the smaller one to make pattern adjustments easier later. You might need different sizes for different types of garments:

For coats, jackets, suits and multi-garment patterns, use the size that most closely matches your chest measurement.

For pants or shorts, select the size which is closest to your waist measurement.

For shirts, as stated above, use your neckband size or ready-to-wear shirt size to pick the right pattern size.

Read the design ease note on page 13; then complete the chart opposite by filling in your sizes.

Boy
About 4'–4'10" (1.22–1.47 m) tall. The just-developing figure that has out-grown Children's sizes.

Teen-Boy
About 5'1"–5'8" (1.55–1.73 m) tall. Young man's figure that falls between Boys' and Men's sizes.

Man
About 5'10" (1.78 m) tall. Man of average adult build.

	Inches	BOY			Centimeters			Size	Inches	TEEN-BOY			Centimeters		
	7	**8**	**10**	**12**	**7**	**8**	**10**	**12**		**14**	**16**	**18**	**20**	**14**	**16**	**18**	**20**
Chest	26	27	28	30	66	69	71	76		32	33½	35	36½	81	85	89	93
Waist	23	24	25	26	58	61	64	66		27	28	29	30	69	71	74	76
Hip (Seat)	27	28	29½	31	69	71	75	79		32½	34	35½	37	83	87	90	94
Neck	11¼	11½	12	12½	28.5	29.3	30.5	31.7		13	13½	14	14½	33	34.3	35.5	36.7
Neckband Size*	11¾	12	12½	13	30	31	32	33		13½	14	14½	15	34.5	35.5	37	38

	Inches												MAN Size	Centimeters											
	34	**36**	**38**	**40**	**42**	**44**	**46**	**48**	**50**	**52**	**54**	**56**	Size	**34**	**36**	**38**	**40**	**42**	**44**	**46**	**48**	**50**	**52**	**54**	**56**
Chest	34	36	38	40	42	44	46	48	50	52	54	56	Chest	87	92	97	102	107	112	117	122	127	132	137	142
Waist	28	30	32	34	36	39	42	44	46	48	50	52	Waist	71	76	81	87	92	99	107	112	117	122	127	132
Hip (Seat)	35	37	39	41	43	45	47	49	51	53	55	57	Hip (Seat)	89	94	99	104	109	114	119	124	129.5	134.5	139.5	145
Neck	13½	14	14½	15	15½	16	16½	17	17½	18	18½	19	Neck	34.3	35.5	36.7	38	39.3	40.7	42	43.3	44.5	45.7	47	48.3
Neckband Size *	14	14½	15	15½	16	16½	17	17½	18	18½	19	19½	Neckband Size *	35.5	37	38	39.5	40.5	42	43	44.5	46	47	48	49.5

ready-to-wear measurement used for reference

Choosing a size...children

Step 1
Take Body Measurements

Begin by reading the Measuring Tips on page 11, then take the child's actual measurements by following the directions on the chart below. Fill in the chart as you measure, so you'll have a record for Steps 2 and 3.

Step 2
Find the Figure Type

There are four figure types for children, shown opposite, plus patterns in Babies' sizes. Use the child's height, general shape and proportions to help you find the most suitable type. The capsule descriptions will help you.

Notice that these figure types describe the child's body and build rather than the age. Also, Toddlers' and Children's patterns suit both boys and girls in many cases, so these types apply to both. Fill in the figure type on the chart.

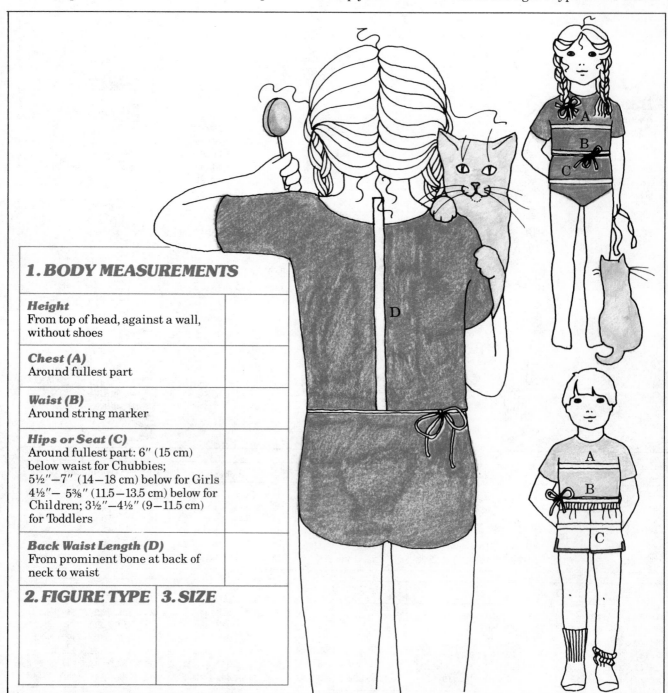

1. BODY MEASUREMENTS

Height From top of head, against a wall, without shoes	
Chest (A) Around fullest part	
Waist (B) Around string marker	
Hips or Seat (C) Around fullest part: 6″ (15 cm) below waist for Chubbies; 5½″−7″ (14−18 cm) below for Girls 4½″− 5⅜″ (11.5−13.5 cm) below for Children; 3½″−4½″ (9−11.5 cm) for Toddlers	
Back Waist Length (D) From prominent bone at back of neck to waist	

2. FIGURE TYPE	3. SIZE

Step 3
Select the Size

Use the charts below to select the child's pattern size.

For Toddlers, choose the size closest to the chest measurement.

For Babies, decide the size according to their weight.

For all others, choose the size most closely matching the chest and back waist length.

Read the note on design ease on page 13, then fill in the pattern size on the chart opposite.

Baby
Designed for infants who are not yet walking.

Toddler
Taller than Baby, but shorter than Child; these patterns have a diaper allowance and often apply to boys and girls.

Child
Has same chest and waist as Toddler, but is taller with wider shoulders and back. Many patterns suit boys and girls.

Girl
About 4' 2"–5' 1" (1.27–1.55 m) tall. The young figure, without bust development.

Chubbie
The girl who weighs more than the average for her age and height.

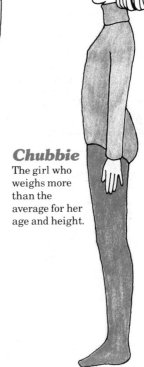

Inches						
TODDLER:						
Size	½	1	2	3	4	
Chest	19	20	21	22	23	
Waist	19	19½	20	20½	21	
Hip	20	21	22	23	24	
Back Waist Length	7½	8	8½	9	9½	
Approximate Height	28	31	34	37	40	
CHILD:						
Size	2	3	4	5	6	6x
Chest	21	22	23	24	25	25½
Waist	20	20½	21	21½	22	22½
Hip	22	23	24	25	26	26½
Back Waist Length	8½	9	9½	10	10½	10¾
Approximate Height	35	38	41	44	47	48
GIRL:						
Size	7	8	10	12	14	
Chest	26	27	28½	30	32	
Waist	23	23½	24½	25½	26½	
Hip	27	28	30	32	34	
Back Waist Length	11½	12	12¾	13½	14¼	
Approximate Height	50	52	56	58½	61	
CHUBBIE:						
Size	8½c	10½c	12½c	14½c		
Chest	30	31½	33	34½		
Waist	28	29	30	31		
Hip	33	34½	36	37½		
Back Waist Length	12½	13¼	14	14¾		
Approximate Height	53	56	58½	61		

Centimeters						
TODDLER:						
Size	½	1	2	3	4	
Chest	48	51	53	56	58	
Waist	48	50	51	52	53	
Hip	50.7	53.3	56	58.3	61	
Back Waist Length	19	20.3	21.5	23	24	
Approximate Height	71	79	87	94	102	
CHILD:						
Size	2	3	4	5	6	6x
Chest	53	56	58	61	64	65
Waist	51	52	53	55	56	57
Hip	56	58.3	61	64	66	67
Back Waist Length	21.5	23	24	25.5	27	27.5
Approximate Height	89	97	104	112	119	122
GIRL:						
Size	7	8	10	12	14	
Chest	66	69	73	76	81	
Waist	58	60	62	65	67	
Hip	69	71	76	81	87	
Back Waist Length	29.5	31	32.5	34.5	36	
Approximate Height	127	132	142	149	155	
CHUBBIE:						
Size	8½c	10½c	12½c	14½c		
Chest	76	80	84	88		
Waist	71	74	76	79		
Hip	84	88	92	96		
Back Waist Length	32	34	35.5	37.5		
Approximate Height	132	142	149	155		

2

the right pattern size

19

Extra measurement charts

Females

1. BODY MEASUREMENTS

Height From top of head, against a wall, without shoes	
Back Waist Length From prominent bone at back of neck to waist	
High Bust Directly under the arms, around the body	
Bust Around the fullest part	
Waist Over the string marker	
Hips Around the fullest part: 9″ (23 cm) below waist for Misses, Women's, Juniors; 7″ (18 cm) below the waist on others	

2. FIGURE TYPE	3. SIZE
	Dress, Blouse, Jacket, Coordinates _____ Pants, Skirt _____

Males

1. BODY MEASUREMENTS

Height From top of head, against a wall, without shoes	
Neck Around neck at base	
Neckband (garment measurement useful for picking shirt size) Add ½″ (1.3 cm) to Neck measurement	
Chest Around fullest part	
Waist Over string marker	
Hips or Seat Around fullest part: 8″ (20.5 cm) below waist on Men; 7″ (18 cm) below waist for Teen-Boys; 6″ (15cm) below waist for Boys	

2. FIGURE TYPE	3. SIZE
	Jackets, Suits _____ Pants, Shorts _____ Shirts _____

Children

1. BODY MEASUREMENTS

Height From top of head, against a wall, without shoes	
Chest Around fullest part	
Waist Around string marker	
Hips or Seat Around fullest part: 6″ (15 cm) below waist for Chubbies; 5½″−7″ (14−18 cm) below for Girls; 4½″− 5⅜″ (11.5−13.5 cm) below for Children; 3½″−4½″ (9−11.5 cm) for Toddlers	
Back Waist Length From prominent bone at back of neck to waist	

2. FIGURE TYPE	3. SIZE

3 pattern and fabric: the magic mix

Now the fun begins — combining the pattern style that you like with the fabric of your choice! While you may feel that selecting exactly the right fabric to go with your pattern requires a little magic, that's just not so. This chapter shows you that it's really a simple matter of using the information the pattern offers and learning a little about fabrics. The result — you create your own fashion magic!

Your pattern is much more than mere tissue paper. Each pattern is really a mini sewing book because it contains a wealth of sewing information. The catalog pages and the envelope front give you ideas on what to make. And the back of the envelope tells you what and how much to buy for your magic mix, while the instruction sheet inside explains how to turn it all into fashion.

On the pages that follow, you'll see how to use the pattern catalog and the pattern to get started. Then you'll learn some practical tips on selecting the right fabrics, interfacings, lining and notions.

The pattern catalog

From cover to cover, each Simplicity catalog is packed with fashions—for you, for the kids, for your home. Not only does the catalog show every Simplicity pattern currently available, it's also a valuable source of inspiration. You'll find ideas for coordinating separates, combining colors and prints, what fabrics to choose and which accessories to use. New catalogs are issued often

Patterns are grouped together in various ways, including special pattern categories, garment styles, size or age ranges, fashion images, home decorating and crafts as follows:

Pattern categories—such as Jiffy®, E.S.P.® and Yes I Can!™ patterns designed to be fast, easy to sew, or for beginners.

Fashion images—for instance, Designer Fashions and Young Sensations.

Home decorating and crafts—including curtains, spreads, pillows, toys, bags and costumes.

If you're interested in seeing what the newest fashions are, turn to the front of each section, just behind the tab. That's where Simplicity introduces all of its latest patterns.

during the year to keep you up to date on the latest fashions and seasonal styles.

How To Use The Catalog

Finding the pattern you want is easy because there are tab dividers to indicate what kind of patterns appear in each of the catalog sections.

Garment styles—like Sportswear, Dresses and Evening fashions. Some of these sections have sub-divisions for easy reference. For example, the Sportswear tab has one section for Separates and Coordinates, one for Tops, T-Shirts and Blouses, and one for Skirts and Pants.

Size and age ranges—such as Half-Sizes, Women, Children, or Men and Boys.

The last few pages of the catalog contain measurement charts, in both metric and imperial measurements, and size selection advice. Use them as a reference for picking a pattern size.

Perhaps you already know which pattern style number you want. The fastest way to find its catalog page is to look at the numerical index on the inside back cover.

The Catalog Page

Take a look at one of the catalog pages—it's a lot like shopping for ready-to-wear at the store. The catalog page tells you everything you need to know before you buy the pattern by giving you a fashion photo, fashion drawings, a list of fabric types, back views, a yardage chart and any special alerts.

A fashion photo of one view shows how the pattern will look when it's all sewn up. It also provides you with valuable clues on what fabric weights and textures are suitable for the design.

Fashion drawings show what other views or versions are included in the pattern. They're illustrated in different colors, prints or fabric types than the photo to provide you with still more fashion and fabric ideas that will work with the design.

A chart tells you which sizes the pattern comes in and how much fabric is needed for each size, fabric width and view. Yardages for fabrics "with nap" are also included. This chart is especially handy if you've come to the store for fabric and you've forgotten to bring your pattern.

Fabric types that will work best with the style are suggested. You might also find a note about which ones to avoid, for example, "Not suitable for obvious diagonal fabrics." Follow these suggestions and notes to insure successful results.

Special alerts, such as "Sized for stretch knits only," "New, simplified construction," "Pants not included" or "Two sizes in one pattern," as well as other helpful fabric selection information, are also included on the catalog page.

Small drawings show you what the garments look like from the back. They also show zipper locations, pockets and other fashion details not visible from the front.

pattern and fabric: the magic mix

The pattern envelope

You may not have realized that the information on the outside of the pattern envelope is just as important as what's inside the package.

The Envelope Front

Photographs or sketches of each view illustrate fabrics that are suitable for the garment style in weight, texture and design. They also give you tips on how to coordinate your separates and accessorize fashionably.

Identification information includes pattern number, price, size and special category—such as Jiffy®, E.S.P.® (Extra-Sure Pattern) or Yes I Can™ Pattern.

In the store, be sure you've gotten the pattern you asked for by checking the style number, size and figure type on the top of the envelope front.

The Envelope Back

It's a good idea to use the back of the envelope as a convenient shopping list for fabric and all the other supplies you'll need. Here's all the helpful information you'll find.

Number of pattern pieces included in the pattern is listed under the pattern identification number. Your view may or may not use every piece.

Small sketches show what the garment looks like from the back and the location of zippers, if any.

The chart shows the amount of fabric to buy for your size and the view you want to make. Yardages are also given for fabrics of different widths, with or without nap. For example, 45″ (115 cm) wide fabric requires more yardage than fabric that is 60″ (150 cm) wide. And if your fabric is napped—that is, the texture or design must go in one direction on the finished garment—you'll need more yardage than you would for a fabric without nap.

The chart also lists yardages for the lining, interfacing, elastic or trimmings you may need.

Simplicity 9074
$2.00
CANADA $2.25
SIZE 10 MISS

patterns against the back lengths of clothes you already have for possible length adjustments.

Standard body measurements that are needed to select the correct size are given for each size. These are also a convenient reference guide for making your pattern adjustments later.

Capsule garment description explains design details, such as linings, topstitching and pockets, that may not be obvious from the illustration.

Suggested fabric list helps you select a fabric that's right for the style. You'll also find advice on which fabrics are unsuitable, and when to buy extra yardage for napped or plaid fabrics.

9074
13 PIECES

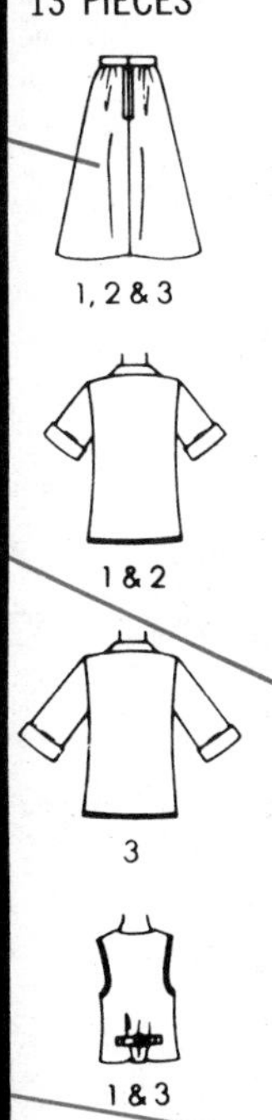

MISSES' SKIRT, BLOUSE AND LINED VEST: Gathered skirt V.1, 2 & 3 has pleats, back zipper, waistband and pockets in side seams. Top-stitched blouse V.1, 2 & 3 with front button closing has shawl collar and set-in sleeves with turn-back cuffs. V.1 & 2 have above elbow length sleeves. V 3 has below elbow length sleeves. Top-stitched, lined vest V. 1 & 3 has front button closing and back buckled belt.

Fabrics–Cotton types: broadcloth, crepe. Linen types. Challis. Silk types. Extra fabric needed to match plaids, stripes, one-way designs. Use nap yardage and nap layouts for one–way design fabrics. Not suitable for obvious diagonal fabrics.

	MISSES						
Sizes	6	8	10	12	14	16	
Bust	30½	31½	32½	34	36	38	Ins.
Waist	23	24	25	26½	28	30	"
Hip–9" below waist	32½	33½	34½	36	38	40	"
Back–neck to waist	15½	15¾	16	16¼	16½	16¾	"
View 1 or 2 Skirt and Blouse–Even plaid or plain fabric							
44" or 45"*	3½	3⅝	3⅞	3⅞	4	1	Yds.
58" or 60"	2¾	2¾	2⅞	2⅞	3⅛	3⅛	"
View 1 Skirt and Blouse–Uneven plaid fabric							
44" or 45"**	3¾	3¾	3¾	4	4¼	4¼	Yd.
View 1 or 2 Skirt and Blouse Interfacing–1⅛ Yds. of 22", 23", 25", 32", 35" or 36" woven or non-woven or fusible							
View 3 Skirt							
35" or 36"*	2⅞	2⅞	2⅞	2⅞	2⅞	2⅞	Yds.
44" or 45"*	2⅛	2⅛	2⅛	2⅛	2⅛	2⅜	"
Interfacing–1 yd. of 22", 23", 25", 32", 35" or 36" woven or non-woven or fusible							
View 3 Blouse							
35" or 35"*	2⅜	2⅜	2½	2½	2½	2⅝	Yds
44" or 45"*	2	2	2	2¼	2⅜	2⅜	"
Interfacing–yd of 22", 23", 25", 32", 35" or 36" woven or non-woven or fusible							
View 1 or 3 Vest							
35" or 36"*	1⅞	1⅞	1⅞	2	2¼	2½	Yds
44" or 45"*	1¼	1⅜	1⅜	1⅜	1⅜	1½	"
Interfacing–½ yd. of 22", 23", 25", 32", 35" or 36" woven or non-woven or fusible							
*without nap **with nap ***with or without nap							
Skirt length	29	29	29	29	29	29	Ins
Skirt width	68	69	70	71½	73	75	"

Notions: Thread. Skirt: 7" zipper, seam binding or stretch lace. Blouse: Five ½" buttons. Vest: Four ¼" buttons, one 1" buckle.

	MISSES						
Sizes	6	8	10	12	14	16	
Bust	78	80	83	87	92	97	cm
Waist	58	61	64	67	71	76	"
Hip–23cm below waist	83	85	88	92	97	102	"
Back–neck to waist	39.5	40	40.5	41.5	42	42.5	"
View 1 or 2 Skirt and Blouse–Even plaid or plain fabric							
115cm*	3.20	3.30	3.40	3.60	3.60	3.70	m
150cm*	2.50	2.50	2.60	2.60	2.80	2.80	"
View 1 Skirt and Blouse–Uneven plaid fabric 115cm**	3.40	3.40	3.40	3.70	3.90	3.90	m
View 1 or 2 Skirt and Blouse Interfacing–1.00m of 55, 60, 64, 82 or 90cm woven or non-woven or fusible							
View 3 Skirt							
90cm*	2.70	2.70	2.70	2.70	2.70	2.70	m
115cm*	1.90	1.90	1.90	1.90	1.90	2.20	"
Interfacing–0.90m or 55, 60, 64, 82 or 90cm woven or non-woven or fusible							
View 3 Blouse							
90cm*	2.10	2.20	2.30	2.30	2.30	2.40	m
115cm*	1.80	1.80	1.90	2.10	2.10	2.20	"
Interfacing–0.90m of 55, 60, 64, 82 or 90cm woven or non-woven or fusible							
View 1 or 3 Vest							
90cm*	1.70	1.70	1.80	1.90	2.10	2.30	m
115cm*	1.20	1.20	1.20	1.20	1.30	1.30	"
Interfacing–0.50m of 55, 60, 82 or 90cm woven or non-woven or fusible							
*without nap **with nap ***with or without nap							
Skirt length	73.5	73.5	73.5	73.5	73.5	73.5	cm
Skirt width	173	176	178	182	186	191	"

Notions: Thread. Skirt: 18cm zipper, seam binding or stretch lace. Blouse: Five 1.3cm buttons. Vest: Four 1.3cm buttons, one 2.5cm buckle.

Sewing notions are all the extras, such as buttons, zippers and seam bindings, that you'll need to complete the garment. The envelope lists the quantity and size to buy. It's best to buy them along with your fabric to save time and insure a close color match.

Finished garment measurements, such as pants side length or the width of a lower skirt edge, are useful when making pattern adjustments for your height. Compare your measurements to those listed for your size on the chart to see if any pattern pieces should be adjusted before cutting your fabric. Also check the finished back lengths listed on some

Metric equivalents are provided on a separate chart, opposite the Imperial chart. Included in this listing are the standard body measurements, the amount of fabric and trims to buy, the finished garment measurements and notions needed.

The Cut And Sew Guide

The sheet of instructions inside the pattern envelope guides your sewing every step of the way—from laying out and cutting the pattern to working at your sewing machine.

Fashion drawings show all views or versions that are included in the pattern. These are simplified line drawings of the color pictures or photographs on the front of the pattern envelope. Each pattern view has a number, for example V1, so you can find the view you plan to make.

Pattern piece drawings are silhouettes of each pattern piece. They have identifying letters and names to help you recognize them. They also tell you which pieces are needed for each view so you can find the ones you'll use for your cutting layout. Pieces with no view number are used for every view. For your convenience, there's a list that summarizes which pieces are needed for making each view.

Simplicity 8756
1ST SHEET FRONT
This pattern includes Time-Saver™ Stretch Knit Methods.

Pattern pieces
16 pieces given
BLOUSE - A B C D E F
VEST - G H K L M
SKIRT - N P R S
SHAWL - T

BLOUSE

A FRONT C BACK B FRONT BAND D COLLAR E SLEEVE F CUFF

Preparation

A · PREPARE THE PATTERN
Press pattern pieces.
Don't trim margins.
If necessary alter pattern.

TO LENGTHEN
Cut pattern between printed lines.
Place on paper, spread pattern amount needed; then pin.

TO SHORTEN
At printed line, pin a pleat half the amount to be shortened.

B · PATTERN MARKINGS

STRAIGHT GRAIN
Place on fabric an even distance from selvage.

FOLD GRAIN
Place on fold of fabric.

CUTTING LINE

LENGTHEN OR SHORTEN LINES

STITCHING LINES

NOTCHES

SEAM ALLOWANCE usually ⅝" (1.5cm)

DOTS—Small • medium ●

C · FABRIC AND CUTTING LAYOUTS
Press fabric. Always check washing or cleaning directions with fabric. If necessary, shrink fabric before cutting
Place pattern pieces on fabric as shown in cutting layouts.

FOR DOUBLE THICKNESS
Fold fabric with RIGHT side INSIDE.
Place pattern on WRONG side of fabric.

FOR SINGLE THICKNESS
Place pattern on RIGHT side of fabric.

FOR NAP OR ONE-WAY DESIGN FABRICS
Use "with nap" cutting layout.

BEFORE CUTTING
Pin all pattern pieces on fabric as in cutting layout. Cut pattern and fabric on cutting lines.
The metric equivalent is in parenthesis

D · MARK AND SEW
Keep pattern pinned to fabric.
Transfer markings. Un-pin pattern and read each piece as you sew.

STAY-STITCHING
Machine-stitch thru single thickness of fabric to prevent stretching of bias or curved edges . . . done on seam line or ⅛" (3mm) from seam line in seam allowance.

Stay-stitching is shown only in the first illustration.

Pin, hand or machine baste seams . . . match same numbered notches . . . stitch ⅝" seams (1.5cm) unless otherwise stated . . . press seams open unless otherwise stated.

SEE SIMPLICITY SEWING BOOK FOR MORE DETAILS.

Preparation explains the important things you need to know about before cutting your fabric. There's a guide to pattern markings such as solid and broken lines, grainlines and foldlines, notches and dots. It also tells how to adjust pattern length, how to prepare your fabric before folding, how to staystitch and how to stitch seams.

Cutting layouts show you how to position the pattern pieces properly and cut out the fabric with the least amount of waste. A key is provided to tell you whether to place the pattern pieces right side up or face down. Layouts are given for different pattern sizes on various fabric widths. Find the diagram for your view, pattern size and fabric width and draw a circle around it. This will help you locate it quickly and accurately when you lay out your pattern later on. If you are using napped, pile or one-way design fabric, be sure the diagram you circle is marked "with nap."

Special notes explain how to cut unusual pieces or extras, such as bias strips, and in some cases, how to cut interfacing.

Step-by-step sewing directions show and tell how to sew the garment the easiest way. These directions are set up by the *Unit System*—a method that completes all stitching on one section or unit, such as a bodice or skirt, before going on to another. It saves time and minimizes handling.

Cutting

*GENERAL NOTE: When pattern pieces extend beyond fold of fabric, cut out all pieces except pieces that extend; then open out fabric and on single thickness, cut extending pieces on right side of fabric in position shown.

KEY: ■ black is fabric. □ white is pattern printed side up.
▨ grey is pattern printed side down. ▤ solid outline is fabric cut without a pattern piece.

NOTE: For smaller sizes, pieces interlock more closely.

BLOUSE – WOVEN FABRICS

35'' 36'' (90cm) fabric without nap
size 6

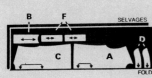

35'' 36'' (90cm) fabric without nap
sizes 8, 10, 12, 14

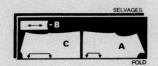

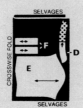

Sewing 8756
Directions
1ST SHEET BACK

Shaded area is right side of fabric.

NON FUSIBLE INTERFACING - When pinning interfacings in place, cut across corners that will be enclosed with seams.

FUSIBLE INTERFACING - Before fusing interfacing, cut across corners that will be enclosed with seams and trim 1/2" (1.3cm) from all edges.
This will eliminate bulk in seam allowance since interfacing cannot be trimmed after it is fused in place.
Follow manufacturer's directions carefully.

BLOUSE

NOTE: Blouse is sized for woven fabrics only.

UNIT 1

front

To reinforce front, stitch along stitching lines, stitching thru small dots, as shown. Slash between stitching.
Clip diagonally to small dots, as shown.

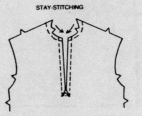
STAY-STITCHING

linea de costura
ligne de couture
seam line

costura
de 1.5 cm

½
seam

1

3

3

cutting line
ligne de coupe
linea del corte

buttonhole
boutonnière
ojal

Simplicity

0000
Miss
size 10

A
blouse front

devant de la blouse
frente de la blusa

cut two
coupez deus
córtense 2 piezas

7 pieces given
7 pièces données
7 piezas incluidas

printed in U.S.A.

8

buttonhole
boutonnière
ojal

center front line
ligne du milieu du devant
linea del centro del frente

place on straight grain of fabric
placer sur le droit fil du tissu
colóquese en el hilo de la tela

2

dart — fold along solid line
stitch along broken line
pince — pliez le long de la ligne continuelle
piquez sur la ligne brisee
pinza — plieguese por la linea
cosase por la linea de guiones

couture
de ½

view   1 pocket line
vue   1 ligne de la poche
vista   1 linea del bolsillo

buttonhole
boutonnière
ojal

linea del corte
ligne de coupe
cutting line

linea de costura
ligne de couture
seam line

alarguese o acórtese aqui
allongez ou raccourcissez ici
lengthen or shorten here

buttonhole
boutonnière
ojal

pin pattern on fabric according to grain
lines; cut pattern and fabric along
cutting lines
epinglez le patron sur le tissu en suivant le droit-fil.
coupez le patron et le tissu le long des lignes
de coupe
préndase el patrón a la tela siguiendo el hilo
recórtese el patrón y la tela a lo largo de las lineas
de corte

waistline
taille
cintura

fold line
ligne de pliure
linea del doblez

linea del corte
ligne de coupe
cutting line

dobladillo angosto
ourlet étroit
narrow hem

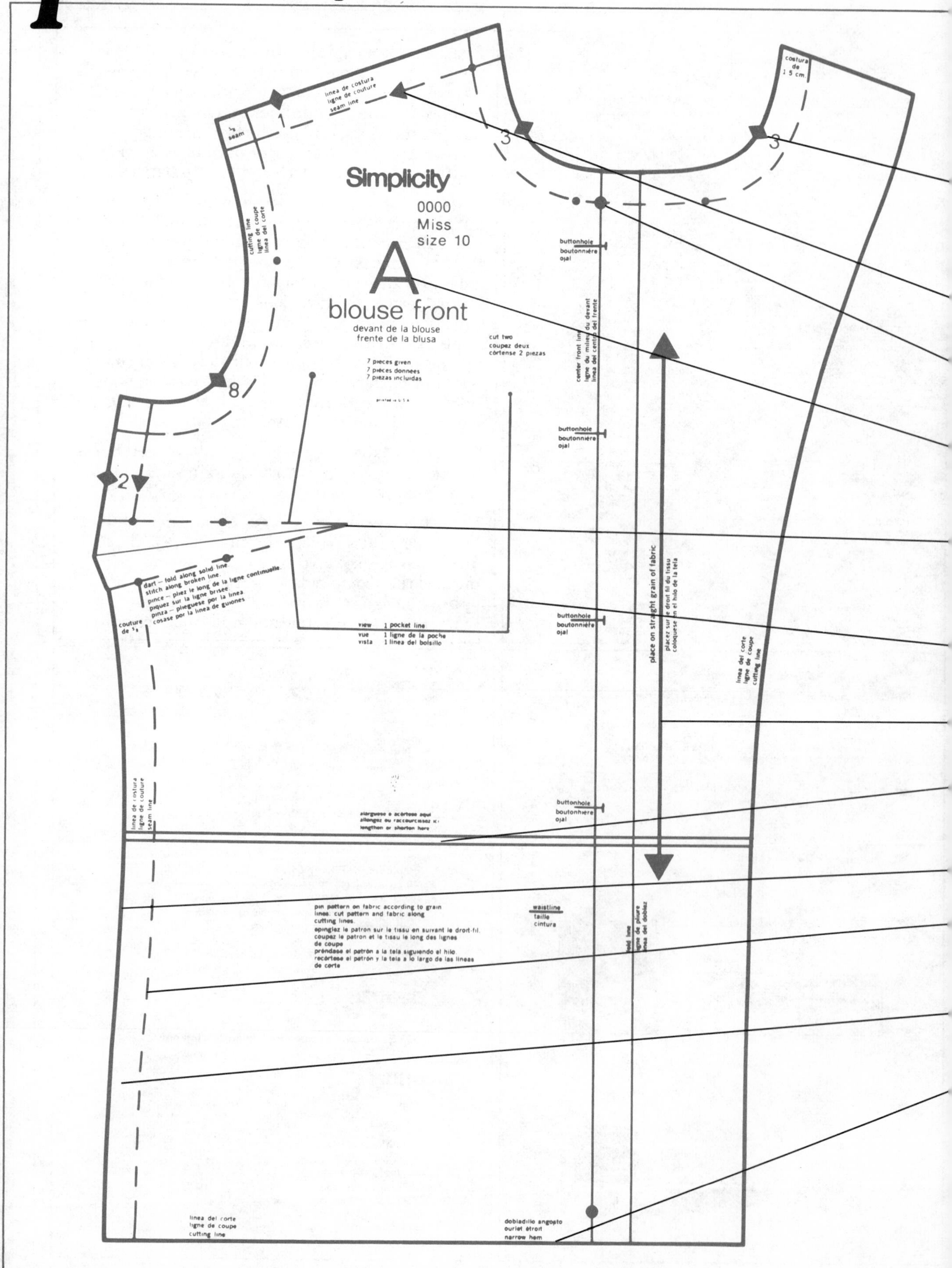

The Pattern Piece

Each pattern piece contains written directions and symbols such as dots and arrows—a kind of shorthand that's easy to learn and speeds your sewing because it shows you which edges to match and where to position details.

Notches are diamond-shaped symbols located on the cutting lines. Each notch or set of notches is numbered in the order you should stitch seams. To match notches, look back at the pattern piece, find notch numbers and match fabric edges with notches of the same number.

Directional stitching arrows are located on the seamline and show you which direction to stitch seams so the fabric doesn't stretch.

Dots* are circles which mark points to be matched before stitching and the placement of details, such as darts, tabs and belt loops.

Letters are printed on each pattern piece so you can tell one from the other. The top of the letter always points to the top of the pattern piece.

Darts* are usually shown as V-shaped broken and solid lines with dots. To sew, fold the dart on the solid line, match the dots and stitch on the broken line. Darts are used to shape fabric so that it fits over your body curves.

Solid lines* show where to position pockets, buttonholes, the waistline, center front and center back, or where to fold the fabric.

Grainline arrow is used for positioning pattern piece on the correct fabric grain (see above, right).

Lengthen or shorten here lines are two parallel lines which indicate where to make the pattern piece longer or shorter so the finished length will be right without distorting the garment shape.

Cutting lines are solid lines along the outer edge. Follow these lines when you cut your fabric.

Seamlines are broken lines, usually ⅝″ (1.5 cm) from the cutting line. When you sew a seam, you are actually stitching two layers of fabric together on the seamline.

Seam allowance is the area between the seamline and cutting line.

Hem tells you how much fabric to turn up for the hem.

Straight grainline arrows indicate pieces that must be placed parallel to the edge of your fabric.

Curved grainline arrows indicate pieces that are placed along folded fabric edges.

Pleat or tuck lines are usually a combination of solid and broken lines.

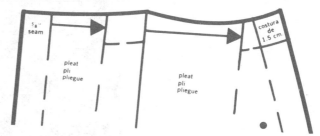

Gathering or ease lines show where to sew the gathering or easing stitches.

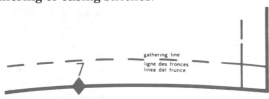

Clip arrow shows where to clip into the seam allowance to make it easier to sew.

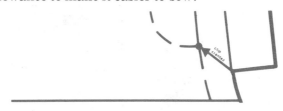

*The symbols with an asterisk (*) eventually get transferred onto your fabric; you'll learn more about this on pages 86-88.

3

pattern
and
fabric:
the
magic
mix

Fabric makes the fashion

There's a wealth of fabrics to sew today and each one has its own personality. It pays to know about them before they dazzle you with their charms. In a very practical way, some fabrics will suit your purposes much better than others.

Fiber Facts

Every fabric claims its origin from one basic unit—the fiber. Natural fibers, cotton, silk, linen, and wool, come from plants or animals, while other fibers, the

On the other hand, manmades can be admired for consistency of texture and easy care features. Because they're not as absorbent as natural-fiber fabrics, they rate lower on the comfort scale.

Blends combine the best features of naturals and synthetics and are here to stay. Usually, you can expect a blend to react according to the properties of the fiber present in the largest amount.

The number of fiber tradenames has blossomed over the years. No wonder if you're feeling con-

Woven fabrics, like the plain and twill weaves below, have yarns that crisscross.

Knitted fabrics, or knits, have interlocking loops of yarn, as the double knit below shows.

Non-woven fabrics, such as felt, quilt batting and certain types of interfacing, are the result of fusing or felting the fibers together in a random arrangement.

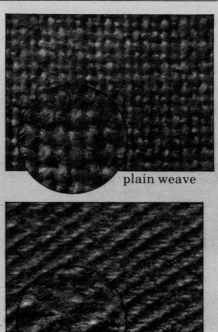
plain weave

double knit

twill weave

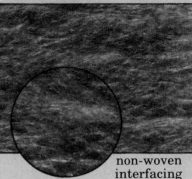
non-woven interfacing

synthetics, are manmade. Of the many synthetics, rayon, acrylic, polyester and nylon are some common examples.

Are naturals and synthetics different to sew? Yes. Most natural fabrics tend to be slightly easier to handle than synthetics, but they also wrinkle more. Clothes made of natural fabrics cannot be surpassed for comfort, durability and overall wearability.

You'll find that the characteristic irregularities in natural textures make them both beautiful and interesting fashion fabrics.

fused! The chart opposite will help straighten things out. It includes some tradenames for today's most popular fibers. The chart also lists some common fabric types, special fiber properties and typical care requirements of each.

Fiber To Fabric

Before fibers become fabrics, they're first made into yarns. These yarns are usually woven, knitted, or fused into fabrics commonly used for sewing.

Fabric Finishes

Now you know that fibers are made into yarns, and yarns into fabric, but the story doesn't end here. The raw fabric still needs further treatment, or finishing, to improve its appearance, handling and safety. These finishes will influence how you'll handle and care for your fabric, so it's smart to become familiar with the ones most often used.

Colorfast: Prevents color from rubbing off or fading.

Crease- or wrinkle-resistant: Reduces tendency to crease; helps fabric shed wrinkles when it hangs.

Flame retardant: Resists spread of flames, required by law on children's sleepwear and home furnishing fabrics.

Mildew-resistant: Retards the growth of bacteria and fungi, especially on cotton, linen, rayon.

Mothproof: Discourages attack from moths and other insects; used on wool and wool blends.

Permanent press: Sheds wrinkles after wearing or washing; needs little pressing.

Preshrunk or shrink-resistant: Keeps later shrinkage to a minimum. If *residual shrinkage* —the amount of shrinkage left after finishing—is more than 3%, preshrink your fabric at home before cutting it out.

Soil release: For easier removal of soil; counteracts tendency of synthetics to attract dirt and oil.

Stain-and spot-resistant: Helps repel and resist absorption of water and oily substances.

Wash and wear: Requires little or no ironing after laundering.

Washable: Will not noticeably fade or shrink when washed.

Waterproof: Fabric treated so no moisture or air can penetrate it.

Water-repellent/water-resistant: Resists absorption of liquids; air can penetrate spaces between yarns but liquids only bead on the surface.

Fiber Facts

	Fiber and Tradenames	Common Fabric Types	Special Properties: Advantages	Special Properties: Disadvantages	Typical Care
NATURALS	**Cotton**	batiste, broadcloth, corduroy, seersucker, terry, denim	absorbent, cool, strong	wrinkles and shrinks (unless treated), weakened by mildew and sunlight	machine wash, tumble dry, can be bleached, iron while damp
NATURALS	**Linen**	handkerchief, lawn, damask, fabrics with nubby textures	absorbent, cool, strong	wrinkles, shrinks, weakened by mildew	dry clean to retain crispness, or wash to soften, iron while damp
NATURALS	**Silk**	chiffon, crepe de chine, organza, broadcloth, linen, raw silk	absorbent, warm, lustrous, drapes beautifully	weakened by sunlight and perspiration	dry clean, though some can be hand washed; iron on wrong side at low temperature
NATURALS	**Wool**	flannel, tweed, melton, jersey, gabardine, crepe, challis	absorbent, warm, flame- and wrinkle-resistant, good insulation	shrinks, attracts moths, knits tend to stretch during wear	dry clean, though some can be machine washed; steam iron with a press cloth on the right side
MANMADES	**Acetate** ◇ Acele® □ Arnel® •• Avicolor® □ Celaperm® ΔΔ Chromspun®	taffeta, satin, tricot, silk-like fabrics	silk-like luster, drapes well, dries quickly, low in cost	fades, relatively weak, exhibits static cling, wrinkles	dry clean or gently machine wash, tumble dry (low), iron at low temperature
MANMADES	**Acrylic** □□ Acrilan® • Creslan® ◇ Orlon® ΔΔΔ Zefkrome® ΔΔΔ Zefran®	pile fabrics, double knits, fleece, wool-like fabrics	warm; resists wrinkles, mildew, moths and oily stains	sensitive to heat, pills, has static cling	machine wash, tumble dry, needs no ironing
MANMADES	**Nylon** ◇ Antron® ◇ Cantrece® ★ Crepeset® ◇ Qiana®	tricot, velvet, two-way stretch knits (swimwear), wet-look ciré	strong, warm, lightweight; resists moths, wrinkles and mildew	has static cling, pills, holds body heat	hand or machine wash, tumble dry, iron at low temperature
MANMADES	**Polyester** ◇ Dacron® □ Fortrel® ΔΔ Kodel® ◇◇ Trevira®	double and single knits, gabardine, jersey, crepe, cotton-, silk-, and wool-like fabrics	strong, warm, very wrinkle-resistant, holds shape and a pressed crease, resists moths and mildew	has static cling, pills, stains are hard to remove, holds body heat	machine wash, tumble dry, needs little or no ironing
MANMADES	**Rayon** •• Avril® •• Avron® ★★ Coloray® ★ Enka® ★★ Fibro® ★ Jetspun® •• Rayflex® ★ Zantrel®	challis, matte jersey, linen-like fabrics	absorbent	relatively fragile, holds body heat, wrinkles, shrinks	dry clean or gently machine wash, iron at moderate temperature, can be bleached
MANMADES	**Blends**	combination of two or more fibers	meant to bring out the best properties of each fiber included		care determined by most sensitive fiber included

• American Cyanamid Company
★ American Enka Company
□ Celanese Corporation
★★ Courtaulds North America
ΔΔΔ Dow Badische Company
◇ E.I. du Pont de Nemours & Company, Inc.
ΔΔ Eastman Kodak Company
•• FMC Corporation
◇◇ Hoechst Fibers Company
□□ Monsanto Textiles Company

Fabric makes the fashion

Great-looking garments depend on the right combination of pattern and fabric. There's a seemingly endless variety of fabrics to choose from which will suit your pattern perfectly. Selecting fabric is a matter of using good fashion and sewing sense. Just take what you know about patterns and fabric and put them together. Here are some ways to simplify your fabric decisions.

Study the Pattern Design

Look carefully at the photo or drawings on the pattern envelope front. They show the garment made up in suitable fabrics. They also provide ideas on coordinating colors and prints. Ask these questions about the pattern design:

What's the fashion image? Is it country casual or city sophisticated, sporty or dressy, trendy or classic? Fabrics have images, too, so it's important to combine a pattern and fabric that portray the same image. Silk, for example, is an elegant fabric—a fabulous choice for a soft, bow-tied blouse, but all wrong for casual wear.

What's the silhouette? Is it soft and flowing? If so, you'll want a fabric that's supple enough to echo the contours of your body and move with you. Is it crisp, with clean lines? If so, choose a fabric with enough body to hold the shape of the design.

Is it designed for knits or wovens? This is important because most knits stretch and most wovens don't. Therefore, knit patterns are cut slightly smaller than patterns designed for wovens and are often made to pull on, with no darts or zippers. A fabric with stretch is a must with a pattern "sized for stretch knits" — a woven fabric just won't do!

Check With the Experts

Study the pattern envelope back. It's a foolproof guide to choosing fabrics—especially for beginners. On the back of the envelope, you'll find a list of fabric suggestions. Choose one of these and you can't go wrong! On page 37, you'll find explanations and photos of fabric types often recommended.

Look at ready-made clothes that are similar to your pattern. Take mental note of the fabrics, colors, textures and weights that are used for a particular style.

Your favorite fashion magazine can also provide inspiration. Cut out photos that impress you and take them along when you shop for fabric.

image - active sports

fabrics - cotton knit, stretch terry

silhouette - soft

Be a smart shopper

Buying blindly can waste a lot of valuable time and money. You not only want to buy the right amount of fabric—you also want to know what you're getting.

Check the Quality

Don't be afraid to handle fabrics. Look for a firm and uniform weave, even dyeing, and wrinkle-shedding properties.

Stretch a Knit

Knit patterns are designed for fabrics with a specific amount of like isn't marked this way, use the Pick-A-Knit® Rule on the envelope back to decide whether the knit has the right amount of stretch. To use this rule, fold the fabric crosswise. Hold it against the left end of the rule and stretch the knit to see if the amount indicated will go to the end of the rule easily. When you let the fabric relax, it should regain its original size and shape.

Buy the Right Amount

You'll find yardage requirements for fabric, lining, interfacing, etc. on the pattern envelope back. The amount to buy will depend on your size, the view you want to make, the width of the fabric and whether or not the fabric has a nap or one-way design.

Fabrics come in different widths—some are 45″ (115 cm) wide, some 60″ (150 cm), etc. You will need more yardage of a narrow fabric than a wide one.

Fabrics with fuzzy surfaces (corduroy, terry, fake fur), twill weaves (chino, denim), shine

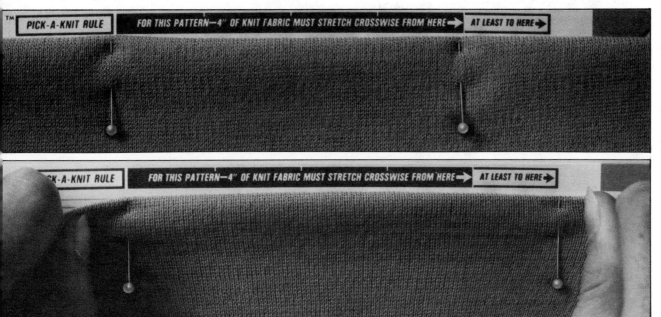

stretch. Some knit fabric manufacturers are using Simplicity's stretch standards on the bolt end of their fabrics to identify the amount of stretch in that particular fabric. For example, if your pattern calls for a Stretch 1 knit, look for knits marked "Stretch 1" on the bolt end. If the fabric you

Look at the Facts

Today's fabrics combine good looks with easy care. But they can stay good-looking only if you treat them the way the manufacturer suggests. You'll find fiber content and care requirements on the bolt end or a hangtag. A federal law requires retailers to supply consumers with a label stating this information. Ask for the label at the fabric counter and sew it into the finished garment.

(satin), or knit construction have a shading effect—they look darker in one direction than in the other. These fabrics, and those with a one-way design, require a "with nap" cutting layout. This takes more fabric than a "without nap" layout because the tops of all pattern pieces face the same way.

For plaids or large designs that must be matched, add an extra motif for each yard of fabric.

On page 36, you'll find a handy fill-in list for the pattern and fabric details you'll need to know when shopping. It's a good idea to take this type of list to the store so you don't forget anything.

3

pattern
and
fabric:
the
magic
mix

Interfacing, lining and notions

While it's true that fabric makes the fashion, a really super fashion may call for something more—the support or shaping of interfacing, for instance, or the polished look of a lining. Every fashion will need some notions to bring it to life. You'll find interfacing, lining and notions indicated on the back of the pattern envelope. To save time and insure good color matches, buy everything (pattern, fabric and all the extras) at once.

Sew-in and fusible are the two basic types of interfacing available. Fusible interfacing is bonded, rather than sewn, to your fabric with your iron and a combination of steam, heat and pressure. Either type may be woven or non-woven. Test a fusible interfacing first on a scrap of garment fabric, following the manufacturer's instructions. Non-fusible interfacings should be preshrunk if you intend to wash the garment. See Chapter 7 for information on how to interface.

Lining

If you are sewing a vest, jacket or coat, a lining may be required. The lining gives a neat finish to the inside of a garment, helps the garment keep its shape during wear, reduces wrinkles and sometimes adds warmth. The yardage requirements are listed on the pattern envelope back. Light-

Fabric and Use	Interfacing	
	For a soft effect	**For a crisp effect**
Very light to lightweight fabrics (voile, gauze, crepe, challis, calico, chambray, interlock knit, jersey, single knit, batiste) Blouses, shirts and dresses	Batiste; Organza; Sew-in sheer, regular, or stretch very lightweight non-woven	Organdy; Sew-in or fusible lightweight non-woven or woven; Fusible knit
	Do not use fusibles on lightweight silks, fine sheers, chiffon or seersucker	
Medium weight fabrics (linen, denim, poplin, flannel, gabardine, satin, duck, chino, velour, stretch terry, double knit, sweater knit) Dresses, lightweight suits, active sportswear	Sew-in or fusible medium weight woven; Regular or stretch light to medium weight non-woven; Fusible knit	Sew-in or fusible lightweight canvas; Sew-in or fusible medium weight woven or non-woven
	Do not use fusibles on rainwear fabrics	
Heavyweight fabrics (corduroy, tweed, worsted, camel hair, melton, sailcloth, canvas, gabardine, coatings) Jackets, suits, coats	Soft, lightweight canvas; Sew-in or fusible regular medium weight non-woven	Sew-in or fusible medium weight woven; Crisp medium or heavyweight hair canvas; Fusible heavyweight non-woven
Leather types (suede, suede cloth)	Crisp or soft canvas; Fusible or sew-in medium weight non-woven or woven Do not use fusibles on real leather	
Waistbands	Fusible non-woven precut strips; Woven stiffener sold by the width; Sew-in or fusible medium to heavyweight woven or non-woven interfacing; Pre-interfaced commercial waistbands	
Crafts (belts, hats, bags, camping gear, home decorating items)	Sew-in regular non-wovens in all weights; Fusible medium to heavyweight woven or non-woven	

Interfacing

An interfacing is one of the great unsung heroes of good fashion. It hides inside most well-made garments, between the outer fabric and the facing. You may not be able to see it, but it's there, giving shape and firmness to collar, cuffs, lapels, neckline, waistband or an edge such as a jacket opening (see the shading on the outfit above). The pattern envelope back tells you how much, if any, to buy.

Use the chart above as your guide to choosing interfacing types and weights for specific fabrics.

When shopping, check the compatibility of your fabric and interfacing. The interfacing should always be lighter in color and weight than the fabric it will support. To double-check both these points, drape the fabric over the interfacing. Does the interfacing provide the right amount of firmness? Does it show through the fabric? To avoid dry cleaning or washing problems, be sure both fabric and interfacing require the same care.

weight fabrics work best with polyester lining or china silk. For medium weight fabrics, use acetate sheath lining, medium weight crepe or silk surah. Line heavyweight fabrics with sturdy taffeta, satin or crepe-back satin. The lining and your fabric should have the same care requirements.

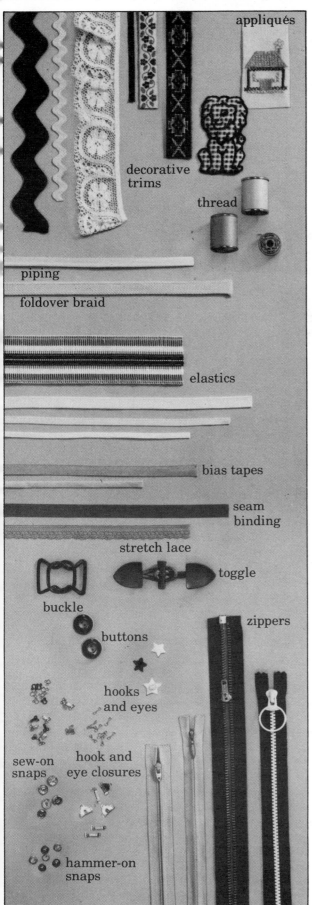

appliqués

decorative trims

thread

piping

foldover braid

elastics

bias tapes

seam binding

stretch lace

buckle

toggle

buttons

zippers

hooks and eyes

sew-on snaps

hook and eye closures

hammer-on snaps

Notions

You'll need a few extras, called notions, to sew up your garment. The ones that follow are most common.

Decorative trims: A wide variety of lace, rickrack, middy braid and embroidered bands. Some lace and eyelet trims are pregathered or ruffled.

Appliqués: Decorative patches used to add a special touch. You'll find both fusible and sew-on types.

Thread: See page 44 for a detailed discussion of thread types. Match the thread fiber to the fabric fiber, or use polyester or cotton-covered polyester thread. Choose a shade slightly darker than or the same as your fabric for the best color blend.

Piping: Fabric-covered cord inserted in seams for a decorative effect.

Foldover braid: Folded braid trim used to bind edges.

Elastic: Comes in various types and widths. The packaged type states what kind of garment the elastic is for, such as non-shrinkable for swimwear, non-roll for waistbands, soft stretch for infants' clothes and lingerie, decorative for waistbands. Buy the width and amount listed on the envelope back.

Bias tape: Single-fold or double-fold tape with pre-folded edges in various widths; for binding an edge, making a casing or hemming a curve.

Seam binding and stretch lace: Use straight-grain seam binding to finish straight edges or to stabilize seams that might otherwise stretch. Bias seam binding or stretch lace should be used on curved edges and knits.

Buckles: May be made of metal, bone or plastic, and are available either with or without a prong.

Toggles: Loop-and-bar type fastener with a leather or leather-like trim, used instead of buttons and button-holes for edges that lap or meet.

Buttons: Choose either a sew-through type (with 2 or 4 holes) or shank type (with a loop or hole under the button). Buy the size listed on the pattern envelope.

Zippers: Your pattern will specify what size to buy — usually 7″ (18 cm) for pants and skirts, 11″ (28 cm) for trousers, and 20 or 22″ (51 or 56 cm) for dresses. It will also say whether a special type, such as an invisible, separating or heavy industrial zipper, is needed.

Hooks and eyes: Metal hooks come with two kinds of eyes—straight eyes, used to fasten lapped edges such as waistbands, and loop eyes, used to fasten edges that meet such as the back neck opening at the top of a zipper.

Hook and eye closures: Large, sturdy hook and straight eye, used for garment areas that take a lot of stress — for example, a waistband.

Sew-on snaps: Ball-and-socket type fastener used on edges that lap, such as cuffs. Good for areas that don't receive much stress.

Hammer-on snaps: Have prongs which grip the fabric when hammered on or applied with a plier-like tool.

Shopping guide

Here's a guide to help you
buy all the things you'll need at one time.

As you shop, buy the items
you'll need in this order:
- pattern
- fabric
- lining
- interfacing
- notions, trims

Check the pattern:
Size . . . does it come
in yours?
Silhouette and
lines . . . will they
flatter you?

Check the fabric:
Color and texture . . . will
they flatter you?
Weight and type . . . are
they suitable for the
pattern design?

CONTENT AND CARE

Basics

**Pattern
number** _____
size _____
view _____

Fabric width _____
with nap
without nap
(circle one)

Extra fabric needed
for plaids, stripes,
large prints
(circle one)

How Much to Buy

Quantity/Size

Fabric _____
Lining _____
Interfacing _____
Trims _____
Elastic _____

Thread _____
Zipper _____
Buttons _____
Seam binding _____
Others _____
_____
_____

Get the Facts

Fabric type _____
Fiber content _____
Care (wash or dry-clean, etc.) _____
_____

Remember to ask for a care label
Fabric construction (knit or
woven) _____
Manufacturer's name and address

_____
_____

Where purchased _____   **Attach
swatch**

familiar fabric types

To help you create the right mix of pattern and fabric, the back of every pattern envelope lists suggested fabric types. These are common terms that refer to fibers, weaves or weights.

Cotton types: Basic weaves and plain-surfaced fabrics traditionally used for sportswear, warm-weather wear and work clothes. Once woven only of cotton, now these weaves can also be synthetics or blends. On the medium weight side, you'll find denim (1), poplin, chino and corduroy; broadcloth, batiste, chambray (2), seersucker and gingham are lighter and softer.

Linen types: Coarse or finely woven fabrics with a slightly lustrous surface. These vary from the lighter handkerchief and shirt linens (3) to the heavier weights used for skirts, dresses and jackets (4). Synthetic fibers now simulate the sought-after look of true linens.

Silk types: Shiny, smooth fabrics made of synthetics or silk and usually reserved for dressy clothes or elegant blouses. The flowing, lightweight types include crepe de chine (5), organza and chiffon. The heavier ones range from textured brocades (6) to shiny satins.

Wool types: Warm fabrics for cold-weather clothes, made of all wool or the new synthetics and blends. These can be everything from lightweight challis (7) or flannel to very heavy coat-weight melton or tweeds (8).

Knits: Stretchable fabrics consisting of interlocked loops. The selection varies from lightweight single knits (9), jerseys and tricots to heavier double knits and novelty knits (10) in almost any fiber or blend.

Sheers: Fabrics you can see through. Silk types include chiffon (11) and organza; cotton types, leno (12), organdy and gauze.

4 sewing tools

Sewing, like all crafts, has special tools of the trade...for stitching and cutting, measuring and marking, as well as fitting and pressing. This chapter describes all the ones you'll need, plus those extras that are nice to have. This includes everything from the sewing machine to a place to sew. Here are some ideas for your sewing space.

38

a sewing place

Your sewing deserves a special place. If you're lucky enough to have a spare room, super! If not, a perfect sewing spot can be created in almost any room. Find a corner you can convert quickly to a sewing place whenever the urge to sew strikes you. Or, consider building a sewing center like this, painted to blend with the decor of the room.

A sewing center may be the answer if you are cramped for space. This one piece of furniture has all the ingredients for convenient sewing. Since cutting and sewing require different work surfaces, this center has a flip-top that goes from cutting height to sewing table height. And, at each level you have ample room to spread out. There are even places in the center to store all your sewing paraphernalia: a shelf beneath, two swing-out bins (one designed for your machine),and four deep drawers. It's yours for the making. To order the plans,send 75¢ (cash, check or money order) to *Woman's Day,* FTSC 111577, Box 1002, Greenwich, Conn. 06830. Ask for the "Flip-Top Sewing Center To Build" and include your name and address.

(Left) Center with top flipped to sewing height. (Above Right) The flush door for the top, 36″ x 72″ (91.5 x 183 cm), swivels on bolts and locks into position. (Right) Center with top flipped to the cutting-table height.

Designed by Ira Grandberg, photographed by the Woman's Day Studio. Reprinted by permission of Woman's Day Magazine. Copyright © 1977 by CBS Publications, Inc.

A convertible sewing corner

Claim a sewing corner for your own, perhaps carved out of your family room or bedroom. To make your corner convert quickly and easily from an active sewing area to an attractive corner, use furniture and accessories that can conceal most of your creative clutter and equipment.

Now it's a neat corner (Insert) with a cloth-covered table (hiding the sewing machine beneath its skirts), a framed print and a bold fabric shade.

Now it's a sewing studio (Below) with a sturdy sewing table, large shelves for fabric storage (concealed by the shade) and smaller ones for notions (stashed behind the picture).

What Your Sewing Corner Needs

• Colorful, inexpensive containers for storing sewing supplies—plastic food storage bins, straw baskets, apothecary jars and kitchen cannisters.
• Deep and high enough shelves for bulky items like sewing books, patterns and fabrics.
• A shallow or see-through box for small things like threads, buttons, hooks and eyes.
• Lighting, overhead and directly on the table.
• A straight-backed chair with a comfortable seat.
• An iron and an ironing board.
• A wastebasket nearby to save you steps.

Tools of the trade

Now, there's a tool to help you with just about every conceivable sewing step. The basic must-have tools—such as a sewing machine, needles and thread—are better than ever. The helpful extras, part of the gadget explosion, have never been so numerous and simple to use. To make your sewing fun and as easy as possible, get the best tools you can find. Make a point of keeping an eye on the notions counter for new ones.

Stocking Up

Since the sewing machine is obviously the most important purchase, don't overlook the special attachments and features that can turn even the simplest sewing machine into a stitching power-house! But the machine can't do the job alone. You'll need other tools for cutting patterns and fabric, measuring and marking, adjusting your pattern to fit, hand-sewing and pressing, to give your sewing a professional look.

Here's a handy checklist of the must-have items for each of the tool categories. Use it as a shopping aid. Then, after you've stocked up on the basics, round out your tool supply with a few of the nice extras. Your favorite sewing notions counter is constantly displaying new items designed to help make sewing more enjoyable. The pages that follow will show you what's available now to speed your sewing along.

Smart Shopper's Guide
- Look for warranties on expensive items—sewing machine, iron, and scissors.
- Ask for a demonstration if you're not sure how the item works.
- Buy measuring tools with metric and standard measurements.
- Buy brand names to be sure of quality.

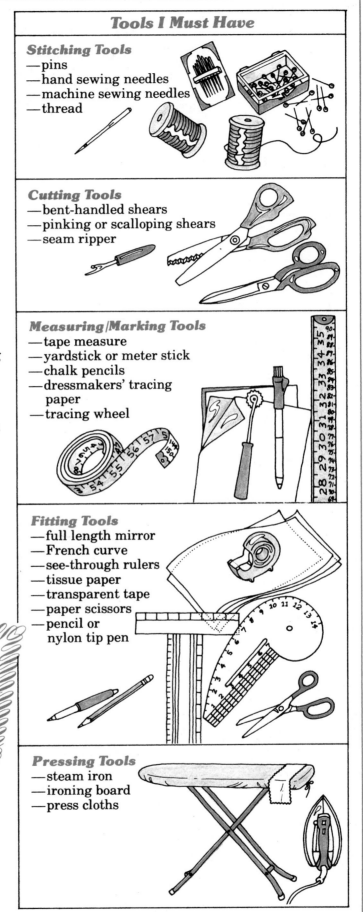

Tools I Must Have

Stitching Tools
—pins
—hand sewing needles
—machine sewing needles
—thread

Cutting Tools
—bent-handled shears
—pinking or scalloping shears
—seam ripper

Measuring/Marking Tools
—tape measure
—yardstick or meter stick
—chalk pencils
—dressmakers' tracing paper
—tracing wheel

Fitting Tools
—full length mirror
—French curve
—see-through rulers
—tissue paper
—transparent tape
—paper scissors
—pencil or nylon tip pen

Pressing Tools
—steam iron
—ironing board
—press cloths

The sewing machine

The modern sewing machine can do almost anything but cut and press! It's the most valuable piece of equipment you'll buy—in terms of both money and performance—so buy the machine that best fills your individual needs.

Shopping Decisions

The type of machine to buy depends on how much you'll be sewing, your budget and your space. When shopping, ask yourself these questions:

Types of Machines

Straight stitch machines can sew forward and backward; zigzag and buttonhole attachments are often available. You can buy this type of machine as a used model.

Zigzag machines make straight and zigzag stitches; buttonhole and decorative stitches are often built-in features.

Stretch stitch or reverse cycle machines are really zigzag machines that can also make stretch stitches by moving the fab-

Free-arm machine has a narrow sewing surface that allows you to sew cuffs, children's wear and other small areas easily. Many convert to a flat-bed type.

Built-in decorative stitches can be set by touching a button or turning a dial.

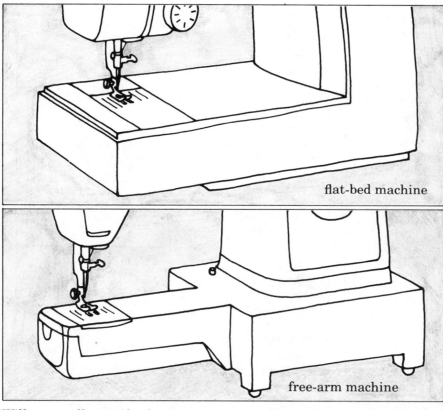

flat-bed machine

free-arm machine

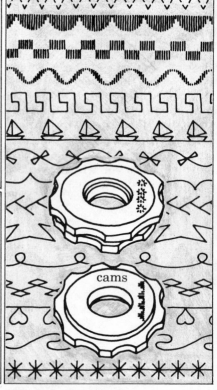

cams

Will you really use the features and accessories that come with it? They add to the expense! Do you have the money and space for a cabinet model or is a portable more your style? Do you really need a new machine? A used one may meet your needs just as well and will be less expensive. But, be sure to buy it from a reputable source.

Before making a decision, it's smart to become familiar with machine types, features and accessories.

ric in a forward-reverse pattern as the needle zigzags.

Features

Console or permanent cabinet combines work space and storage in one piece of furniture.

Portable machine has its own carrying case. If space is limited, this is the most versatile choice. Many portables can be put into a table or cabinet later on.

Flat-bed machine has a large, flat sewing surface.

Decorative stitch cams can be added to some machines. Cams allow you to update your machine by buying more cams at any time. You may want to buy the basic machine now and add other cams as you can afford them.

Built-in buttonhole stitch can be set at the touch of a button; handy if you make buttonholes fairly often.

Basic Accessories

These basic accessories come with most machines:

Straight stitch presser foot is hinged for straight stitching only; it can sew over pins.

Straight stitch throat plate has a small round hole for the needle to pass through; can also be used to straight stitch on zigzag machine.

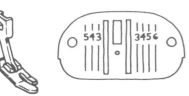

General purpose zigzag foot is used for straight and zigzag sewing of all types.

General purpose throat plate has a wider needle hole; use it with the general purpose zigzag foot for straight or zigzag stitching or when using a twin needle.

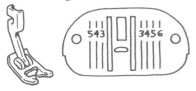

Zipper foot may be positioned either to the right or left of the needle; a must for good zipper application. It is also used for sewing piping and cording.

Handy Accessories

In addition to the basic feet and throat plates, these handy attachments are available for many machines. If they are not included with your machine, you may purchase them separately as you need them.

Binder folds and attaches purchased or self-fabric binding in one step.

Blindstitch foot guides fabric evenly for blindstitching hems.

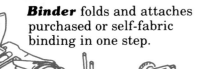

Button foot holds a button in place while the machine sews it on.

Buttonhole attachment is for machines without a built-in buttonholer; it makes buttonholes in various sizes.

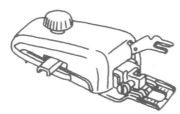

Buttonhole feet help you stitch uniform buttonholes; they can be metal, see-through plastic or long gauge type.

Buttonholer makes a buttonhole to fit the size of button inserted in it; only for some machines.

Cording foot allows cord to be fed through and stitched to fabric at the same time.

Darning and button plate is used with the darning foot on machines where the feed dog can't be lowered.

Darning and embroidery foot is for machine embroidery and repairing rips in fabrics. To use this, you must be able to lower the feed dog on your machine. If you can't lower it, use a darning and button plate.

Edge stitcher holds two edges together for narrow, overlapping seams and trim applications; also guides topstitching.

Even feed or dual feed foot prevents slippage by moving both layers of fabric at the same speed; good for matching plaids, stripes.

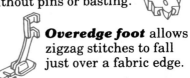

Eyelet plate allows you to turn fabric in a circle while sewing embroidery and eyelets.

Hemmer foot turns under and sews a narrow hem at the same time.

Invisible zipper foot is a plastic foot used to insert invisible zippers without pins or basting.

Overedge foot allows zigzag stitches to fall just over a fabric edge.

Quilting foot guides quilting stitches and top-stitching up to 2″ (5 cm) from edge.

Roller foot rolls hard-to-feed fabric like vinyl under the needle.

Ruffler gathers or knife-pleats a fabric edge alone or while sewing a seam.

Seam guides, either magnetic or screw type, guide fabric as you stitch.

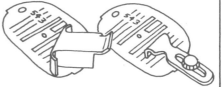

Stitching Tools

Pins, needles and thread are the basic stitching tools. It pays to have a selection of these and other stitching aids at hand, no matter what you're sewing.

Pins with colored heads are easy to see and handle. Use fine, non-rusting dressmaker pins for fine fabrics, ball-point pins for knits.

Pin cushions come in all shapes and sizes. Some have an emery bag to sharpen pins and needles and remove rust. Pin cushions with a wristband are convenient.

Hand-sewing needles range in size from 1 (largest) to 10 (finest). The needle should not pierce too large a hole in the fabric; use the chart below to select the correct size needle for your fabric.

Types of hand needles include:
• *Ball-point*—a rounded point pushes aside fabric threads instead of piercing them; used for sewing on knits.
• *Sharps*—medium length; for general sewing.
• *Wedge-shaped*—for leather and leather-like fabrics.
• *Betweens*—short; for fine tailoring and quilting.

Types of machine needles include:
• *Universal ball-point*—specially tapered for both knits and wovens.
• *Ball-point*—a rounded point pushes aside fabric threads instead of piercing them; for knits.
• *Sharp*—for general sewing on woven fabrics.
• *Wedge-shaped*—for leather and leather-like fabrics.
• *Twin and triple needles*—for decorative stitching; use with general purpose throat plate.

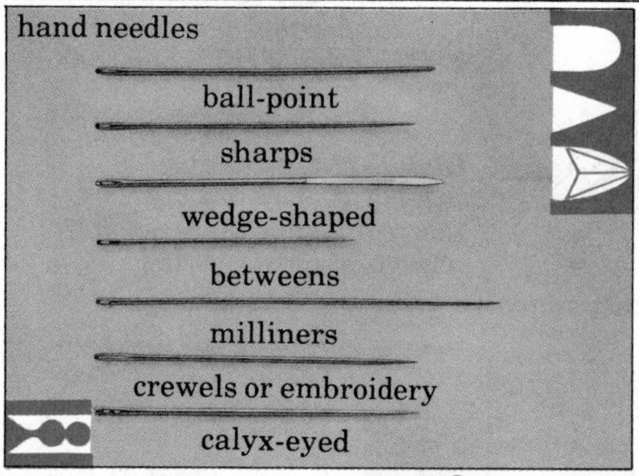

hand needles
ball-point
sharps
wedge-shaped
betweens
milliners
crewels or embroidery
calyx-eyed

Fabrics		Needle Size	
Lightweight: tricot, sheers, chiffon, organdy, challis, crepe, jersey, interlock knits		**Hand:** 10-8	**Machine:**
		Fine	9-11
Medium Weight: corduroy, flannel, satin, velvet, linen, medium weight double knits, sweater knits, denim, quilted fabrics		8-6	
		Medium	11-14
Heavyweight: sailcloth, upholstery fabric, coating, canvas, duck		5-1	
		Coarse	16-18

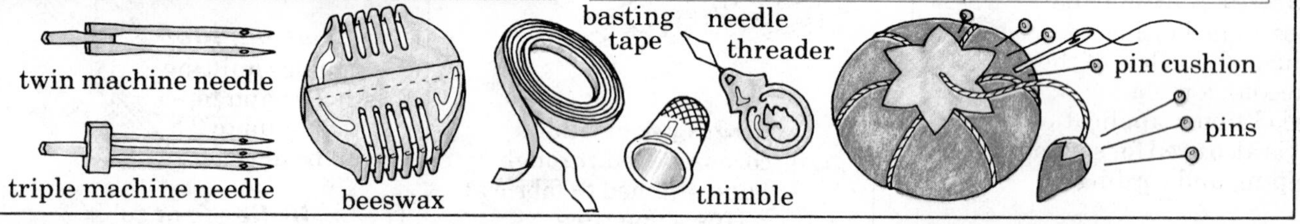

twin machine needle
triple machine needle
beeswax
basting tape
needle threader
thimble
pin cushion
pins

Thimbles may be metal or plastic and are useful for hand sewing. Select one that fits the middle finger snugly and use it to push the needle through the fabric.

Needle threader can be used for both hand and machine needles. Push wire through needle eye. Insert thread through wire; then pull wire and thread back through the eye of the needle.

Basting tape has adhesive on both sides to hold layers of fabric together for matching designs or stitching. It also holds zippers in place for stitching.

• *Milliners*—long and slender; for basting and hand shirring.
• *Crewels or embroidery*—medium length; with long eyes for embroidery floss.
• *Calyx-eyed*—open at the top for quick threading.

Machine needles range in size from 9 (finest) to 18 (largest). Sizes 11 and 14 are the most often used. The needle should be small enough to pierce the fabric without leaving a hole, but have a large enough eye for the thread. Use the chart above to select the correct size needle for your fabric.

Polyester or cotton-covered polyester thread is recommended for all fabrics; must be used on synthetics. Choose thread the same shade as or one shade darker than the fabric. Available types include:
• *Extra-fine*—for lightweight fabrics and machine embroidery.
• *Regular*—for general sewing.
• *Extra-strong*—for buttons, carpets and hand sewing heavyweight fabrics.
• *Buttonhole twist*—for topstitching, hand-worked buttonholes and sewing on buttons.
• *Quilting*—comes in cotton-covered polyester.

Cutting Tools

Mercerized cotton thread is used on fabrics with little or no stretch. Available in regular sewing thread for light and medium weight fabrics, button and carpet thread, quilting thread and basting thread.

Silk thread is used on silk, wool and silk-like synthetic fabrics. Available in regular sewing thread and in buttonhole twist.

Invest in good quality scissors and shears for easy and accurate cutting. Look for these features:
• a warranty.
• stainless steel blades that are held together by a screw so you can keep blade tension tight.
• blades that cut all the way to the point. Test this in the store.
• lightweight, plastic contour handles—they're comfortable to use! Scissors and shears will last indefinitely if you only use them to cut fabric and keep them sharpened.

Sewing and embroidery scissors with 4 or 5 inch (10 or 12.5 cm) long, pointed blades are handy for cutting buttonholes open and snipping thread ends.

Pinking or scalloping shears cut a zigzag or scalloped edge for finishing seams, etc. Never use them to cut out a garment because they don't give an accurate outline. Left-handed models are available. When they become dull, have them sharpened professionally.

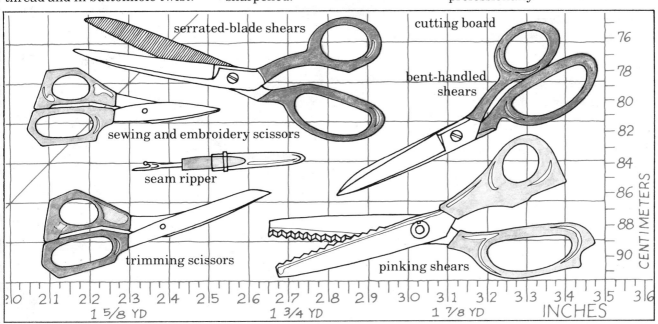

serrated-blade shears — cutting board — bent-handled shears — sewing and embroidery scissors — seam ripper — trimming scissors — pinking shears — 76 78 80 82 84 86 88 90 CENTIMETERS — 20 21 22 23 24 25 26 27 28 29 30 31 32 33 34 35 36 — 1 5/8 YD — 1 3/4 YD — 1 7/8 YD — INCHES

Novelty threads include transparent nylon for use on sturdy fabrics, elastic for machine shirring and metallic thread for decorative stitching.

Beeswax strengthens and lubricates thread. It prevents tangling, making it easier to sew on buttons and do other hand sewing. To apply, pull thread through the grooves in the container.

Bent-handled shears are the best to use for cutting out fabric; the blades rest flat on the cutting surface so you do not have to lift the fabric. The 7 or 8 inch (18 or 20.5 cm) lengths are the most common. Left-handed models are also available.

Serrated-blade shears are excellent for knits; the serrated lower blade prevents the fabric from slipping.

Trimming scissors are good for general trimming and clipping. The 6 inch (15 cm) length is best.

Seam ripper is handy for removing stitches.

Cutting board opens flat to enlarge and protect your cutting surface, then folds compactly for storage. Fabrics can be pinned to the cardboard surface to prevent slipping. The newest boards have inch and metric markings to help you determine if the fabric is on-grain and to keep pattern grainline straight.

Measuring and marking tools

Many measuring devices now include metric equivalents in preparation for the pending changeover to the metric system.

Sewing tapes have printed measurements and guidelines for even topstitching, buttonhole placement and securing pattern adjustments. Read the package instructions before using them. You can stitch through some; others must be separated into strips and then stitched along the edge, on the fabric only.

Hem guide lets you measure and press hems up in one step. One side is for straight hems; the other, for curved ones. It's also helpful for adjusting pattern hems. A small, narrow version is good for straight hems on sleeves and pants.

Sewing gauge is a 6 inch (15 cm) ruler with a movable indicator.

Transparent rulers come in many shapes and sizes. Use them with a tracing wheel or chalk pencil to mark lines for pattern adjustments, darts, pleats or tucks.

Tape measure is essential for taking body measurements. Select a flexible one that will not stretch or tear, and has metal-tipped ends. Numbers should be printed on both sides.

Yardstick or meter stick should be used to measure fabric and check grainlines. Buy a smooth one that will not snag fabric.

Skirt markers are a quick way to mark an even hem. The pin type is most accurate, but requires a helper. The bulb type with powdered chalk allows you to work alone.

Chalk pencils come in white, pink and blue. They can be sharpened to a point to give a thin, accurate line. Some have a brush for erasing; test chalk pencil on your fabric to see if it brushes off.

Tailor tacker with chalk inserts marks both layers of fabric at once.

Dressmaker's tracing paper is used along with a tracing wheel or sharp pencil to transfer pattern markings to some fabrics. Choose a color close to that of the fabric and test it on a scrap to be sure the color will come out in washing or dry cleaning. It can be used to mark both layers of some fabrics at one time.

Tracing wheels with teeth or a smooth edge are used with dressmaker's tracing paper. To get a better impression and protect your working surface, slip cardboard or a magazine under the fabric before using the wheel.

Tailor's chalk comes in squares of various colors. A handy type has a refillable holder and built-in sharpener. Remove tailor's chalk by brushing the marks.

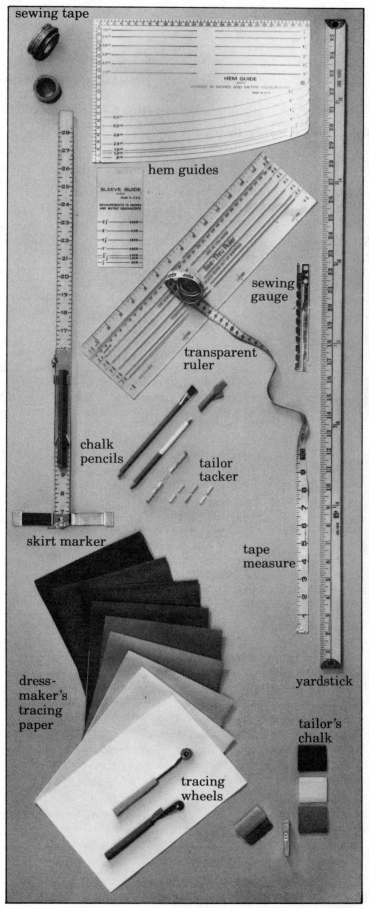

sewing tape

hem guides

sewing gauge

transparent ruler

chalk pencils

tailor tacker

skirt marker

tape measure

dressmaker's tracing paper

yardstick

tailor's chalk

tracing wheels

Fitting tools

Many tools are available to help you make pattern adjustments and fit your garment correctly. Several items you may need for fitting have been described and illustrated on the previous pages: pins • shears and scissors • seam ripper • cutting board • tape measure • yardstick • skirt marker • hem guide • transparent ruler • chalk pencil.

In addition, the following tools help in fitting.

T-square is especially handy for checking grainlines, measuring crotch depth and marking patterns. Some are adjustable. A transparent one is best.

Flexible segmented ruler will help you draw curves that conform to your exact body shape.

Dress form is a wire or foam model with your torso shape. Try the garment on the form to see how it will fit. Many are adjustable so you can change the shape if necessary. A pants/skirt form with a stomach and derrière is also available.

French curve will help you re-draw armholes, necklines and other curves for pattern adjustments. A transparent one is ideal. It's available in small and large sizes.

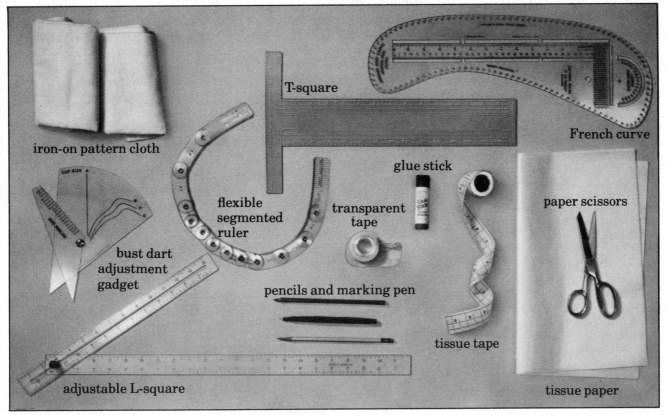

iron-on pattern cloth

bust dart adjustment gadget

flexible segmented ruler

T-square

glue stick

transparent tape

pencils and marking pen

French curve

paper scissors

tissue tape

adjustable L-square

tissue paper

Iron-on pattern cloth or interfacing reinforces the pattern so you can try it on. Adjustments can be marked on it. This is a good way to save a basic fitting pattern.

Bust dart adjustment gadget is a transparent aid for adjusting patterns to fit any bust cup size.

Adjustable L-square is useful for checking crotch depth, drawing grainlines and correcting cutting lines, especially if it's transparent. It can be converted to a T-square or straight ruler.

Transparent tape secures pattern adjustments and mends tears.

Pencil or nylon-tip marking pen is needed to mark changes on the pattern tissues.

Full-length mirror helps you see how your pattern or garment fits.

Paper scissors are used to cut tissue. Never use dressmaker's shears for cutting paper.

Tissue tape and glue stick are a quick way to adjust patterns and mend tears.

Tissue paper may be needed for pattern adjustments or you can substitute brown wrapping paper.

Pressing tools

Careful pressing is essential to a perfectly finished garment. Investing in the proper tools will repay you many times in the professional look of your sewing.

Point presser and pounding block has some features of a tailor's board, with a pounder on the bottom.

Tailor's board, made of hardwood, has many shaped surfaces for pressing points and curves. Use it with or without a cover.

Sleeve board is really a small double ironing board. Use it to press small areas.

Pounding block or clapper is a shaped length of wood used to pound and flatten seams and faced edges as they are steamed. Use it for tailoring woolens and hard-to-press fabrics.

Press cloths may be placed between the iron and your fabric to add extra moisture and prevent iron shine. Types include:
• *see-through* disposable or regular press cloths
• *cheesecloth* (or man's handkerchief instead)
• *drill cloth*—firm and heavy for extra protection
• *wool* (often combined with drill cloth)—prevents flattening the texture of woolens
• *muslin*—used with fusibles

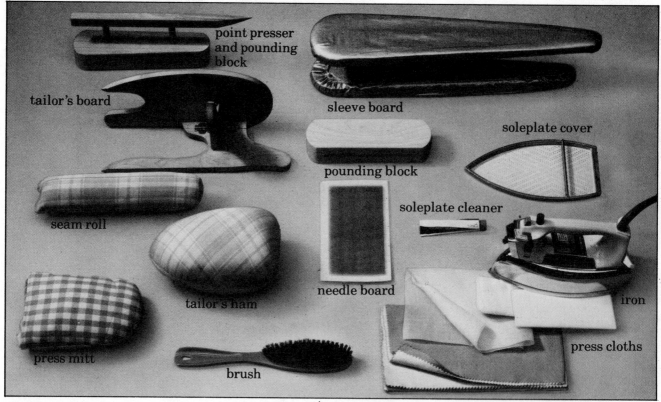

point presser and pounding block

tailor's board

sleeve board

soleplate cover

pounding block

soleplate cleaner

seam roll

needle board

tailor's ham

iron

press mitt

press cloths

brush

Seam or sleeve roll is a narrow cylinder used for pressing seams and small areas. It prevents ridges from forming on the right side of the garment.

Tailor's ham, a firm, rounded cushion, covered half in wool and half in cotton, should be used for pressing curved seams, darts and other shaped areas.

Press mitt, used like a tailor's ham for small areas, has pockets to fit your hand or sleeve board.

Needle board is made of canvas covered with upright wires. Press napped and pile fabrics face down on the wires to prevent matting.

Combination steam and dry iron is essential for successful sewing results. A button for extra steam is very handy. Compact, lightweight irons are now made specially for sewing. Follow the directions for use and keep the soleplate clean.

Ironing board may be adjusted to various heights. It should be well padded, with a clean, heat-resistant cover.

Other pressing aids include:
• *distilled water filter* for the iron
• *soleplate cover*—used instead of a press cloth
• *soleplate cleaner*
• *brush*—used after pressing napped fabric to raise the nap

5 *making your pattern fit*

Since no two people have the same shape, patterns are made to fit general figure types and sizes. Even though you've chosen the correct size, your pattern might need a few adjustments to fit you the way you'd like —especially if it's a closely-fitted style.

Be sure to find out whether your pattern needs adjusting **before** cutting into your fabric. There are three ways to do this. One way is to compare the pattern to a garment in your wardrobe. Choose a style that fits well and is similar to your pattern. First, pin out any pattern darts and pin up the hem. Then, spread the garment flat. Lay the pattern on top, matching shoulder seamlines. To compare width and waist shaping, see where the pattern side seamline falls in relation to the garment seam. Also, compare the necklines and overall length.

The second way to check fit is to try the pattern on. You'll need a friend to help you with this. Press the pattern with a warm, **dry** iron. Wear your usual undergarments, plus the shoes you'll wear with the finished garment. Then:

• Tie a string around your waist and at the base of your neck.

• To find the center front and back, hang a plumb line (a pencil tied to another string) from neck string.

• Pin all darts or pleats from the outside. Then pin pattern together, lapping seam allowances. Leave side seams open for a bit at the underarm. Pin up the hem.

• Slip the pattern on and pin it to your undergarments along center front and back.

• Check the length, circumference, darts and seams.

• Slip the sleeve on and hold it, without pinning, so all underarm seams match. Check width, length and position of dart, if any.

• Pin-mark any changes. Remove the pattern. Then draw changes on the pattern.

The third and most accurate way to see how your pattern will fit is to compare all of the pattern body measurements to your own. On the following pages, you'll find out how to do this in three simple steps—measure, compare, adjust.

Measure—compare—adjust

step 1
measure up—
females

From page 13, get the measurements you took to find your pattern size and enter them on the chart below. You'll need a few other measurements to see exactly how your pattern will fit. Follow the directions below to measure the other key body areas and enter them on the chart. Then, turn to page 56 for comparing your pattern measurements to your own.

personal body measurements

Figure Type _____

Date _____

Pattern Size for Skirts, Pants _____

Dresses, Jackets, Tops, Coordinates _____

Height	Bust	Waist	Hips	Back Waist Length

Shoulder to Bust (A) From shoulder at base of neck to bust point		**Upper arm (G)** Around arm at fullest part between shoulder and elbow	
Front Waist Length (B) From shoulder over bust point to waist		**Thigh (H)** Around upper leg at fullest part	
Shoulder Length (C) From base of neck to shoulder point		**Back Skirt Length (I)** From center back at waist to desired length	
Back Width (D) Across back, 5″ (12.5 cm) below base of neck or 4½″ (11.5 cm) on Young Junior/Teens		**Pants Side Length (J)** From waistline to desired length along outside of leg	
Arm Length (E) From shoulder point to wristbone, over slightly bent elbow		**Crotch Depth (K)** From side waist to chair (sit on a flat chair and use a ruler)	
Shoulder to Elbow (F) From shoulder point to middle of slightly bent elbow		**Crotch Length (L)** From center back waistline between the legs to center front waistline	

pattern body measurements —females

Young Junior/Teen

Inches

Size	5/6	7/8	9/10	11/12	13/14	15/16
Front Waist Length	14⅝	15¼	15⅞	16½	17	17½
Shoulder to Bust	8⅜	8¾	9⅛	9½	9⅞	10¼
Shoulder Length	4	4⅛	4¼	4⅜	4½	4⅝
Back Width	12½	12¾	13⅛	13½	13⅞	14¼
Arm Length	21⅜	21¾	22⅛	22½	22⅞	23¼
Shoulder to Elbow	11⅞	12⅛	12⅜	12⅝	12⅞	13⅛

Centimeters

Size	5/6	7/8	9/10	11/12	13/14	15/16
Front Waist Length	37	38.7	40.3	42	43.3	44.5
Shoulder to Bust	21.3	22.3	23.3	24	25	26
Shoulder Length	10.3	10.5	10.7	11	11.5	11.7
Back Width	31.7	32.3	33.3	34.3	35.3	36
Arm Length	54.3	55.3	56.3	57	58	59
Shoulder to Elbow	30.3	30.7	31.3	32	32.7	33.3

Junior Petite

Inches

Size	3jp	5jp	7jp	9jp	11jp	13jp
Front Waist Length	15¼	15⅝	16	16⅜	16¾	17⅛
Shoulder to Bust	8¼	8½	8¾	9	9¼	9½
Shoulder Length	4¼	4⅜	4½	4⅝	4¾	4⅞
Back Width	13¼	13½	13¾	14	14¼	14½
Arm Length	20⅝	20⅞	21⅛	21⅜	21⅝	21⅞
Shoulder to Elbow	12½	12⅝	12¾	12⅞	13	13⅛

Centimeters

Size	3jp	5jp	7jp	9jp	11jp	13jp
Front Waist Length	38.7	39.7	40.7	41.5	42.5	43.5
Shoulder to Bust	21	21.5	22.3	23	23.5	24
Shoulder Length	10.7	11	11.5	11.7	12	12.3
Back Width	33.5	34.3	35	35.5	36	36.7
Arm Length	52.3	53	53.5	54.3	55	55.5
Shoulder to Elbow	31.7	32	32.3	32.7	33	33.3

Junior

Inches

Size	5	7	9	11	13	15
Front Waist Length	16	16⅜	16¾	17⅛	17½	17⅞
Shoulder to Bust	9½	9¾	10	10¼	10½	10¾
Shoulder Length	4½	4⅝	4¾	4⅞	5	5⅛
Back Width	13⅜	13⅝	13⅞	14¼	14⅝	15⅛
Arm Length	22	22¼	22½	22¾	23	23¼
Shoulder to Elbow	13¼	13⅜	13½	13⅝	13¾	13⅞

Centimeters

Size	5	7	9	11	13	15
Front Waist Length	40.7	41.5	42.5	43.5	44.5	45.5
Shoulder to Bust	24	24.5	25.3	26	26.5	27.3
Shoulder Length	11.5	11.7	12	12.3	12.7	13
Back Width	34	34.5	35.3	36	37	38.4
Arm Length	56	56.5	57	57.7	58.3	59
Shoulder to Elbow	33.5	34	34.3	34.5	35	35.3

Miss Petite

Inches

Size	6mp	8mp	10mp	12mp	14mp	16mp
Front Waist Length	15¾	16⅛	16½	16⅞	17¼	17⅝
Shoulder to Bust	9⅛	9⅜	9⅝	9⅞	10⅛	10⅜
Shoulder Length	4⅝	4¾	4⅞	5	5⅛	5¼
Back Width	13¾	14	14¼	14⅝	15⅛	15⅝
Arm Length	20½	20¾	21	21¼	21½	21¾
Shoulder to Elbow	12½	12⅝	12¾	12⅞	13	13⅛

Centimeters

Size	6mp	8mp	10mp	12mp	14mp	16mp
Front Waist Length	40	41	42	43	43.7	44.7
Shoulder to Bust	23.3	23.7	24.3	25	25.5	26.3
Shoulder Length	11.7	12	12.3	12.7	13	13.3
Back Width	35	35.5	36	37	38.4	39.7
Arm Length	52	52.7	53.3	54	54.5	55.3
Shoulder to Elbow	31.7	32	32.3	32.7	33	33.3

Miss

Inches

Size	6	8	10	12	14	16	18	20
Front Waist Length	16⅝	17	17⅜	17¾	18⅛	18½	18⅞	19¼
Shoulder to Bust	9⅞	10⅛	10⅜	10⅝	10⅞	11⅛	11⅜	11⅝
Shoulder Length	4⅝	4¾	4⅞	5	5⅛	5¼	5⅜	5½
Back Width	13¾	14	14¼	14⅝	15⅛	15⅝	16⅛	16⅝
Arm Length	22¾	23	23¼	23½	23¾	24	24¼	24½
Shoulder to Elbow	13½	13⅝	13¾	13⅞	14	14⅛	14¼	14⅜

Centimeters

Size	6	8	10	12	14	16	18	20
Front Waist Length	42.3	43.3	44	45	46	47	48	49
Shoulder to Bust	25	25.5	26.3	27	27.5	28.3	29	29.5
Shoulder Length	11.7	12	12.3	12.7	13	13.3	13.5	14
Back Width	35	35.5	36	37	38.4	39.7	41	42.3
Arm Length	57.7	58.3	59	59.7	60.3	61	61.5	62.3
Shoulder to Elbow	34.3	34.5	35	35.3	35.5	35.7	36	36.5

Half-Size

Inches

Size	10½	12½	14½	16½	18½	20½	22½	24½
Front Waist Length	17	17⅜	17¾	18⅛	18⅜	18⅝	18⅞	19⅛
Shoulder to Bust	10½	10¾	11	11¼	11½	11¾	12	12¼
Shoulder Length	4½	4⅝	4¾	4⅞	5	5⅛	5¼	5⅜
Back Width	14½	15	15½	16	16½	17	17½	18
Arm Length	22¼	22½	22¾	23	23¼	23½	23¾	24
Shoulder to Elbow	14	14⅛	14¼	14⅜	14½	14⅝	14¾	14⅞

Centimeters

Size	10½	12½	14½	16½	18½	20½	22½	24½
Front Waist Length	43.3	44	45	46	46.5	47.3	48	48.5
Shoulder to Bust	26.5	27.3	28	28.5	29.3	30	30.5	31
Shoulder Length	11.5	11.7	12	12.3	12.7	13	13.3	13.5
Back Width	36.7	38	39.3	40.7	42	43.3	44.5	45.7
Arm Length	56.5	57	57.7	58.3	59	59.7	60.3	61
Shoulder to Elbow	35.5	35.7	36	36.5	36.7	37	37.5	37.7

Woman

Inches

Size	38	40	42	44	46	48	50	52
Front Waist Length	19⅝	19⅞	20⅛	20⅜	20⅝	20⅞	21⅛	21⅜
Shoulder to Bust	12	12¼	12½	12¾	13	13¼	13½	13¾
Shoulder Length	5	5	5⅛	5⅛	5¼	5¼	5⅜	5⅜
Back Width	16¼	16¾	17¼	17¾	18¼	18¾	19¼	19½
Arm Length	23¾	24	24¼	24½	24¾	25	25¼	25½
Shoulder to Elbow	14⅜	14½	14⅝	14¾	14⅞	15	15⅛	15¼

Centimeters

Size	38	40	42	44	46	48	50	52
Front Waist Length	50	50.5	51	51.7	52.3	53	53.5	54.3
Shoulder to Bust	30.5	31	31.7	32.3	33	33.5	34.3	35
Shoulder Length	12.7	12.7	13	13	13.3	13.3	13.5	13.5
Back Width	41.3	42.5	43.7	45	46.3	47.5	49	49.5
Arm Length	60.3	61	61.5	62.3	63	63.5	64	64.7
Shoulder to Elbow	36.5	36.7	37	37.5	37.7	38	38.4	38.7

Maternity

Inches

Size	6	8	10	12	14	16
Front Waist Length	16⅝	17	17⅜	17¾	18⅛	18½
Shoulder to Bust	9⅞	10⅛	10⅜	10⅝	10⅞	11⅛
Shoulder Length	4⅝	4¾	4⅞	5	5⅛	5¼
Back Width	13¾	14	14¼	14⅝	15⅛	15⅝
Arm Length	22¾	23	23¼	23½	23¾	24
Shoulder to Elbow	13½	13⅝	13¾	13⅞	14	14⅛

Centimeters

Size	6	8	10	12	14	16
Front Waist Length	42.3	43.3	44	45	46	47
Shoulder to Bust	25	25.5	26.3	27	27.5	28.3
Shoulder Length	11.7	12	12.3	12.7	13	13.3
Back Width	35	35.5	36	37	38.4	39.7
Arm Length	57.7	58.3	59	59.7	60.3	61
Shoulder to Elbow	34.3	34.5	35	35.3	35.5	35.7

Measure—compare—adjust

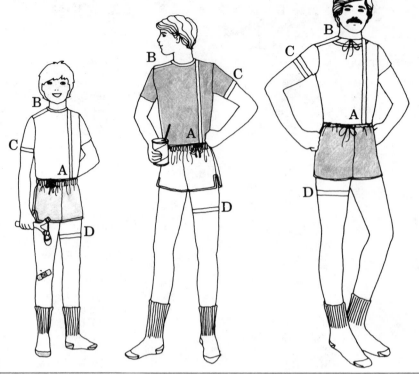

step 1 measure up— males

Fill in the top part of the chart with the measurements you took on page 16 to select your pattern size. Next, take the other measurements described on the chart; the figures opposite show you where to measure. Enter your measurements in the spaces provided. Then, turn to the chart on page 56 to compare the pattern measurements to your own.

personal body measurements

Figure Type _____

Date _____

Pattern Size for Shirts _____

Coats, Jackets _____ Pants, Shorts _____

Suits, Wardrobe Patterns _____

Height	Neckband**	Neck	Chest	Waist	Hips or Seat

Front Waist Length (A) From shoulder at neck base to waist		**Arm Length (G)** From shoulder point to wristbone over slightly bent elbow	
Shoulder Length (B) From base of neck to shoulder point		**Crotch Depth (H)** From side waist to chair (sit on a flat chair and use a ruler)	
Upper Arm (C) Around arm at fullest part between shoulder and elbow		**Crotch Length (I)** From center back waist between the legs to center front waist	
Thigh (D) Around upper leg at fullest part		**Pants Side Length (J)** From side waist to desired pants length	
Back Waist Length (E) From prominent bone at back of neck to waist		**Shirt Sleeve Size**** From prominent bone at back of neck along shoulder, over slightly bent elbow, down to wristbone	
Back Width* (F) Across mid-back		* 6″ (15 cm) below base of neck on Men 4½″ (11.5 cm) below on Teen-Boys 4″ (10 cm) below on Boys ** a ready-to-wear measurement used for reference	

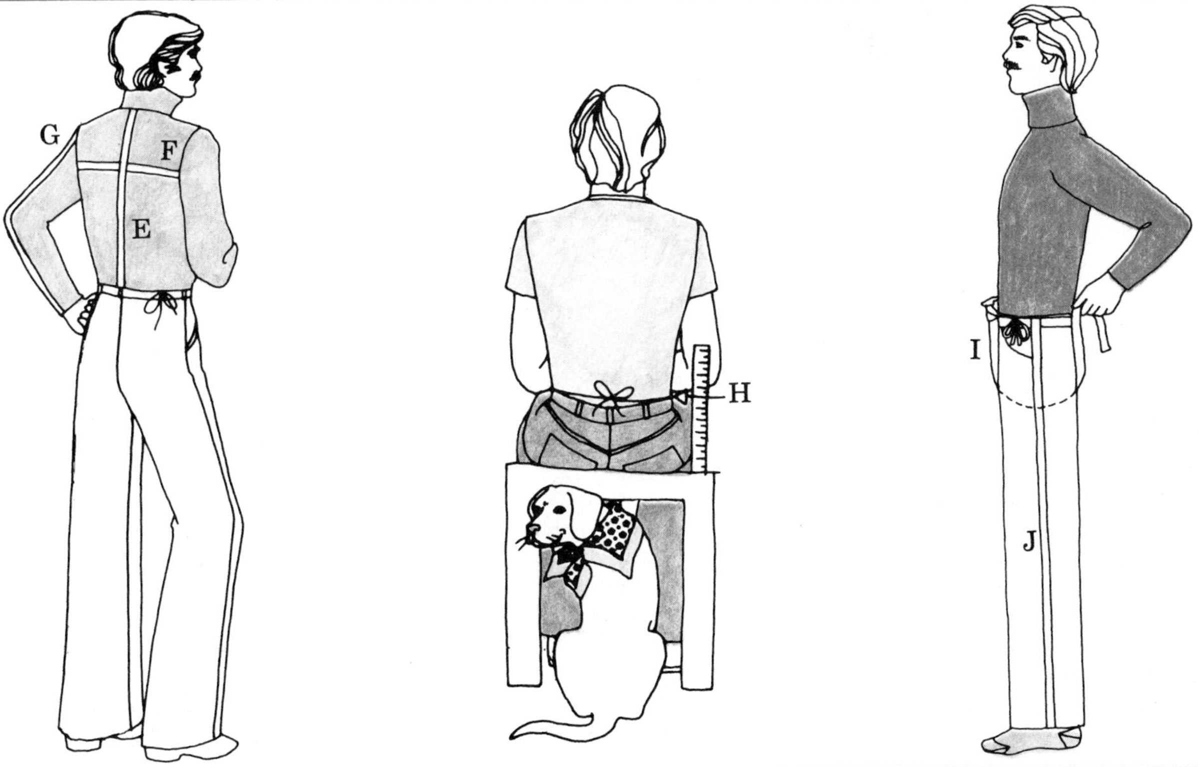

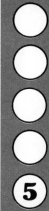

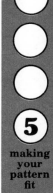

pattern body measurements—males

	Inches					Centimeters			
Boy	**7**	**8**	**10**	**12**	**Size**	**7**	**8**	**10**	**12**
	11⅜	11¾	12½	13¼	Back Waist Length	29	30	31.7	33.5
	12⅜	12¾	13½	14¼	Front Waist Length	31.3	32.3	34.3	36
	4	4⅛	4¼	4½	Shoulder Length	10.3	10.5	10.7	11.5
	11½	11¾	12⅛	12¾	Back Width	29.3	30	30.7	32.3
	16¼	17	18½	20	Arm Length	41.3	43.3	47	50.7
	22⅜	23¼	25	26¾	Shirt Sleeve Size*	57	59	64	68
Teen-Boy	**14**	**16**	**18**	**20**	**Size**	**14**	**16**	**18**	**20**
	14	14¾	15½	16¼	Back Waist Length	35.5	37.5	39.3	41.3
	14⅝	15⅜	16⅛	16⅞	Front Waist Length	37	39	41	43
	4¾	5	5¼	5½	Shoulder Length	12	12.7	13.3	14
	13⅞	14½	15⅛	15¾	Back Width	35.3	36.7	38.4	40
	21⅞	22½	23⅛	23¾	Arm Length	55.5	57	58.7	60.3
	29	30	31	32	Shirt Sleeve Size*	74	76	79	81

		Inches											
Man	**Size**	**34**	**36**	**38**	**40**	**42**	**44**	**46**	**48**	**50**	**52**	**54**	**56**
	Back Waist Length	17½	17¾	18	18¼	18½	18¾	19	19¼	19½	19¾	20	20¼
	Front Waist Length	17¾	18	18¼	18½	18¾	19	19¼	19½	19¾	20	20¼	20½
	Shoulder Length	6⅛	6¼	6⅜	6½	6⅝	6¾	6⅞	7	7⅛	7¼	7⅜	7½
	Back Width	16	16½	17	17½	18	18½	19	19½	20	20½	21	21½
	Arm Length	23⅝	23⅞	24⅛	24⅜	24⅝	24⅞	25⅛	25⅜	25⅝	25⅞	26⅛	26⅜
	Shirt Sleeve Size*	32	32	33	33	34	34	35	35	36	36	37	37
		Centimeters											
Man	**Size**	**34**	**36**	**38**	**40**	**42**	**44**	**46**	**48**	**50**	**52**	**54**	**56**
	Back Waist Length	44.5	45	45.7	46.3	47	47.5	48.3	49	49.5	50.3	50.7	51.3
	Front Waist Length	45	45.7	46.3	47	47.5	48.3	49	49.5	50.3	50.7	51.3	52
	Shoulder Length	15.5	15.7	16	16.5	16.7	17	17.5	17.7	18	18.5	18.7	19
	Back Width	40.7	42	43.3	44.5	45.7	47	48.3	49.5	50.7	52	53.3	54.5
	Arm Length	60	60.7	61.3	62	62.5	63.3	63.7	64.3	65	65.7	66.3	67
	Shirt Sleeve Size*	81	81	84	84	87	87	89	89	91	91	94	94

* a ready-to-wear measurement used for reference

Measure—compare—adjust

step 1
measure up—
children

Find the measurements you took on page 18 to select the right pattern size and enter them on the top part of the chart below. Next, measure the child as directed on the chart. The figures opposite show you how to measure. Write those numbers in the spaces provided. Then, turn to page 56 for the next step.

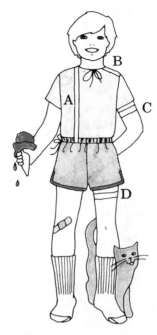

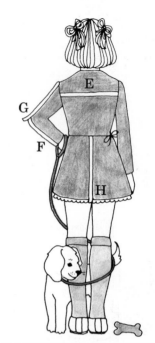

personal body measurements

Date _____

Figure Type _____

Pattern Size _____

Height	Chest	Waist	Hips or Seat	Back Waist Length

Front Waist Length (A) From neck base over chest to waistline			**Shoulder to Elbow (G)** From shoulder point to middle of slightly bent elbow	
Shoulder Length (B) From base of neck to shoulder point			**Back Skirt Length (girls only) (H)** From center back waist to desired length	
Upper Arm (C) Around arm at fullest part between shoulder and elbow			**Crotch Depth (I)** From side waist to chair (sit on a flat chair and use a ruler)	
Thigh (D) Around upper leg at fullest part			**Crotch Length (J)** From center back waistline to center front waistline between the legs	
Back Width* (E) Across mid-back			**Pants Side Length (K)** From waistline to desired length along outside of leg	
Arm Length (F) From shoulder point to wristbone over slightly bent elbow			* 2¾" (7 cm) below neck on Toddlers 3" (7.6 cm) below on Children 4" (10 cm) below on Girls 4½" (11.5 cm) below on Chubbies	

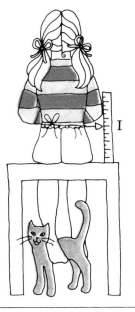

pattern body measurements — children

	Inches						Size	Centimeters					
	1/2	**1**	**2**	**3**	**4**			**1/2**	**1**	**2**	**3**	**4**	
Toddler	8⅜	8⅞	9⅜	9⅞	10⅜		Front Waist Length	21.3	22.5	23.7	25	26.3	
	2⅜	2½	2⅝	2¾	2⅞		Shoulder Length	6	6.3	6.5	7	7.3	
	7¾	8	8¼	8½	8¾		Back Width	19.7	20.3	21	21.5	22.3	
	10	10¾	11½	12¼	13		Arm Length	25.3	27.3	29.3	31	33	
	6½	6⅞	7¼	7⅝	8		Shoulder to Elbow	16.5	17.5	18.5	19.3	20.3	
	2	**3**	**4**	**5**	**6**	**6x**		**2**	**3**	**4**	**5**	**6**	**6x**
Child	9⅜	9⅞	10⅜	10⅞	11⅛	11⅜	Front Waist Length	23.7	25	26.3	27.5	28.3	29
	2⅞	3	3⅛	3¼	3⅜	3½	Shoulder Length	7.3	7.5	8	8.3	8.5	9
	9½	9¾	10	10¼	10½	10⅝	Back Width	24	24.5	25.3	26	26.5	27
	12¾	13½	14¼	15	15¾	16⅛	Arm Length	32.3	34.3	36	38	40	41
	7¾	8⅛	8⅝	9	9½	9⅞	Shoulder to Elbow	19.7	20.7	22	23	24	25
	7	**8**	**10**	**12**	**14**			**7**	**8**	**10**	**12**	**14**	
Girl	12⅜	13	13⅞	14¾	15⅝		Front Waist Length	31.3	33	35.3	37.5	39.7	
	6¾	6⅞	7¼	7⅝	8		Shoulder to Chest	17	17.5	18.5	19.3	20.3	
	3⅝	3¾	4	4¼	4⅜		Shoulder Length	9.3	9.5	10.3	10.7	11	
	11¾	12	12½	13	13½		Back Width	30	30.5	31.7	33	34.3	
	17½	18¼	19¾	21¼	22		Arm Length	44.5	46.3	50.3	54	56	
	10½	10⅞	11⅝	12½	13¼		Shoulder to Elbow	26.5	27.5	29.5	31.7	33.5	
	8½c	**10½c**	**12½c**	**14½c**				**8½c**	**10½c**	**12½c**	**14½c**		
Chubbie	13¼	14⅛	15	15⅞			Front Waist Length	33.5	35.7	38	40.3		
	7¼	7⅝	8	8⅜			Shoulder to Chest	18.5	19.3	20.3	21.3		
	4⅛	4⅜	4⅝	4⅞			Shoulder Length	10.5	11	11.7	12.3		
	12½	13	13½	14			Back Width	31.7	33	34.3	35.5		
	19	20½	22	22¾			Arm Length	48.3	52	56	57.7		
	10¾	11½	12¼	13			Shoulder to Elbow	27.3	29.3	31	33		

Measure —compare —adjust

Pattern Adjustment Chart

| | Body Measurements | | Adjustments |
	Yours	Pattern	(+ or −)
Length & Width			
1. Front Waist Length			
2. Shoulder to Bust (females only)			
3. Back Waist Length			
4. Shoulder Length			
5. Back Width			
6. Arm Length			
7. Shoulder to Elbow (females only)			
Circumference			
8. Bust/Chest			
9. Waist			
10. Hips			
11. Upper Arm (for sleeve width)		*	
12. Neck (males only)			
	Garment Measurement		
Finished Length		(see envelope back)	
13. Back Skirt Length (females only)			

*Measure pattern and subtract 2-2½″ (5-6.3 cm) for plain sleeves

step 2 compare

Now that you know your body measurements, you can see how they compare with the pattern body measurements.

First, write down your body measurements. Then, find the pattern body measurements for your figure type and size on pages 14 and 51 for Females, pages 17 and 53 for Males and pages 19 and 55 for Children. Fill them in on the chart. Note that Back Skirt Length is not given because this measurement varies according to the style. You'll find this on the back of your pattern envelope.
Now, compare the **Yours** and **Pattern** columns and write the difference—plus or minus—in the **Adjustments** column.

You'll need to adjust your pattern if there are any differences in length and width or any greater than 1″ (2.5cm) in circumference. For closely-fitted styles, you may also wish to make smaller circumference adjustments, but that's a matter of choice.

NOTE: You'll find a special Pants Adjustment Chart on page 72.

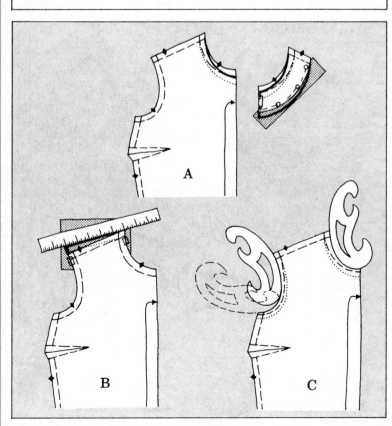

step 3 adjust

Adjustments are easier and turn out better if you remember these guidelines:
• Follow the number order of the chart when making more than one simple adjustment. For special adjustments, work from the top down: neck, shoulders, chest, bust, back, armhole, sleeve, hip, abdomen, derrière.
• If you adjust one pattern piece, you may have to make a corresponding change on a piece that will be stitched to that one. For example, if you adjust a neckline, trace the changes onto the facing to match (A).
• If adjustments distort cutting lines, correct them with a ruler for straight lines (B) or a French curve (C) or free-hand drawing for curves. Taper new lines gradually into the original ones on the pattern piece.
• Afterwards, check corrected seamlines on adjoining pattern pieces to see that all symbols or notches match up and that the pattern piece lies flat.

Simple pattern adjustments

For these basically easy changes — length, width and circumference — find out how much to adjust your pattern from the chart opposite.

Length
Special lines printed on the pattern indicate where to shorten or lengthen. Sometimes, you can also change length at the lower edge.

To shorten: Measure up from the shorten/lengthen line the amount needed and draw a line straight across the pattern at this point. Fold on the printed line, bring the fold to your drawn line, and pin or tape the fold in place. Connect cutting lines affected. To shorten at the lower edge, measure and mark the change; then cut excess away.

To lengthen: Cut pattern apart on the shorten/lengthen line, place paper underneath, and spread the pieces apart evenly the needed amount. Pin or tape in place. Connect the cutting lines.

To lengthen at a lower edge, place paper underneath, extend cutting lines evenly and redraw the bottom edge.

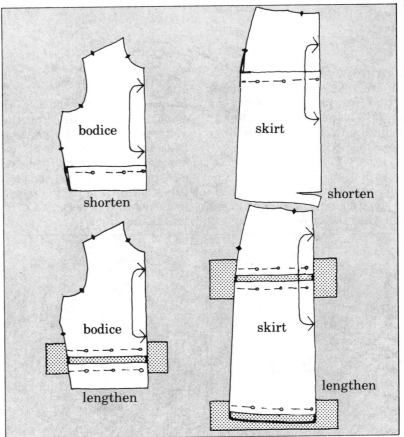

Width
When you're adding to the pattern, you may need to pin or tape extra paper underneath the pieces.

Shoulder length: To adjust up to ¼″ (6 mm), mark the amount inside (to shorten) or outside (to lengthen) the shoulder seam at the armhole on front *and* back patterns. Draw a new cutting line, tapering to the original line at the armhole notch. For adjustments greater than ¼″ (6 mm), see pages 60-61.

Back width: To adjust up to 1″ (2.5 cm), mark ½ the amount needed inside (to decrease) or outside (to increase) the armhole cutting line above the notch on the back pattern only. Draw a new cutting line from the mark, tapering back to the shoulder and underarm. For adjustments greater than 1″ (2.5 cm), see pages 66-67.

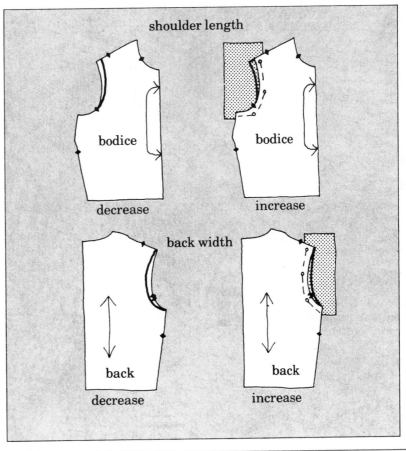

Simple pattern adjustments

Circumference

For circumference adjustments up to 2″ (5 cm), add or subtract at side seams — usually ¼ of the total amount at each side seam allowance, front and back. Because you'll need to do fewer cutting line corrections, it's easier to use the slash-and-spread (or lap) method for some changes. The adjustments below are shown on

Sleeve width: To adjust ½″ (1.3 cm) or less, draw a line from the dot at the sleeve cap to the wrist, parallel to the grainline. Cut pattern apart on this line. Lap (to decrease) or spread (to increase) the cut edges, pinning or taping paper underneath if necessary. Correct the cutting lines.

Hip: To adjust up to 2″ (5 cm), add or subtract ¼ the total amount needed at the side seams, adding paper to the pattern edges if needed. To correct the cutting line, taper it up to the original line at the waist and extend it straight down to the hem, parallel to the old cutting line.

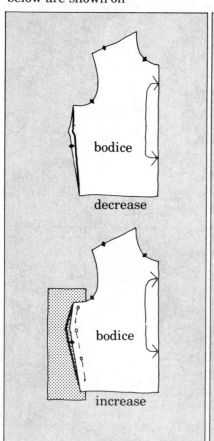

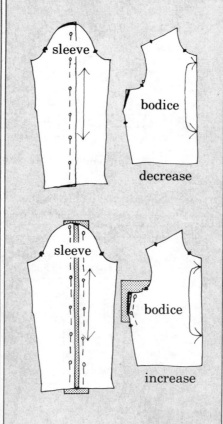

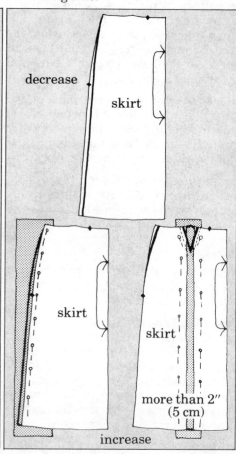

the *front* section only, but you should make the same adjustment on the *back*, too.

Bust: To adjust up to 1″ (2.5 cm), mark ¼ of the total amount needed at the bustline inside (to decrease) or outside (to increase) the side seam. Add paper to the pattern edge if necessary and correct the cutting lines. To adjust more than 1″ (2.5 cm), see page 65 for bust cup adjustments.

Adjust bodice side seams at the underarm to match by subtracting or adding ½ of the total amount changed, tapering to the original cutting line. Also, move armhole notches up (if decreasing) or down (if increasing) by ½ the total amount adjusted. To adjust more than ½″ (1.3 cm), see page 69.

To increase more than 2″ (5 cm), draw a vertical line through the dart, (or through the middle of the pattern if there is no dart), parallel to the grainline, from waist to hem. Cut the pattern on this line. Spread ¼ of the amount needed, adding paper underneath. Make the dart wider and taper side seams up to the waist, removing the extra width added at the waist. Correct the cutting lines.

Waist: To adjust up to 2″ (5 cm), add or subtract ¼ of the total amount at the side waist. Add paper to the pattern edge if needed, and taper cutting lines back to hip.

To adjust more than 2″ (5 cm) on a pattern with waistline darts, distribute the total amount more evenly by changing the waistline darts as well as the side seams. Make darts narrower to add to the waist, and wider to subtract. To change darts, divide the change in half and fix both sides of dart. If you need to adjust more than 2″ (5 cm) and your pattern has no darts, buy the next larger or smaller size pattern when possible. Decrease waistband by folding out ½ of the amount needed at each side marking. Increase by slashing and spreading the waistband ½ the amount needed at each side marking, adding paper underneath. Make new side markings in the center of each tuck or spread. Correct cutting lines.

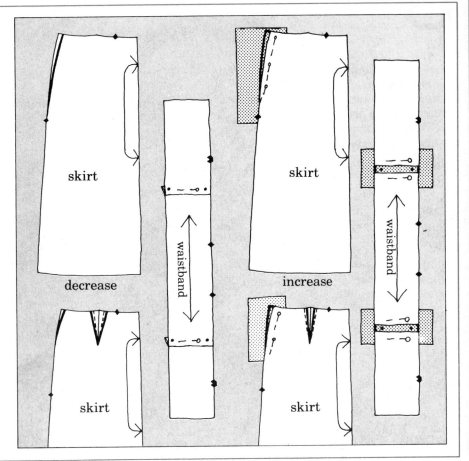

Princess styles: Because there are six seams (excluding the center back seam), circumference changes must be divided equally among all of them. First, divide the total change needed by 6 to get the amount each seam will be changed. Then divide that number by 2 for the amount you should add or subtract at each seam allowance.

To correct the cutting line, taper it up to the original line at the waist and extend it straight down to the hem, parallel to the old cutting line.

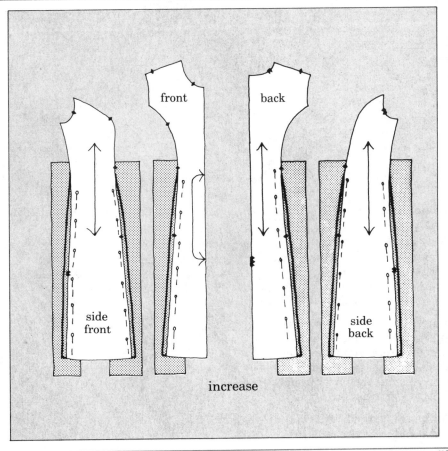

Once you've done the simple adjustments, the pattern will fit your measurements. You can solve specific figure problems, such as one high hip or sloping shoulders, with some special adjustments.

Narrow or Broad

The adjustment method given here applies when the change required is ¼″ (6 mm) or more. To adjust less, see page 57.

For raglan sleeve styles: Draw a horizontal line across the sleeve pattern piece so the line intersects the dart halfway. Cut the pattern apart on this line.

For kimono sleeve styles:

On front and back pattern pieces, draw a diagonal line from the midpoint of the shoulder to the underarm curve. Cut the pattern apart on this line. Lap (to decrease) or spread (to increase) the cut edges, tapering to nothing at

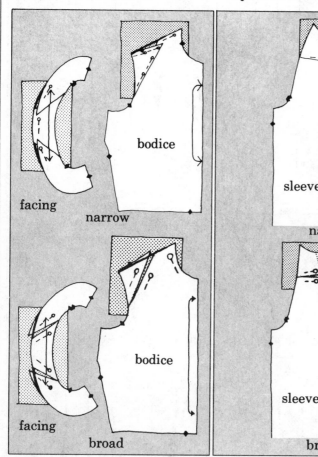

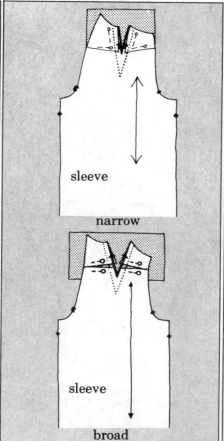

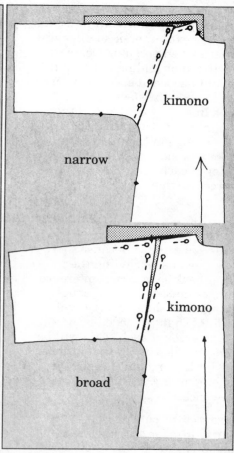

For set-in sleeves and sleeveless styles: Draw a diagonal line from the midpoint of the shoulder seam to the cutting line above the armhole notch, and cut the pattern apart on this line.

Lap (to decrease) or spread (to increase) cut edges the needed amount, tapering to nothing at the armhole seamlines. If necessary, pin or tape paper underneath. Correct the cutting lines.

Make this adjustment on front, back and armhole facing pieces.

Lap (to decrease) or spread (to increase) the pattern apart, tapering both kinds of adjustments to nothing at the armhole seamlines. Pin or tape paper underneath to anchor your adjustment. Correct the dart cutting lines and stitching lines.

the underarm seamline. Pin or tape paper underneath to secure the adjustment. Correct the shoulder cutting line.

Sloping or Square

To see if your shoulder slope differs from the pattern, pin the pattern together and try it on.

Ask a friend to re-pin the shoulder seam (or the dart on some raglan styles) at a slant that fits you better; this will mark the adjustment you should make.

For raglan sleeve styles: If you have sloping shoulders, you'll have to lengthen the dart as much as necessary on the sleeve pattern piece. If there's no dart, take away from sleeve at the cutting line above the notch and taper to neck and underarm cutting lines.

For kimono sleeve styles: Draw a line from the midpoint of the shoulder to the underarm curve. Cut the pattern on this line.

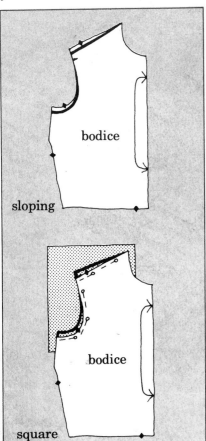

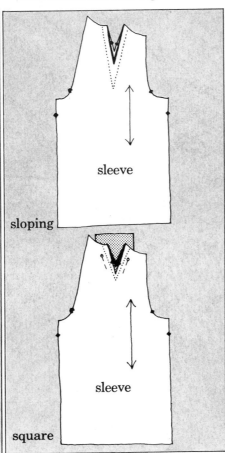

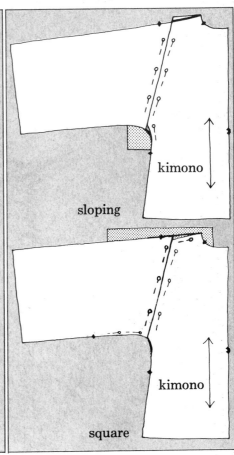

For sleeveless or set-in sleeve styles: Draw a new cutting line as follows: begin ⅝″ (1.5 cm) above the pin marking at the shoulder end and taper to the original line at the neck edge. If you have sloping shoulders, lower the underarm by the amount you lowered the cutting line at the shoulder end. For square shoulders, raise the underarm by the amount you raised the cutting line. Adjust *both* front and back pieces and any armhole facings.

If your shoulders are square, pin or tape paper underneath the dart area and shorten the dart. If there's no dart, add to the sleeve cutting lines above the notch and taper to the neck and underarm cutting lines.

Pin or tape the bodice to paper, and shift the sleeve portion down for sloping shoulders and up for square shoulders. Keep the cut edges even and pin or tape the sleeve portion in place. Correct the cutting lines at shoulders and underarm curves as shown. Adjust *both* back and front pattern pieces.

Necklines

Tight or Large

To see if the pattern neckline fits, pin the shoulder seams together and try the pattern on. Ask a friend to help by clipping into the neckline seam allowance until it lies flat and by pin-marking a new seamline.

For a tight neckline: Pin-mark a new, lower seamline on front *and* back pattern pieces and any

For a large neckline: Pin-mark new neck seamline above the original one on front *and* back pattern pieces *and* on any facings, adding paper underneath if needed. Then draw a new cutting line ⅝″ (1.5 cm) above the new seamline.

For a gaping neckline: See how much to adjust by pinning pattern shoulder seams and side seams together and trying the pattern on. Pinch out the excess.

On the pattern front, draw a horizontal line from middle of neckline to the armhole. Cut on this line.

Lap (to decrease) the needed amount at the neckline, tapering to nothing at the armhole. Pin or tape paper underneath and correct the cutting line. Adjust the neckline facing to match.

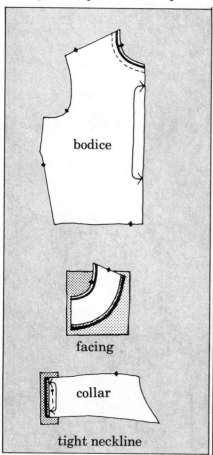

tight neckline

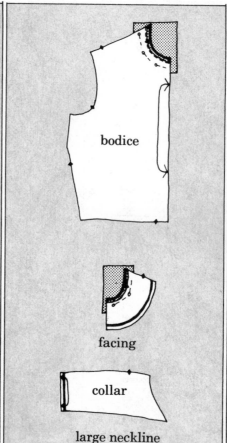

large neckline

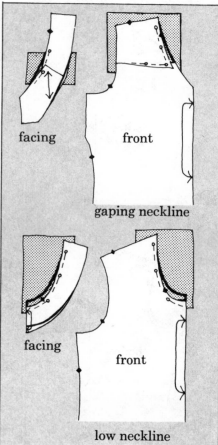

gaping neckline

low neckline

neckline facings. Then draw a new cutting line ⅝″ (1.5 cm) above the new seamline.

The new seamline will have a larger circumference than the original one, so you must also adjust any collar pattern pieces. Measure both the old and new neck seamlines on front and back patterns; subtract to find the difference. Add ½ this amount to the center back of the collar piece.

You must also adjust any collar pattern piece, since the new neck seamline will have a smaller circumference than the old one. Measure the old and new seamlines on front and back; subtract to find the difference. Remove ½ this amount from the collar center back.

For a low neckline: To see how much to raise the neckline, first tape paper under the pattern. Then pin shoulder and side seams together and try it on.

Raise the neck cutting line the desired amount at center front, tapering it into the original one at the shoulder.

Adjust the neckline facing to match the new neckline.

Chest

Hollow or Pigeon Chest

To see how much to adjust, pin the pattern together at the shoulder and side seams and try it on. Clip neck seam allowance. For hollow chest, pinch out the excess length above the bustline where the pattern buckles; this is the amount to be removed. For pigeon chest, slash and pin the pattern to paper as described below; then try it on to see how much length to add.

For raglan sleeve styles: Draw a diagonal line from a point on the center front line at the chest level to midpoint of the raglan seam. Cut pattern apart on this line.

Place paper under the pattern. Lap (to decrease) or spread (to increase) the pattern the amount

For kimono sleeve styles: Draw a diagonal line from a point on the center front line at the chest level to the approximate end of the shoulder.

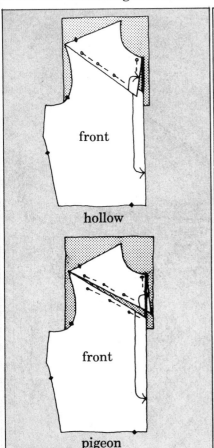

hollow

front

pigeon

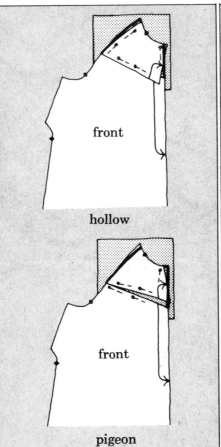

front

hollow

front

pigeon

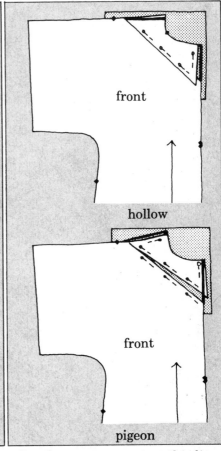

front

hollow

front

pigeon

For sleeveless and set-in sleeve styles: Draw a diagonal line beginning at the point where the armhole and the shoulder seams meet and ending on the center front line at the chest level. Cut the pattern apart on this line.

Place paper under the pattern. Lap (to decrease) or spread (to increase) the pattern the amount needed at center front, tapering to nothing at the shoulder seamline. Then pin or tape the cut edges in place. Correct center front line.

needed at center front, tapering to nothing at the raglan seamline. Pin or tape cut edges in place.

Redraw the center front cutting line and, if necessary, the raglan cutting line to maintain original neckline measurement.

Cut the pattern apart on this line. Place paper under the pattern. Lap (to decrease) or spread (to increase) the pattern the amount needed at center front, tapering to nothing at the shoulder seamline. Pin or tape the cut edges in place.

Redraw the center front cutting line and, if necessary, the shoulder cutting line to maintain original neckline measurement.

Bust

High or Low Bust

These pattern changes are made on the *front* pieces only. Check your Pattern Adjustment Chart on page 56 for the amount of shoulder-to-bust adjustment you'll need to make.

Cut out the bust box and move it up (for high bust) or down (for low bust) the needed amount. Pin or tape paper underneath and correct the cutting lines.

For princess styles: The first step will be to raise or lower the bust curve on the front and side front sections. This will change the overall pattern length, so you must restore the original length.

For high bust, raise the curve by lapping the pieces the needed amount; pin. To restore the original length, cut the pattern on the lengthen/shorten lines; place paper underneath and spread the pattern the same amount the bust curve was raised; pin it in place.

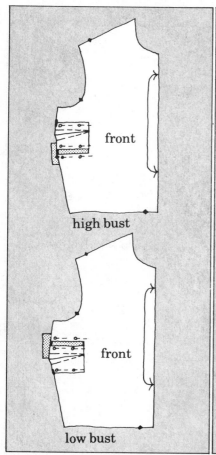

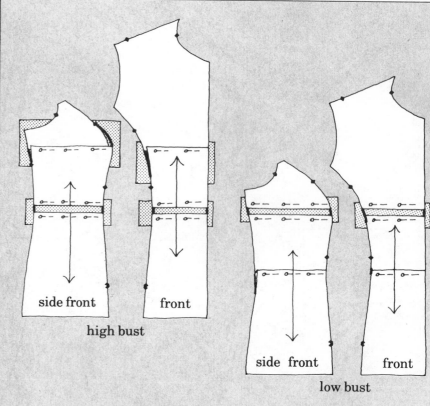

For patterns with a bust dart: Some Simplicity patterns have a printed box around the bust dart. If yours doesn't, make one by drawing lines above and below the dart, perpendicular to the center front and as long as the dart. Connect these two lines through the dart point.

On the side front, draw a line across the pattern at the widest part of the bust curve. Also draw a line at the corresponding point on the front pattern piece. Cut the patterns apart on these lines. Place paper under the patterns.

For low bust, lower the curve by spreading the pattern apart the needed amount; pin to paper. Restore the original length by making a tuck on the lengthen/shorten line the same amount the curve was lowered.

Redraw all affected cutting lines.

Bust Cup

If you are not a B cup size, you may want to adjust the pattern to fit your cup size. Check your Pattern Adjustment Chart on page 56 for the amount to adjust the front waist length and bust circumference.

For patterns with a bust dart:

If there is no bustline printed on the pattern, draw one. Locate the bustline by subtracting pattern measurement #2 from #1 on the

Adjust the front waist length along the bustline slash. Then adjust the bust circumference ½ the amount needed along the vertical slash. Lap (to decrease) or spread (to increase) the edges, tapering to nothing at all seamlines. Pin or tape paper underneath if necessary.

Redraw the dart wider or narrower to restore the original side seam length.

For princess styles: Make changes on front and side front patterns. Adjust front waist length by slashing and spreading (for larger cup) or lapping (for small cup) at the bust curve, as shown on page 64. At the lengthen/shorten line, restore overall length by slashing and lapping (for larger cup) or spread-

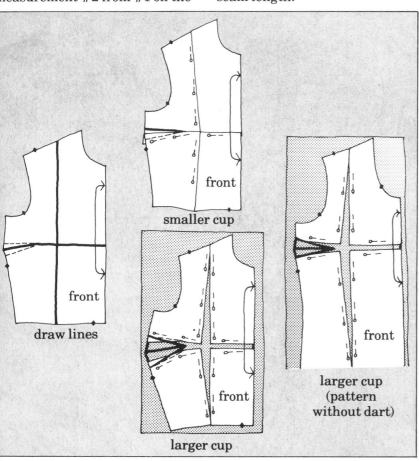

draw lines

front

smaller cup

front

larger cup

front

larger cup
(pattern
without dart)

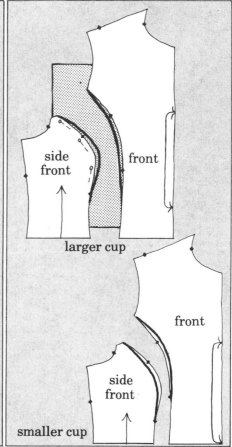

side
front

front

larger cup

side
front

front

smaller cup

Pattern Adjustment Chart (page 56); measure up this distance from the pattern waistline. At this point, draw a horizontal line across the pattern from center front to dart point; continue through dart center to side cutting line. Next, draw a vertical line from the shoulder midpoint to the waist (or hem). On raglan styles, begin this line 1" (2.5 cm) from the end of the dart. Cut the pattern apart on these lines.

On patterns without bust darts: Decrease cup size by making a bust circumference adjustment as shown on page 58. For a larger cup, adjust the same as for patterns with bust darts, above, but also create a dart wide enough to maintain the original side seam length. The dart should end ½" (1.3 cm) from your bust point; to find your bust point, hold the pattern up to your body.

ing (for smaller cup) the same amount as the bust curve.

Then, adjust bust circumference by drawing a new cutting line at the bust curve to add or subtract ¼ the total amount needed at each seam allowance. Taper the new curves into the original cutting lines at armhole and waist.

 # **B**ack

Broad or Narrow

If your Pattern Adjustment Chart (page 56) shows you need to change the back width less than 1″ (2.5 cm), see page 57. Adjust the back pattern piece for 1″ (2.5 cm) or more as follows.

For sleeveless or set-in sleeve styles: Draw a vertical line starting at the shoulder 2″ (5 cm) from the armhole and ending 1″ (2.5 cm) below the underarm. Then draw a horizontal line from the

For princess styles: Line up the armhole edges of the back and side back patterns as shown.

To increase back width, pin or tape paper under the patterns. Add ½ the needed amount outside the cutting line at the armhole notch. Draw a new cutting line from this point, tapering it into the original cutting line at the shoulder and extending it past the

Round or Erect

Try the pattern on to see how much length to add or subtract across the upper part of the back pattern piece. Have a friend slash and spread the pattern as described below or pinch out the excess. Adjust any neck facings to match the new neckline.

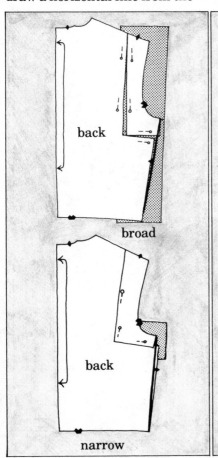

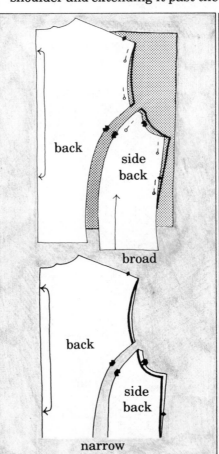

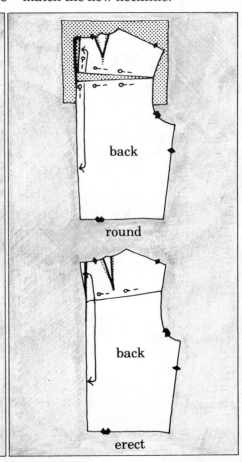

side seam to meet the vertical line. Cut pattern apart on these lines. At the armhole notch level, spread or lap the vertical cut edges ½ the total needed. Pin or tape paper under pattern and correct the side cutting line.

For raglan styles: Adjust same as above, beginning the vertical line above the midpoint of the raglan seam.

For kimono styles: Adjust same as above, beginning near the end of the shoulder.

side seam the same amount added at the armhole notch. Redraw the side cutting line.

To decrease, take ½ the needed amount away from the cutting line at the armhole notch. Draw a new cutting line, tapering it into the original one at the shoulder and stopping short of the side seam the same amount taken away at the armhole notch. Redraw the side cutting line.

For sleeveless or set-in sleeve styles: Draw a line from center back to the middle of the armhole and cut the pattern apart on this line. Spread (to increase) or lap (to decrease) the cut edges at center back, adding paper underneath if needed. Correct the center back cutting line. Restore the original neckline size as follows. Make any darts shorter and wider (for round back) or longer and narrower (for erect back).

If there is no dart, lower (for round back), or raise (for erect back), the shoulder cutting line at the neck edge the amount you changed the neck at center back, tapering the line to the original one at the end of the shoulder.

Spread the back pattern evenly the needed amount, adding paper underneath. Spread the sleeve at the back raglan edge, tapering to the dart (a small pleat may form at the dart). Pin or tape in place. Correct cutting lines.

For kimono sleeve styles:
Draw a vertical line from the end of the shoulder part-way down the back. Then draw a horizontal line below the neckline at mid-back to meet the first line. Cut the pattern apart on these lines.

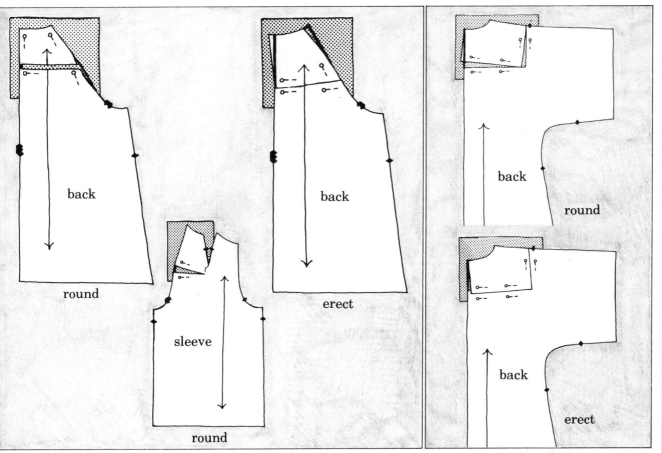

For raglan sleeve styles: Draw a line on the back pattern piece from the center back to the middle of the raglan seam. Cut the pattern on this line. For round back, also draw a line on the back of the sleeve from the middle of the raglan seam to just below the dart.

For erect back, lap the cut edges at center back only, tapering to nothing at the raglan seamline. Correct the center back line. Add to the raglan seam neck edge the amount removed from center back to maintain the original neckline size. Straighten the grainline.

Place paper under the pattern and spread (to increase) or lap (to decrease) the amount needed at center back, tapering to nothing at the shoulder seamline; pin or tape pattern in place.

Redraw the cutting lines.

Tight or Gaping Armholes

To see how much to adjust, pin the pattern together at the shoulder seam and the side seam, leaving several inches unpinned at the underarm. Clip into the armhole

For sleeveless or set-in sleeve styles: Lower or raise the underarm cutting line the needed amount, tapering to nothing at the shoulder. When raising, add paper underneath and correct the side cutting line. Adjust the facing and sleeve armholes to correspond; restore facings to their original width.

Sleeve Cap Ease

You'll need to reduce the ease in the sleeve cap when you're using a fabric that can't be steamshrunk—those with permanent-

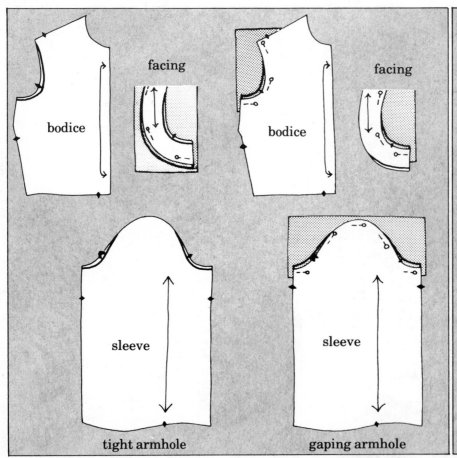

facing

bodice

facing

bodice

sleeve

sleeve

tight armhole

gaping armhole

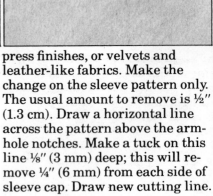

sleeve

reduce ease

seam allowance at the notches so it lies flat; then try on the pattern. Sometimes this can be adjusted at the shoulders; see page 61. Otherwise, mark new underarm cutting line, higher or lower. Make the adjustments above on front and back patterns, plus any armhole facings or sleeves.

For princess styles: Pin the front pattern piece to the side front, and the back to the side back. Then, adjust the same as for sleeveless or set-in sleeve styles.

press finishes, or velvets and leather-like fabrics. Make the change on the sleeve pattern only. The usual amount to remove is ½″ (1.3 cm). Draw a horizontal line across the pattern above the armhole notches. Make a tuck on this line ⅛″ (3 mm) deep; this will remove ¼″ (6 mm) from each side of sleeve cap. Draw new cutting line.

Tight or Loose Sleeves

If your Pattern Adjustment Chart (page 56) shows you must adjust the upper arm circumference ½″ (1.3 cm) or more, use the method below. To adjust less, see page 58.

level, tapering to nothing at lower edge. Pin or tape to paper and correct sleeve cap cutting line.

For loose sleeve, lap the cut edges the amount needed at the underarm level; keep cut edges parallel. Pin correction in place and redraw the cutting lines at sleeve cap and lower edge.

For raglan sleeve styles: Draw a vertical line on the sleeve from the dart point (or mid-neck edge, if there is no dart) to the lower edge. Cut the pattern on this line.

Spread (to increase) or lap (to decrease) the needed amount at the underarm level.

For spreading, add paper underneath and taper the adjustment to

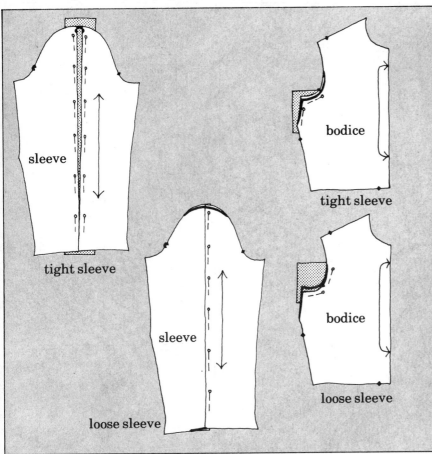

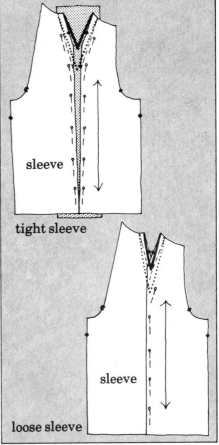

For sleeveless or set-in sleeve styles: Draw a vertical line on the sleeve pattern from the dot at the top to the lower edge. Cut the pattern on this line. For tight sleeve, spread cut edges the amount needed at the underarm

On front and back patterns, lower or raise the underarm curve ½ the amount of the sleeve adjustment. Lower or raise the armhole notches the same amount. Correct the side cutting lines.

nothing at the lower edge. If lapping, keep cut edges parallel. Pin or tape the correction in place. Correct the dart stitching lines, maintaining the original dart length. If your pattern has no dart, you must restore the original neckline size by adjusting the armhole seams at the neck edge: to each seam, subtract or add ½ the amount of the spread or lap, tapering to the original cutting line above the notch.

Protruding Hipbones

To see where to adjust a skirt pattern, try it on and check hipbone locations (left and right sides may not be identical).

On pattern front, move the dart toward the hipbone and widen it to add needed fullness or shaping over the hipbones.

Draw a line across the pattern above the hipline. Cut front pattern on the line. Add paper underneath and spread slash the needed amount, tapering to nothing at center front. Pin or tape to paper. Correct the center front line. Add the amount removed from the waist at the front to the side seam, tapering to the original cutting line. Adjust the back the

Draw a vertical line on the pattern front through center of dart, from waist to hem. Draw a horizontal line across the pattern midway between waist and hipline. Cut the pattern on both lines.

Pinning or taping paper underneath, spread the horizontal cut the needed amount at center front, tapering to the side. Spread the

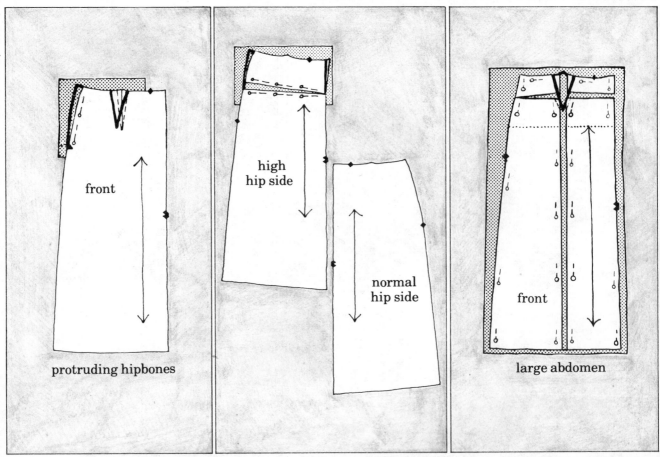

front

protruding hipbones

high
hip side

normal
hip side

front

large abdomen

Pin or tape paper under pattern. To maintain waist measurement, add on at side waistline the same amount you added to the dart. Taper line back to hip.

One High Hip

To see how much to adjust a skirt, tie a string around your waist; measure over each hip from string to floor. The difference is the amount you need to adjust. Make duplicates of the front and back patterns; change front *and* back on the high-hip side as follows.

same way. When cutting out your fabric, remember to cut the patterns and duplicates from a single fabric layer.

Large Abdomen

To see how much to adjust, slash the pattern front as follows. Pin it to paper and try it on. Have a friend spread the slash.

vertical cut the amount needed, keeping the cut edges parallel. Correct cutting lines and the dart stitching lines.

For a one-piece dress, add paper underneath the front pattern. Add ½ the amount needed between waist and hipline at center front and side seams. Correct the grainline, so it's parallel to the new center front seam. If there's no center front seam, add the amount to each side. Draw new cutting lines.

Swayback/Derrière

Swayback

To see how much excess length to remove from the center back, try on the pattern. Have a friend fold or pinch out the excess where the pattern buckles below the waist.

Round or Flat Derrière

To see how much to adjust for round derrière, slash the skirt back pattern as described below and pin it to paper; try it on, having a friend spread it as much as necessary. For flat derrière, try on the pattern and have a friend pin vertical and horizontal folds to make the pattern flat in back.

Spread (to increase), adding paper underneath, or lap (to decrease), the horizontal cut edges the needed amount at center back, tapering to nothing at the side edge. Spread or lap the vertical cut edges evenly the amount needed. Correct the cutting lines.

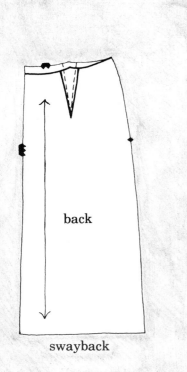

swayback

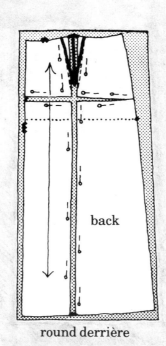

round derrière

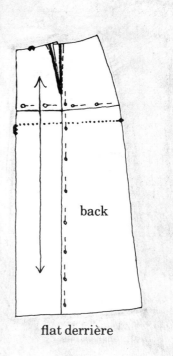

flat derrière

On the skirt back, lower the waistline the amount needed at center back, tapering the new cutting line into the original at the side. This adjustment lengthens the waistline seam; restore the original size by widening the dart.

On the back pattern, draw a horizontal line between waist and hipline, from center back to side edge. Draw a vertical line parallel to the grainline, through center of dart, from waist to hem. Cut the pattern on these lines.

Make the dart wider or narrower to maintain the original waist size. Adjust the dart length.

Pants adjustments

Pants patterns are a breeze to fit, thanks to our simple 3-step method—1. Measure 2. Compare and 3. Adjust.

1. Measure

First, read the Measuring Tips on page 11. Then fill in the six body measurements in the **Yours** column on the chart below. Pages 12-18 and 50-55 show where and how to take body measurements.

Crotch depth: Measure *front* pattern piece from natural waist to crotch line. If a crotch line isn't printed on the front, draw one from the crotch point to the side seam, perpendicular to the grainline.

If the natural waistline is above the pattern waistline seam, as on some trouser styles, first pin the waistband piece to the pants piece, matching seamlines. Then measure from the waistline marking or seamline to the crotch line.

Crotch length: Stand a tape measure or flexible ruler on edge and measure along the center front and center back seams from the natural waist (see crotch depth, left) to the crotch points. Don't include seam allowances. Add front *and* back measurements.

Thigh: Measure front and back pieces at the thigh between the seamlines, the same distance below the waist as you took your body measurement. Add front *and* back measurements.

Pattern Adjustment Chart

	Measurements				Adjustments (+ or −)
	Yours	Plus Ease*	Total	Pattern	
1. Crotch depth		¼ to ½″ (6 mm to 1.3 cm)			
2. Crotch length		up to 1½″ (3.8 cm)			
3. Waist				**	
4. Hips				**	
5. Thighs		2″ (5 cm)			
6. Pants length				***	

*For wovens; for stretchable knits, allow less ease
**See pages 14-19
***See envelope back

front

back

Next, add the minimum wearing ease to the measurements indicated; record these numbers in the **Total** column.

To fill in the **Pattern** column, find the pattern body measurements for waist and hip on pages 14-19. For pants length, use the measurement on the pattern envelope back. Find the remaining pattern measurements as follows.

Some pants styles, such as hiphuggers, don't come all the way up to the natural waistline. Compare the pattern pieces with a regular pants pattern or pair of pants, matching them at the hip. Then, measure your pattern from the point above it where the natural waistline would fall.

2. Compare

After you've filled in the **Pattern** column, compare these measurements with those in the **Total** column. If the total is more than the pattern, you'll need to add to the pattern; if less, you may need to make the pattern smaller.

3. Adjust

Before adjusting, see the guide lines on page 56. Then, make pattern adjustments in the order listed on the chart opposite, since one change may affect another.

Crotch depth: Adjust both front *and* back patterns on the shorten/lengthen line located above the crotch line. Use the general directions on page 57 to shorten or lengthen.

Waist and hips: Adjust the same as for skirts on pages 58 and 59.

Thigh: Adjust the thigh circumference on front *and* back patterns. To increase, pin or tape pattern to paper. Add or subtract ¼ the total needed at thigh level on each leg seam. Draw new cutting lines, tapering up to hip and crotch, extending straight down to lower edge.

Smile or frown: Wrinkles that "smile" in front or back result when pants are too tight in the crotch. If they have wrinkles that "frown," they're too long and loose in the crotch area. First, adjust the pattern for crotch depth and length. If pants still "smile" or "frown," add paper under pattern and redraw the crotch curve.

Straighten and lengthen it for "smile," moving crotch point out and down *slightly.* Also correct leg cutting line, tapering to original.

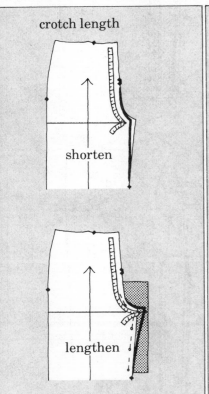

crotch length

shorten

lengthen

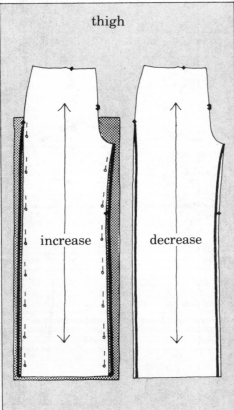

thigh

increase

decrease

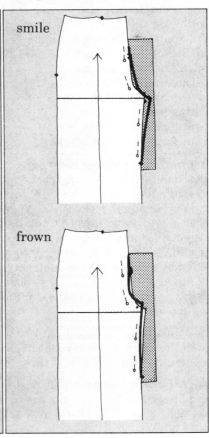

smile

frown

Crotch length: If you adjusted crotch depth, re-measure the pattern to see if the crotch length needs fixing. You can divide the adjustment equally between the front and back, or add more to the back and less to the front, depending on your figure. To adjust the front, measure along the center front seamline, from the waistline to where the amount needed meets the level of the crotch line. To add, pin pattern to paper and extend crotch line. Redraw crotch and leg cutting lines, tapering to original lines. Repeat for back.

Pants side length: Follow the general directions for lengthening or shortening on page 57. Use the adjustment line printed on the front *and* back pants legs.

For "frown," draw a deeper and shorter curve, moving the crotch point in and up *slightly.* Also correct the inner leg seam.

Other adjustments: Adjust for protruding or high hips, large abdomen, swayback, and round or flat derrière the same as for skirts, pages 70-71.

Adjusting men's patterns

The basic techniques for adjusting patterns are the same for men and women. See the Simple Adjustments on pages 57-59 and the Special Adjustments which begin on page 60. In this section, we'll focus on fitting men's jackets and pants patterns.

Jackets

Simple adjustments: To adjust the length, use the shorten/lengthen lines on the pattern. Be sure to adjust:

- all jacket body pattern pieces — front, back and side sections
- all sleeve pattern pieces — upper sleeve and under sleeve
- facing pattern pieces
- lining pattern pieces
- interfacing pattern pieces

After making any length changes, reposition buttonholes and pockets, if necessary, to maintain the right proportions. To adjust jackets with three pieces at waist and hips (A), you'll be changing 4 seams for a total of 8 seam allowances. Divide the total change needed by 8. Then, add or subtract this amount at all side seams. Draw new cutting lines, tapering to the original ones above the waist.

Since you chose the jacket pattern to match the chest measurement in size, you shouldn't have to adjust this area.

Special adjustments: The most common special adjustments are for the shoulders (pages 60-61) and the back (pages 66-67).

To adjust a gaping collar (B), estimate how much to adjust from experience with ready-made jackets. Draw a new foldline on the upper collar pattern ½ the needed amount in from the original line. Decrease under collar at center back the same amount.

On the jacket front pattern, take away ¼ the total needed from the shoulder seam at the neck edge, tapering the new cutting line to the original at the armhole. Adjust the back, front facing and interfacing patterns to match.

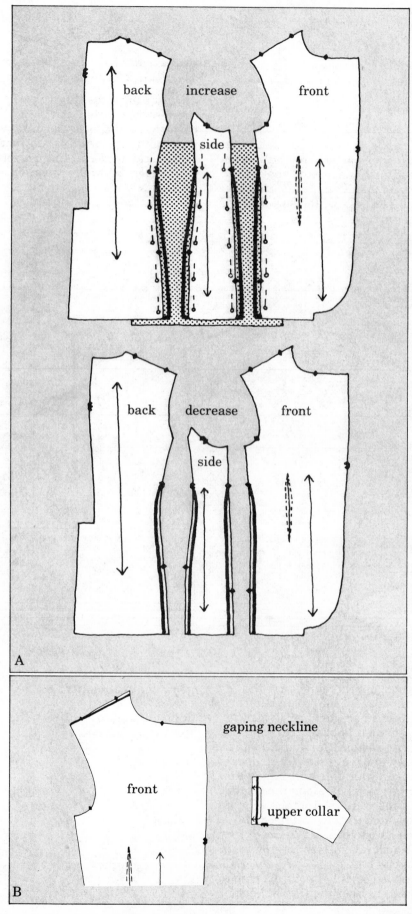

Pants

Fitting men's pants is a lot like fitting women's. You can use the Pants Adjustment Chart on page 72 to decide what pattern changes are needed.

Other pants, like jeans, ride low on the hips, with the top of the waistband 1–2″ (2.5 – 5 cm) below the natural waist; the illustration on the pattern envelope will give you a clue. To see how far down the waistband will be, compare the pattern with a pair of ready-made regular pants *or* compare

Remember, too, to pin any yoke or pocket pieces to the pants pattern before measuring or adjusting (E). To adjust crotch depth, crotch length, hip, thigh width and pants side length, follow the directions on page 73.

making your pattern fit

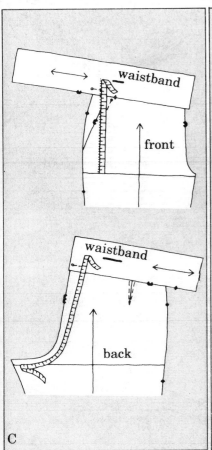

C

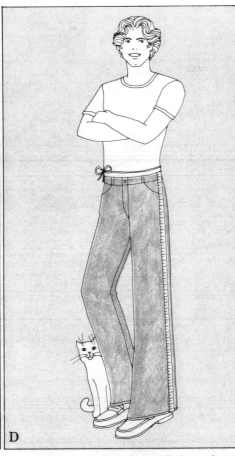

D

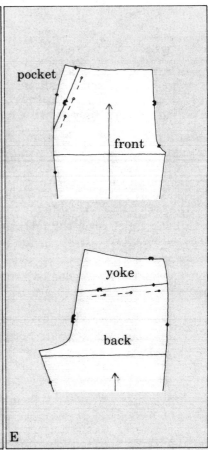

E

Simple adjustments: Measuring and adjusting the pants pattern depends on locating the natural waist properly. On regular men's pants patterns, the top of the waistband rests at the natural waist. To measure crotch depth and length on a regular pattern, pin waistband to pants piece, matching seamlines. Then measure from waistline mark on waistband (C).

the pattern's finished side length (on back of pattern envelope) with the finished side length of a regular pants pattern. Then take the body measurements, starting at that distance below natural waistline (D).

Special adjustments: To adjust men's pants for a round or flat derrière or large abdomen, follow the directions for skirts on pages 70-71. When adjusting for a large abdomen, be sure to change the fly, front pockets and pocket facings, in addition to the front pattern piece.

Adjusting children's patterns

Most children's patterns are loose-fitting styles, so you only have to adjust for length. Do this at the hem if it's fairly straight, or draw your own shorten/lengthen lines perpendicular to the grainline at the locations shown (A); adjust as on page 57.

Chubbie Sizes

If your child takes Chubbie patterns, but the style you like doesn't come in this size range, it will probably fit all right if the style is loosely-fitted.

For a fitted style, buy the size closest to the chest and waist measurements, and adjust the length.

Growth Allowance

There's no need to make a child's clothes too big now so they'll fit next year. A few easy pattern adjustments can provide good fit, plus growing room.

Tucks: If the pattern has a straight hem, add 3″ (7.5 cm) to the hem allowance. Later, baste a 1½″ (3.8 cm) tuck in the hem allowance before turning up the hem; press tuck up. Then, sew the hem as usual. After releasing the tuck for a growth spurt, cover the old hem crease with trim (B).

You can also add a tuck to a dress with a waist seam. Adjust the bodice front and back patterns by extending the waist length 1-3″ (2.5-7.5 cm). Machine-baste tuck on the inside seamline half as wide. Join bodice to the skirt; press tuck up. To release tuck later, remove and restitch lower portion of zipper. Cover fade marks with a sash (B).

Elastic: On dresses, add ½″ (1.3 cm) to side waist of back bodice and skirt sections, tapering to original cutting lines. Sew dress, then sew bias tape casing along back waist seam. Insert elastic cut as long as child's back waistline plus 1″ (2.5 cm); secure ends in side seams. If there's a zipper, cut elastic and tape in half and place ends at center back. Insert zipper (C).

On skirts and pants with waistbands, add ½″ (1.3 cm) to each side of back at waist and waistband. Sew notched edge of waistband to waistline. Use elastic ¼″ (6 mm) narrower than finished band; cut it the length of the child's back waistline. Zigzag elastic to inside of back waistband, stretching it to fit. Complete the waistband (D).

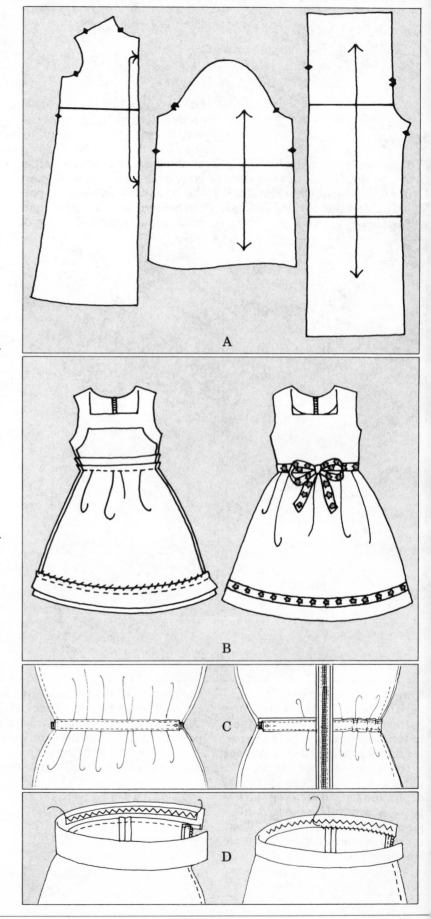

6 layout, cutting and marking

Once you've bought your fabric and notions, you can put them all together and create your very own fashion. These steps ease you right into sewing.

For starters, see if your fabric needs preshrinking or dry cleaning and check to see that the grain is straight. When you lay out the pattern on the fabric, you'll see how the pattern pieces relate to the actual garment. Then mark your fabric, transferring guide lines and symbols which help you match up the pieces to sew.

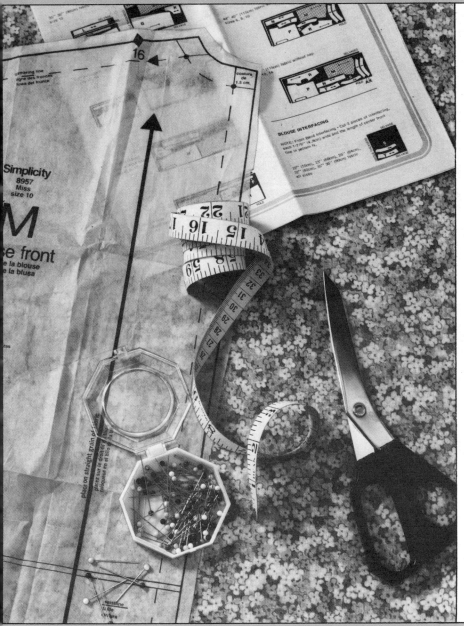

preliminaries

Take the time now to prepare your fabric and pattern. Preshrinking the fabric and straightening the grain and the ends guarantee you a garment that won't shrink or lose its shape later on. Sorting and pressing the pattern pieces simplifies layout and cutting.

Preshrinking the Fabric
If your fabric is not labeled "preshrunk" or "sponged," wash or dry clean it as the manufacturer recommends. It's also a good idea to preshrink zippers and trims along with your fabric. That way, they won't pucker the garment by shrinking later.

Fabric Terms
Get acquainted with some basic fabric terms. Look closely; most fabrics have a *right* and *wrong* side. The finished edges which don't ravel are called *selvages*. The *cut edges* may ravel.

Fabric Grain
Grain refers to direction on fabric, either lengthwise, crosswise or bias (see page 78). The terms that follow all describe grain.

Lengthwise grain: Also called the *straight* grain, this refers to the direction of threads or ribs parallel to the selvages. Garments are laid out along the lengthwise grain because it is the least stretchy and the most stable.

Crosswise grain: This is the direction of the crosswise threads which run across the fabric from selvage to selvage, perpendicular to the lengthwise grain (A). On a knit, it's called the *crosswise course* and is perpendicular to the ribs. This direction stretches more than the lengthwise grain.

Bias grain: This is any diagonal direction. *True bias* is the diagonal edge formed when fabric is folded so that lengthwise and crosswise grains match (A). Bias grain has the most stretchability.

printed off-grain, such as some plaids or stripes, or fabrics that are finished off-grain, such as some permanent press types, should be avoided since they cannot be straightened. If you happen to buy one of these, follow the fabric design during layout, rather than the grainline.

Straightening Fabric
Before you lay out your fabric, you must straighten the ends. Then check the grain and straighten it if necessary.

• For *twill, loose, napped or pile weaves,* unravel a few crosswise threads until one can be drawn off the entire width. Then trim away the resulting fringe (C).
• For many *even weaves,* clip one selvage and pull one or two crosswise threads gently, pushing the fabric along the threads with your other hand. Continue across to the opposite selvage; then cut along the pulled thread (D).

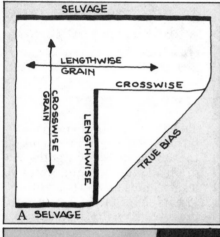

SELVAGE

LENGTHWISE GRAIN

CROSSWISE

CROSSWISE GRAIN

LENGTHWISE

TRUE BIAS

A SELVAGE

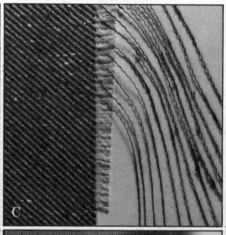

C

E

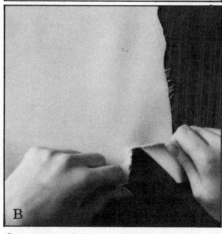

B

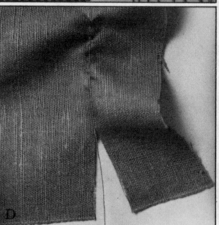

D

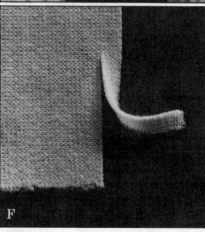

F

On-grain fabric: The fabric must be on-grain—with lengthwise and crosswise yarns exactly perpendicular to each other—for a garment to fit and hang properly without bagging or sagging.

Off-grain fabric: The fabric is *off-grain* if it was distorted while being processed or put on the bolt. If this happens, the fabric must be straightened before you can cut it out. Otherwise, the garment will have off-kilter seams, pulls and a drooping hem! Fabrics that are

Fabric ends are straight when the cut edge follows a single thread from selvage to selvage. Check both crosswise ends to see whether they were cut along a thread. If not, there are several ways to straighten the ends:
• On *plain, firm weaves* (but not linen), snip through one selvage; then tear fabric quickly (B) and snip through the other selvage. If fabric doesn't tear easily, don't force it! Try another method. After tearing, you may have to flatten the torn edges by pressing.

• On *woven plaids, checks or crosswise stripes,* cut along one of the crosswise bars (E).
• On *knits,* cut along the crosswise course (F). Since knits have no selvages, check to see that the lengthwise edges are straight; if not, cut along a lengthwise rib.

A

B

C

D

Check the fabric grain after you've straightened the ends. To see if it's on-grain or off-grain, fold the fabric in half lengthwise. Then try to line up the ends with a table corner or the markings on a cutting board. If fabric is on-grain, the crosswise edges form a right angle with the selvages (A) and line up with the table or markings on the cutting board. With an off-grain fabric, the edges are slanted (B). When choosing a knit, take a look at the grain before you buy to be sure it hasn't been pulled out of shape. Remember, you cannot straighten a knit—just be sure the lengthwise and crosswise edges have been cut as straight as possible, as explained opposite.

Straighten off-grain fabric in one of the following ways:

• *Steam press.* Fold the fabric in half lengthwise with right sides together. Pin the selvages together, pin the crosswise ends together and place the fabric on a flat surface. Diagonal wrinkles and puckers will form (C). To eliminate them, dampen the underside of the folded fabric with a sponge and steam press on the top side. Move the iron in the lengthwise and crosswise directions only, never diagonally. Don't press the folded edge because the crease might be difficult to remove later on.

• *Pull the fabric diagonally* in the opposite direction of the off-grain slant. Start at a corner (D) and pull hard on the diagonal along the entire length and width of the fabric. If your fabric is very wide or very long, ask a friend to help.

Sorting Pattern Pieces

Remove everything from the pattern envelope. Check the Cut and Sew Guide to see which pattern pieces you'll need for your view (A). Then, sort out the pattern pieces you'll need and put the rest back into the envelope.

You'll find that a smooth pattern is easier to work with than one that is folded and wrinkled. First press each piece with a warm, dry iron (C). Never use steam; it makes the tissue shrink and pucker. Look at

size (D), a pocket pattern might say "cut four," a waistband might say "interface," or the pattern might give cut-away lines for different hem lengths. It's important that you note all these now, before getting into the actual cutting and sewing.

One final preliminary, an important one, is to make any necessary pattern adjustments before you cut out your fabric. Chapter 5 tells

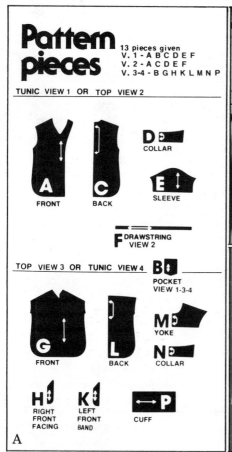

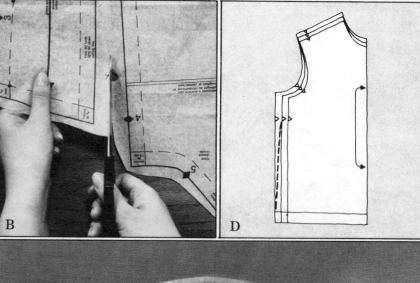

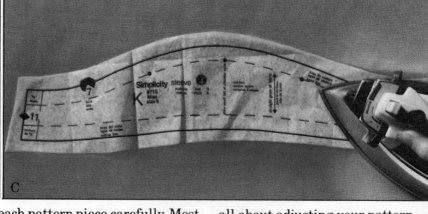

Usually, several pattern pieces are grouped together on the tissue. Cut apart the ones you'll need, leaving margins around each (B). They may be handy if you make any pattern adjustments—just mark your change right on the margins. When you cut out the fabric, you'll cut along the pattern cutting line, eliminating the remaining margins.

each pattern piece carefully. Most of the symbols and phrases you'll see are explained on page 29. But there might be special notes, too. For example, a piece may include cutting lines for more than one

all about adjusting your pattern. You may not have to adjust the pattern at all, especially if you use Simplicity multiple-size patterns, such as E.S.P.® or "Fashions in Large Sizes." They have cutting lines on each pattern piece for two to four sizes. So, if you are a two-size figure—a size 8 bust and a size 10 waist—simply taper the cutting lines from one size to another at the appropriate places (D).

Laying out the pattern

Positioning the pattern on the fabric is a little like doing a jigsaw puzzle, but with one big difference—the Cut and Sew Guide shows you exactly how everything fits so there's no guesswork involved!

A large work surface will be needed for you to work comfortably and accurately. A cutting table, or any large table with a cutting board placed on it, is ideal. If you don't have a large table, put the cutting board on a bed. As a last resort, even the floor will do.

Find the cutting layout for your fabric width, nap, pattern size and view you are making and circle it (A). Be sure that the layout is labeled for fabrics *with nap* if you're using a napped or one-way design fabric. This special layout will show all the pattern pieces with their tops facing in the same direction. As you lay out the pattern, refer to the cutting layout, then back to the fabric and the pattern. Be sure you're looking at the right layout each time.

Folding the Fabric

The cutting layout shows how to fold the fabric. The right side should be inside unless it has a special design that you want to see clearly for matching purposes. Fold pile and napped fabrics with the nap side out so the fabric doesn't shift as you cut.

A lengthwise fold is the most common one. The fabric is folded in half lengthwise so that the selvages and crosswise edges line up evenly (B).

A crosswise fold is generally used only for fabrics *without nap.* Match the selvages to be sure the fold is on the true crosswise grain (C). Napped fabrics can't be cut with a crosswise fold because the nap of the two layers won't run the same way. But sometimes, the full width of the fabric is needed for large pattern pieces. For this type of layout, fold the fabric in half crosswise and cut along the fold. Turn one layer around so that the nap runs in the same direction on both layers and place the two layers of fabric back together again (D).

For a single fabric thickness, the fabric is not folded at all. Just spread it out on your cutting surface, with the *right side face up* (E).

A combination of lengthwise fold and single thickness means the fabric is not folded in half; it's folded only partway. The selvages are parallel, instead of on top of each other. To be sure the fold is on-grain, use a ruler to measure from selvage to selvage in two places to make sure the selvage edges are the same distance apart (F).

For two lengthwise folds, the fabric is folded twice so the selvages meet in the center (G). For any type of fold, pin the selvages together to prevent them from shifting. Don't let the fabric hang over the edge of the table or it might stretch out of shape. Fold it up neatly.

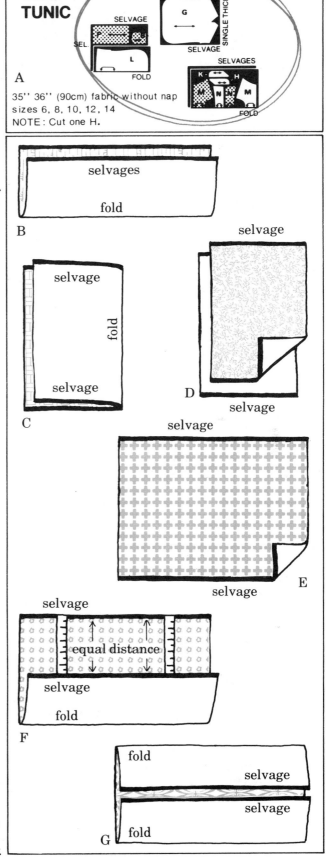

Positioning Pattern Pieces

The cutting layout shows how to fold your fabric and position the pattern pieces. Some pieces are white; others are shaded. This shading is explained before the first cutting layout by a key like the one below.

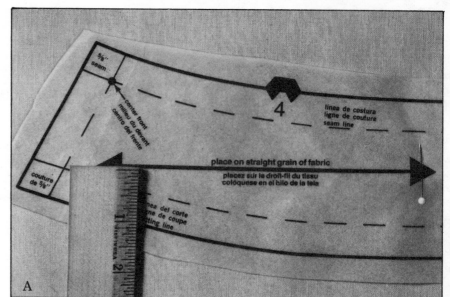

█ black is fabric

▓ grey is pattern printed side down

☐ white is pattern printed side up

▬ solid outline is fabric cut without a pattern piece

Position the pattern exactly as the layout shows, beginning with the large pieces. Place pieces with curved grainline arrows first, on the fabric fold. Place pieces with a straight arrow so the arrow is parallel to the selvages. Measure from each end of the arrow to the selvages, or the fold, and shift the pieces a bit until the distances are the same (A). Pin the pattern piece at each end of the arrow so it doesn't shift off-grain.

Pin the edges of pattern pieces in place through both layers of fabric, inside the cutting line or foldline. Use ball-point pins for knits. First, pin diagonally into the corners and smooth the pattern from the pinned area. Then add pins along the edge every 2-3″ (5-7.5 cm), parallel to the cutting line (B). Do not let pins extend past the cutting edge. Pick up only a bit of fabric and pattern with each pin. Overlapping margins will be cut away later.

Instead of pins, save time by placing a few weights (C) or cans on the pattern pieces; then hold the pattern edges flat as you cut.

Special notes may be printed near your cutting layout or on the pattern piece which explain:
● how to cut fabric without a pattern piece, like bias strips
● when to cut more than one
● when the same piece is used to cut fabric, interfacing or lining
● how to cut pieces that are shown extending beyond the fold

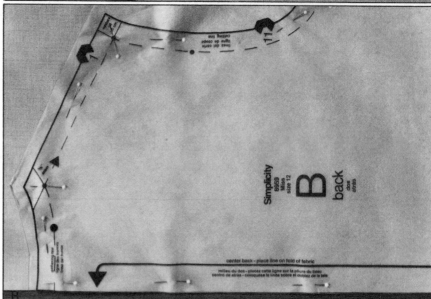

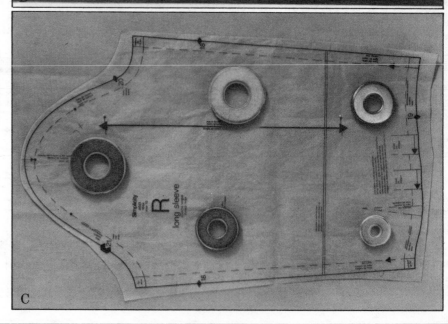

Special Layouts

Napped fabrics and fabric with designs that must be matched—plaids, bold stripes, large or medium-sized checks and large prints or border prints—require special layouts to look their best.

Napped Fabrics

For *layout* purposes, "napped" refers to fuzzy-surfaced, pile or shiny fabrics, knits and other fabrics with one-way designs or shading. From different directions, the colors may look darker or lighter. Because the nap must run one way, the Cut and Sew Guide provides a "with nap" layout so the tops of all pieces face one way (A).

Fabrics to Match

Plaids, bold stripes, big and medium-sized checks, border prints or any large design motif must be matched at seams; you'll have to arrange your pattern pieces differently than your cutting layout shows to do this.

Positioning bars or motifs:

The most prominent bar or motif should be placed at an attractive location on the main garment sections. Position the designs this way:

• Prominent vertical bars and large squares or motifs at the center front and back of the garment, and at the center of sleeves, yokes, and collars.

It's not always possible to match every seam, but try to match:
• Crosswise bars and designs at all vertical seams, such as center front, back and side seams.
• Bars on center back of collar or yokes to garment, if possible.
• Lengthwise bars or designs, where possible (plaids will not match vertically unless both seamlines are on the same slant).
• The design on pockets, flaps, etc. to the design on the garment.
• Set-in sleeves to the bodice front at armhole notches.
• Kimono sleeve seams below the shoulder notch.
• Two-piece outfits at the point where they overlap—top to bottom, jacket to vest, etc.

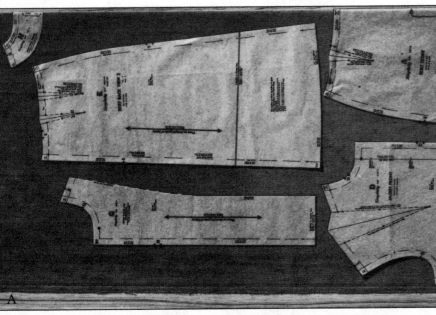

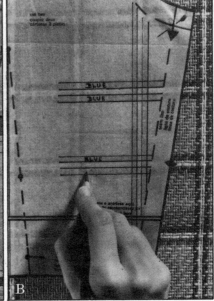

To lay out fuzzy fabrics, first determine the direction of the nap. If you stroke the fabric *with* the nap, it feels smoother and the color is lighter than *against* the nap. Lay out velvet or velveteen with the nap running up, to show off its deep rich color. Corduroy, suede cloth and deep pile fabrics wear better when the nap runs down.

Knits or shiny fabrics, such as satin, reflect light differently from each lengthwise direction. Lay out the fabric in whichever direction you prefer.

One-way designs have an obvious this-end-up look. Decide which way is up before doing the layout.

• Dominant horizontal bars at straight or slightly curved hemlines; keep in mind that a big horizontal bar can be unattractive across the fullest part of the bust, abdomen or hips.
• Hemlines along the bottom edges of a large border print or below large motifs.
• Pattern pieces on a complete large motif without breaking it up, where possible.

Since people usually see the front, position this section first. Be sure grainline arrow is parallel to the selvages or to the bars of a plaid. Then position the remaining pattern pieces so that the adjoining pieces match at seams.

Designs will not match at raglan seams, shoulder seams, darts, above bust darts on side seams, above the bust on princess seams, at the back armhole seam or in a gathered or eased area.

To match adjoining pieces, trace the design of the fabric onto the pattern at the notch and indicate colors (B). Then place the pattern piece to be joined on top of the first piece, lapping seamlines and matching notches. Trace the design onto the second piece. Then place it on the fabric so that the traced design matches the fabric.

Plaids and Stripes

The layout of plaids and stripes depends on whether the design is even or uneven. In an *even* plaid or stripe, the arrangement of bars (stripes) is the same on both sides of the main bar, creating a perfectly balanced design repeat (the easiest kind to match).

In an *uneven* plaid or stripe, the arrangement or color of bars is different on either side of the main bar.

To see what your fabric is, fold it on the center of a main lengthwise bar. See if the design and colors repeat evenly on either side of it. Do the same for the main crosswise bar. If all bars on both fabric layers match, the fabric is even; if not, it's uneven (A).

For even plaids or stripes, you may use a "without nap" layout unless the fabric is brushed or napped; then use a "with nap" (one-way) layout. Although cutting a single fabric layer is more accurate, a double layer may be used if you align the plaid design first (B). Pin the fabric or use basting tape to keep it from shifting.

For uneven plaids or stripes, use a "with nap" layout. An uneven plaid can be made to go around the figure in one direction or in opposite directions from the center, producing a symmetrical, mirror-image effect.

To lay out a plaid so it goes *around the figure* (C), fold fabric at the center of a main bar or group of bars. Position pattern pieces that must be cut on the fold. Then cut other pieces from a single layer of fabric. Place the foldline of pants fly openings on the center of a main bar. Be sure to place sleeves so the plaid goes in the same direction on both sleeves.

For a *mirror-image* effect (D), the pattern must have a center front and back seam or closure. To lay out, work with a single layer of fabric. The main pieces (the garment front and back) must be cut once, then reversed and turned upside down before they are cut again. Place center seams or center front lines at the center of a main bar or group of bars. Position the center of the sleeve on a main bar and cut it out. Then, reverse and turn pattern piece to cut the second sleeve. Make sure plaid moves in the same direction as corresponding side of bodice.

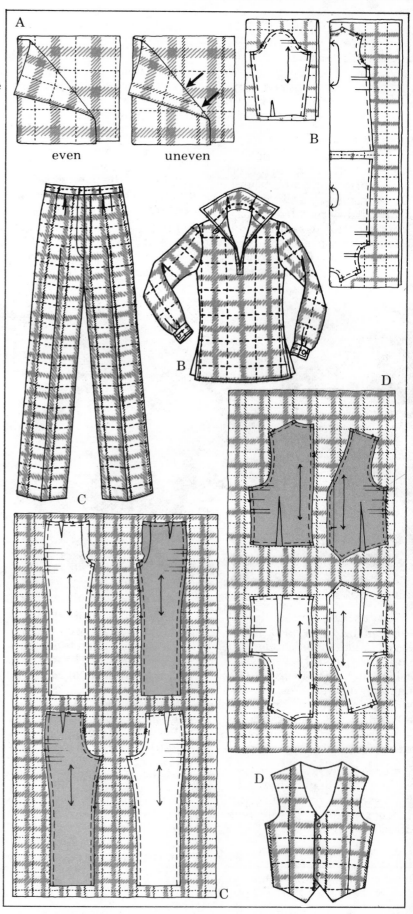

even   uneven

Border Prints

Borders are edgings designed right into fabrics. Although they're naturals for hemlines, there are other clever ways to sew with border prints.

Horizontal borders: For hemlines and other horizontal uses of borders, follow these hints (E):

● Decide on finished garment length; then position hemline on border edge where it looks best.

● Pattern edges where a border will be placed must be on the

Vertical borders: These work best on pattern pieces with straight vertical seams or edges (F), unless the border is used for small details, such as cuffs.

● When placing a border along a front opening, match the border motif at front seamlines.

● Lay all pattern pieces on the straight, lengthwise grain. Place pieces that use the border first (F).

● Position the main motif to avoid breaking up its design.

● Place the remaining pieces on straight grain, beyond the border.

Sheets and Towels

Today, brightly designed fabrics are often found in linen and domestics departments. Since designer sheets and towels have become such pacesetters in color and design, they have zoomed out of the linen closet right into many fashion wardrobes!

Pre-hemmed items have some advantages over fabrics by the yard. Their width makes it possible to skip some of the seams required by normal-width fabrics. The

straight grain or should be straightened (E). Use only patterns with slightly curved edges or you may distort the style when straightening the edge.

Lay out pattern pieces on the crosswise grain. First position pieces that use the border—front (E), then back and other pieces, centering dominant motifs. Match borders at side seams where possible. Place remaining pieces where they look best, either on, below, or above the border.

Large Scale Prints

Bold designs have a big fashion impact, whether they are florals, geometrics or scarf prints.

There are two ways of handling a large scale or scarf print. You can treat the fabric as you would an allover print if the motifs or squares are not too large—6″ (15 cm) square or smaller. Or, center a main motif or square to make the design the main focus of attention (G).

hemmed edges are helpful for curtains and other home decorating items. Towels also have the bonus of finished edges, some with woven borders or fringe that can be used at garment edges.

A twin sheet contains over 5 yards (4.60m) of fabric, making the cost per yard (m) very low. To use borders of sheets and towels, follow the previous directions for border prints and large-scale prints to plan your layout.

Cutting and marking

cutting

Before you cut into the fabric, check the following list to see if you're ready to cut:

☐ fabric has been preshrunk
☐ fabric ends have been straightened
☐ fabric is on-grain
☐ fabric is folded as layout shows
☐ all pattern pieces for your view are pinned in place
☐ grainlines are parallel to the selvages, or on a fold

Traditionally, a right-handed person cuts with the pattern on the left; left-handed, on the right. What's important is using the position that gives you the greatest accuracy.

Cut with long, even strokes exactly on the cutting line. Take shorter strokes when cutting around curves. Cut around notches, using the tips of the shears, unless you plan to use the quick snip-marking method, shown opposite. Leave pattern pieces pinned to the fabric after cutting.

• *Solid lines* for folding pleats or front edges, placement lines for buttonholes and pockets
• *Stitching lines* like the ones on fly front zipper openings
• *Center front and back,* unless these are located on seamlines
• *Curved seamlines* for beginners to help them stitch accurately
• *Darts,* along stitching line, at dots and at the point

Marking Methods

Since there are several good marking methods, the one to use depends on your fabric type and the method that works for you.

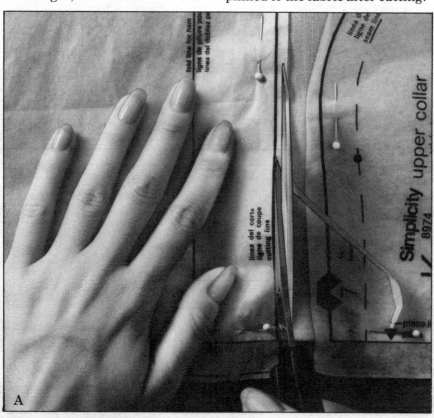

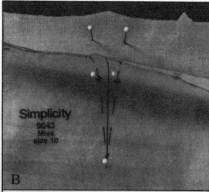

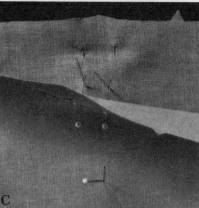

☐ pieces shaded on the layout are placed printed side down
☐ room has been left on the fabric for any pieces labeled "cut four"
☐ special notes for cutting pieces without a pattern have been studied and understood
☐ all pins are inside cutting lines

How to Cut

It's easy to cut out the pattern using bent-handled shears; don't use pinking or scalloping shears. Just hold shears straight, with the edge of the blade resting on the working surface. Use your hand to keep pattern flat (A).

marking

Marking means transferring the pattern symbols to the wrong side of the fabric. If a garment section, such as a collar, will be interfaced, mark the interfacing instead.

What to Mark

Pattern symbols help you match up the garment sections for seaming and to sew details, such as darts, accurately. These are the ones to mark:
• *Dots,* including those on dart stitching lines

Pins: On many smooth fabrics, the fastest way to mark is simply to stick pins straight through the pattern and both fabric layers at dots and foldlines (B). Carefully pull the pattern over the pinheads, holding pins in place (B). Turn the piece over and push pins through the fabric at the pinpoints on this side, too. Separate the layers carefully and secure the pins by sticking the points back in the fabric (C).

Chalk and pins: For most flat-surfaced fabrics, chalk and pin marking is fine. Dressmaker's chalk pencils and bars of tailor's chalk are available in several colors. Use the color that most closely matches your fabric. Before marking, test colors first on a fabric scrap to be sure the marks don't show through on the right side. For accurate marking, make sure that the pencil point or bar edge is sharp.

Tracing paper and wheel:

Fairly flat-surfaced fabrics can be marked with tracing paper and a tracing wheel. This method doesn't give good results on nubby or very bulky fabrics. Select a color that matches your fabric as closely as possible. Use it only on the wrong side of the fabric because these marks don't always come off. Test first on a scrap to be sure marks won't show on right side.

On most fabrics, you can mark two layers at once to save time. Heavyweight fabrics must be marked one layer at a time to get a

Snip marking: Tiny clips in the seam allowances of nearly any fabric type are a fast way to mark the ends of darts, foldlines, center front and back, as well as dots and notches (C). Make clips ⅛" (3 mm) deep at the edge through the pattern and fabric. Use this method only on garments you're sure won't be let out during fitting.

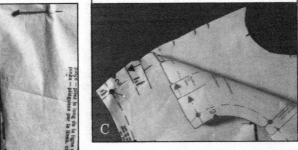

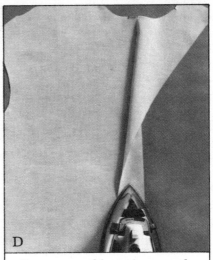

C

A

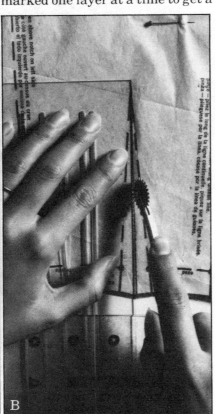

B

D

First, stick pins straight down through the pattern symbols and all fabric layers. Turn the fabric over so the pinpoints face up. For long lines and darts, draw a line connecting the pins with a chalk pencil or bar and ruler (A). Mark dots with a line crossing the stitching line and darts with a line across the end. Pull away the pattern piece carefully, holding the pins in the fabric. Mark the other layer with chalk. Remove the pins and separate the layers.

clear impression. To avoid marring the surface of the table you are working on, place a magazine or piece of cardboard underneath the fabric and pattern.

To mark, place the tracing paper under the pattern with the carbon sides facing the wrong side of both fabric layers. Remove any pins in the way and roll the tracing wheel over the symbols to be marked. Use a ruler to help you trace straight lines. Mark a line across the stitching line at dots and a line at the end of darts (B).

Press marking: A pressed crease used along with snip marking is another shortcut way to mark a foldline. Make a tiny clip in the seam allowance at each end of the foldline. Then remove the pattern tissue and separate the fabric layers so you can press each one separately. Fold the fabric with wrong sides together, using the clip marks as guides. Then press the fold (D).

Speed hand basting: Basting is a quick, safe way to transfer markings to the right side of a garment. With pattern on wrong side of *one* fabric layer, pin close to the area to be marked. Hand-baste along the pattern markings, taking tiny stitches on the pattern side and large stitches on the fabric side (A).

Remove the pattern piece gently so as not to rip it. Use this method to mark grainlines, center fronts and backs, pleat and fold lines, fly fronts and placement lines for trims and pockets.

Tailor's tacks: These are loops of thread which can be used to mark any fabric at dots or at intervals on straight lines. They are especially good for thick or textured fabrics, as well as delicate types such as satin, lace and sheers.

Use a long, unknotted double thread. Take a small stitch through the pattern and both fabric layers, leaving a long thread tail. Take a second stitch over the first to form a large loop. Then cut the thread, leaving another long thread tail.

After all tacks have been made, clip the loops. Carefully remove the pattern (B). Separate the fabric layers and clip the threads between them. You'll have thread tufts on each layer (C).

Transferring symbols to the right side of the fabric: Most of the time, you only need to mark symbols on the wrong side of the fabric. But sometimes these markings must be transferred to the right side. Zipper stitching lines, pocket placement lines, buttonholes and pleats are construction details that can be marked this way. You can mark on the right side with pins, speed hand basting or machine basting.

For machine basting, loosen the top thread tension so that stitches will be easy to remove. First mark on the wrong side with pins, chalk or tracing paper. Then stitch along the marked line, using the longest stitch (D). The stitches will show on the right side.

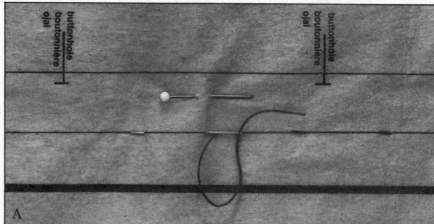

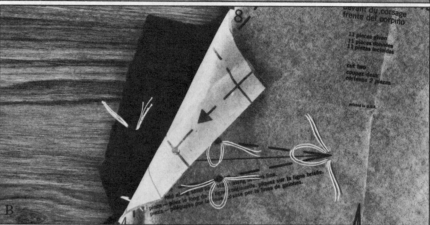

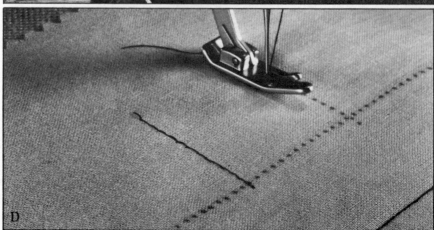

7 sewing today:

it's better than ever

You couldn't have picked a better time to sew. The fashion climate is just right. After years of rules, fashion has become everything for everybody—the point now is *freedom*! You are *free* to wear what suits you best, and the patterns you'll find now wholeheartedly reflect this more realistic attitude!

Simplicity keeps coming up with new ways to help you sew happily with fantastic results. Suddenly, the gap between home sewing and ready-to-wear has closed. Now you can sew the way clothing manufacturers do, thanks to the pattern designs, modern machines, new techniques and better notions; they're being designed to make sewing simpler all the time.

In the following seven color pages, you'll get a close look at the excitement of today's sewing scene.

(Left) Simply done! Three easy-fit pieces with a minimum of sewing details—and all the stitching is done by machine! This outfit is designed to give you the *most fashion* for the *least amount* of time and effort. Dress it up or down for lots of wearability, or add pieces to it as your fashion moods change.

Patterns for successful sewing

If you browse through a Simplicity pattern, you'll see clear, easy-to-follow instructions, of course, but now there's even more! Many Simplicity patterns fit into categories which zero in on a special feature or a particular sewing need. You'll find patterns that are planned to take less time to sew; others focus on fit, showing you how to adjust a pattern easily; still others are designed especially for knit fabrics and include the latest knit sewing techniques. Be sure to check out the catalog and the pattern glossary, so you'll know what the special categories are and what they have to offer. Here is a sampling of five of them:

Jiffy ® patterns are designed for anyone who wants results in a hurry. Chances are you could make up a Jiffy® tonight and wear it to work tomorrow! A Jiffy® is easy to sew, with never more than *five total* pattern pieces. And for even speedier sewing, a Super Jiffy® has no more than *three* pieces!

Fuss-Free Fit ™ patterns are just what you need if you think you might have to make an adjustment or two. They pinpoint areas to be measured, then show you how to measure yourself and make the necessary adjustments right on the pattern. Why wait until all the sewing is done— nip the problem early!

E.S.P ®, those Extra-Sure Patterns that offer you foolproof sewing, also contain three complete sizes to *assure* you of a good fit. And, there are lots of timesaving tips to speed your sewing along.

Yes I Can! ™ patterns include special information for the beginner. There's a learn-to-sew booklet, so questions about sewing can be answered as they arise. The instructions are simplified for the novice and have more illustrations to show how every step should be done, clearly and quickly.

Designer Fashions come directly from famous fashion experts! You'll spot many well-known names and the distinctive details and styles that make these fashions stand out.

(Near Right) This terrific-looking dress takes only three pattern pieces—it's a Super Jiffy®! (Center) An E.S.P.® dress that's as sure as a pattern can be with complete instructions for every step, plus special shortcut methods. (Far Right) For more sewing help, Yes I Can!™ patterns, like these smart separates, include a booklet that explains sewing talk, the special terms and techniques, to beginners.

*T*imesaving shortcuts

Since time to sew is often at a premium, it's nice to know how to make the most of your spare minutes. Start by being your own efficiency expert. There are many areas where you can take sewing shortcuts. Try the newer, faster techniques tested by experts.

Here are just a few of those professional tips—you'll find many more throughout this chapter. Each shortcut method is boxed off to catch your eye and alert you to another idea that saves you time and work in sewing.

(Right) Two for one! When you use the timesaving shortcuts, you may find you can sew yourself a handsome quilted coat and still have time left over to sew your child a quilted vest! A Jiffy® pattern, pre-quilted fabric and simple edge finishes help to make it all possible here.

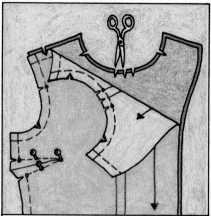

Why cut around all those notches when snips will do? Use scissors tips to make ¼″ (6 mm) snips, marking ends of darts, center lines and foldlines (see page 87).

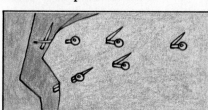
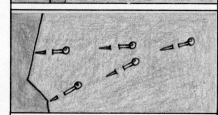

Instead of marking darts, dots and foldlines with tracing paper, chalk or tailor's tacks, try using pins to mark. It's easier, quicker, and it works (see page 86)!

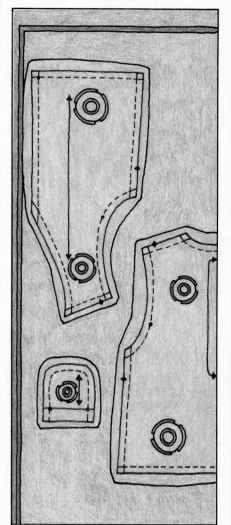

Instead of pinning pattern pieces to the fabric, use weights to keep the pattern in place while you cut. You can buy weights at a notions counter or use small cans of food from your cupboard (see page 82).

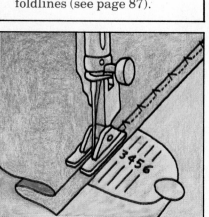

If you're in a hurry, why do anything by hand that you can do by machine? Your machine can baste, overcast, make buttonholes and even hem for you (see pages 100, 106, 141, 161).

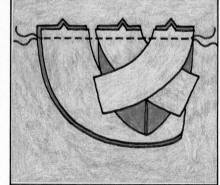

Try continuous stitching! Instead of pinning, stitching and pressing each step separately, pin all you can at once and stitch seams without breaking your stitching. Then cut apart and press.

Let your machine do it!

Today's home sewing machines offer more convenience features than ever before. Machine techniques and methods previously known only to ready-to-wear manufacturers are now accepted for home sewing as well. They reduce the amount of time-consuming handwork and provide extremely durable finishes that often blend into the design details more than hand finishing could.

No wonder it's always been faster to turn out a dress in a factory than at home! Manufacturers have machines for every step! Certainly a garment takes its first shape in a straight stitch machine, but that's only the beginning. There are separate machines for sewing buttonholes, hems, sleeves and pants legs. Others overedge-stitch, bind, embroider and sew on buttons. Today most new home sewing machines can do all this and more! And you need only one machine, with perhaps some added attachments.

In addition, today's home machines offer other features—electronic speed and stitch memory, needle-threading and automatic bobbin-winding, buttonholes, hemming and dual-feed mechanisms so fabrics won't slip and slide.

With all the new features, you can use your machine to save time and money just the way the manufacturers do. Consider these stitching tricks the very next time you sew:

• Stitch in the ditch of an existing seam to hold facings in place (see page 127). No hand-tacking!

• Make blindstitched hems using a blindstitch foot and the stitch built into your machine (see page 141). No hand-hemming needed!

• Sew buttons on by machine—the two or four-hole kind only—to save time and keep them anchored securely (see page 108).

• Stitch seams and finish the edges all at one time with a built-in overedge stitch (page 161).

• Sew elastic directly into a waistband (see the No-roll Method, page 110) and skip the step of working the elastic through a casing.

• Stitch a neckline facing to the zipper tape before you stitch the zipper into the garment (see page 128). No need to tack by hand.

The machine does it all. Sew super fashions like these in a breeze! Sportswear, career clothes, on-the-go separates are all so much easier to sew, thanks to new machine sewing techniques. (Left) Sew jogging suits with the quick knit seaming methods shown on page 161. That way you can sew them both in less time with no handwork at all. (Right) Machine stitching handles all the important details on these two fashions: the reversible Jiffy® jacket with topstitched pockets and trim, and the soft dress with topstitched placket opening, cuffs and hem.

Fuse it!

Now that fusibles have come into their own, you might be surprised at the many times you don't have to sew at all, but can fuse instead!

Fuse That Hem!

Often a fusible web makes not just an easier hem, but a more attractive one as well, especially on a knit fabric (see page 141). A hand-sewn hem on a delicate knit may have telltale stitches which show up on the outside.

Fuse That Interfacing!

Now you can choose from several types of interfacing that can be fused in place rather than sewn in. There are as many interfacing weights as fabric weights as well as woven, non-woven and knit types, with or without stretchability. Why not fuse whenever you can (see page 143) and save all that hand-sewing time for something more creative!

Fuse That Appliqué!

You can buy appliqués with fusible backing or you can cut fusible web to match the appliqué shape and iron it onto your fabric! No need to always baste or sew!

Remember, when you choose to fuse, test the fusible on a scrap of the garment fabric first, following the manufacturer's instructions (see page 134 for additional information on fusing).

(Below) It's impossible to tell at a glance whether the self-fabric bands on this jacket were interfaced with the new fusibles or with regular interfacing sewn in stitch by stitch. What a marvelous time-saver! And, the pants waistband is just firm enough, thanks to another fusible — precut waistband interfacing (see pages 134 and 143).

sewing method handbook

Here's where you'll find the most up-to-date sewing methods for bands, facings, hems, zippers and much, much more. Besides the step-by-step instructions, there are easy-to-follow photos and illustrations for every method.

All the how-to information for the basic techniques is in this 80-page handbook, plus many timesaving methods. To spot these shortcuts, just check the brown instructions in the boxes for the streamlined way to do many sewing tasks.

The major subjects, such as Seams, are all alphabetically arranged to help you find them quickly and easily. They're also listed on the right-hand tabs so you can flip through the pages to find the instructions you need.

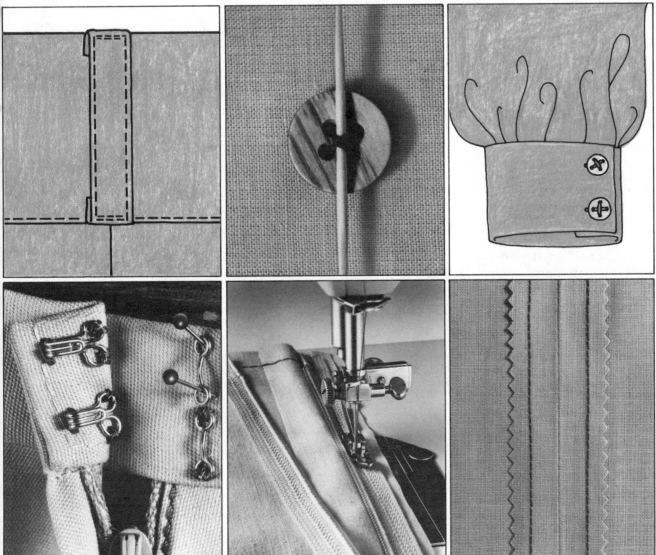

Bands

Contrasting or self-fabric bands are always in style and make neat finishes for necklines, armholes and front closings.

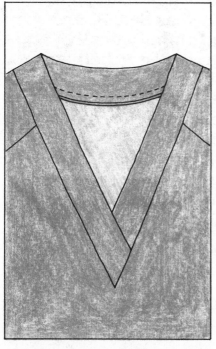

Lapped V-neck Band

This type of band makes a perfect neckline finish for knits and is not difficult to sew. To begin, reinforce the front neck seamline at the V, using small machine stitches (A).

With wrong sides together, fold the band in half lengthwise. Pin or baste the raw edges together. On the outside, pin the band to

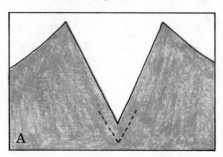

the neck edge, keeping the raw edges even. Match markings, especially at the point of the V. Leave the right end of band free beyond the last mark. Starting at the left-hand end of the band,

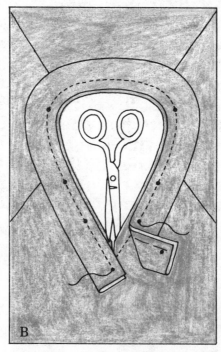

stitch the seam, stretching the band to fit the neck edge as you sew. End stitching at next to last mark on the right side of the seamline. To make the band easier to finish, clip into the garment neckline to the reinforcement stitches at the V. Do not clip band (B).

Turn the band up and slip the ends to the inside through the clip (C).

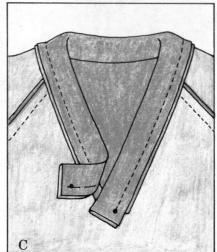

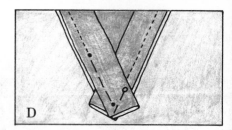

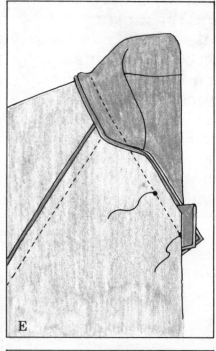

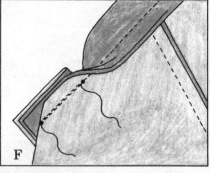

Working from the wrong side of the garment, lap the free end of the band over the stitched end. Match markings at the point of the V. Pin or baste the free end in place (D). Finish stitching seam, ending at the point of the V (E).

To finish the neckline, stitch the loose end of the band to all the seam allowances on top of the previous stitching (F).

Front Placket

This classic style is often used for front openings on blouses, shirts, tops and dresses. The two straight band sections are joined at the bottom of the front opening. There are several different ways to make front placket bands. Here's the quickest method.

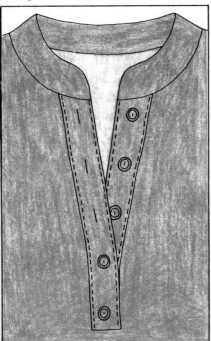

Machine-stitch the front along the marked stitching lines to reinforce the corners and act as a stitching guide for the band sections. Then slash the center front halfway between the rows of stitching, clipping diagonally into the corners up to the stitching (A).

Interface the band sections following the pattern directions.

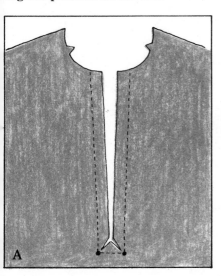

On the side of the band that is interfaced, press under the seam allowance on long edge and trim to ¼″ (6 mm). Then stitch the right side of the uninterfaced portion of each band to the wrong side of the opening (B).

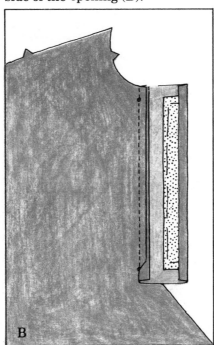

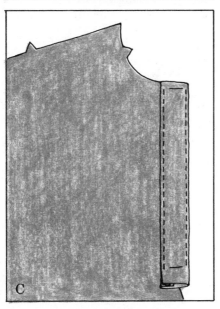

Trim the seam and press it toward the band. Pin the pressed edge in place along the seam on the outside and topstitch close to both long edges (C).

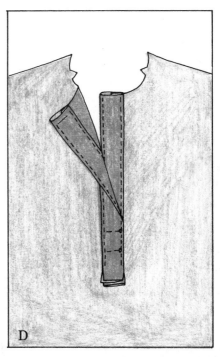

Slip the ends of the bands through to the wrong side. On the inside, lap left band over right (right over left for men) and pin (D).

Pin the ends of the lapped bands to the triangle of fabric at the lower edge of the opening and stitch through all thicknesses (E). Press ends down. Finish according to the pattern instructions.

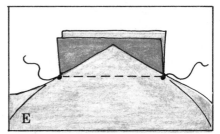

Basting

Basting is used to hold fabric layers together temporarily for stitching or fitting. Hand basting is the method usually taught to beginners. However, there are faster, less tedious machine methods that are just as effective.

Hand Basting

For firm holding power, use *even basting*. Make running stitches about ¼" (6 mm) long by weaving the point of a long, fine needle in and out of the fabric (A). *Uneven basting* is for areas that don't need to be held as securely. Make stitches ¼" (6 mm) long, spaced about ½" to ¾" (1.3 to 2 cm) apart.

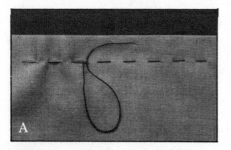

Slip Basting

Make sure that stripes or plaids match at seams by slip basting. With fabric right side up, press one seam allowance under and lap it over the adjoining section, matching seamlines and fabric design. Pin at right angles. Bring the needle to the right side at the folded edge, through all three fabric layers. Then, insert the needle just opposite the fold, through the single fabric layer. Bring the needle back up through the fold, about ⅜" (1 cm) to the left of the previous stitch (B). Continue to slip baste the seam in place. Remove the pins. To sew the seam, fold the fabric with the right sides together and machine stitch along the basting line.

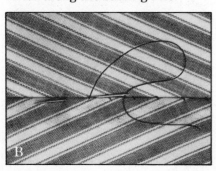

Pin Basting

A hinged presser foot will allow you to stitch right over pins—just slow down a bit as you stitch over them.

Place pins perpendicular to the seamline 1-3" (2.5-7.5 cm) apart (closer together for eased or gathered seams, farther apart for flat seams). The tips should take small bites of fabric exactly at the seamline. Keep pin heads away from the presser foot and machine stitch along the basting line (C).

Machine Basting

For a quick fitting, machine basting is an ideal way to stitch a garment together. Pin fabric layers together, matching markings. Loosen the upper thread tension considerably and use your longest stitch length. Use a different color thread in the bobbin to make it easy to recognize and remove later. Don't backstitch at the ends. For removal, clip the needle thread every inch (2.5 cm) or so; then pull the bobbin thread (D).

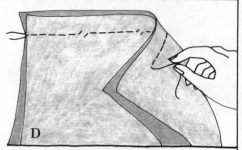

Some newer machines will do speed basting with a stitch up to 2" (5 cm) long (E); others may have a chainstitch feature (F). These types of basting are much faster to remove than conventional machine basting. Check your sewing machine manual to see if you have these special features.

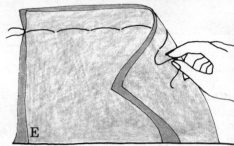

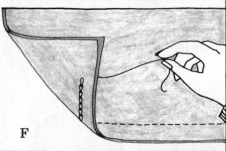

Fuse Basting

This is a fast way to hold areas in place for hand finishing or topstitching. Cut a strip of fusible web the desired length. Sandwich it between two fabric layers and fuse (G), following the manufacturer's instructions.

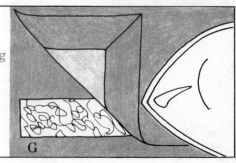

Belts

To make a traditional belt, sew a fabric covering over belting or stiff interfacing. There's also a stitch-free way to do this, and there are timesaving ideas for making other belt styles, too.

Covered Belt

Cut stiffener the desired belt width and the length of the waist measurement plus 6″ (15 cm). Cut a right-angle point at one end.

Cut a lengthwise fabric strip ¾″ (2 cm) longer than the stiffener. Use the selvage as one edge if possible. Cut strip double the stiffener width plus 1″ (2.5 cm) if selvage is used, 1¼″ (3.2 cm) if not. For a strip without the selvage, turn under ¼″ (6 mm) on one long edge and stitch.

Hand-sewn: Fold the fabric strip lengthwise, with right sides together, so that the raw edge is ¼″ (6 mm) from the finished edge or selvage. Pin and stitch one end in a ¼″ (6 mm) seam, backstitching to secure it (A). Trim the corner. Then press the seam open and turn the belt right side out. Press seam flat, forming a point.

Center the stiffener over the belt, inserting the pointed end of the stiffener into the fabric point (B).

Fold the raw edge of the fabric over the stiffener and press. Then fold the finished edge or selvage over the raw edge; press. Pin it so that the fabric is pulled snugly over the stiffener, but is not pulled off-grain. Whipstitch the edges securely in place (C).

Fused: Press one end of fabric strip under ¼″ (6 mm). Center stiffener on wrong side of fabric, with point towards pressed edge. Fold fabric over point; fuse with a triangle of fusible web (D).

Fold the long edges over the stiffener, with the selvage edge on top. Fuse each edge in place separately with a long strip of web (E).

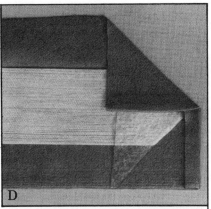

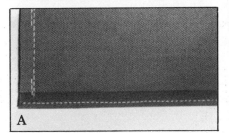

Attaching a buckle: Make a small oval hole in the belt 1½″ (3.8 cm) from the straight end. Overcast hole and insert prong. Fold edge back and stitch (F).

Eyelets: Try on the belt and mark several holes 1″ (2.5 cm) apart. Apply hammer-on metal eyelets or make thread eyelets by making small holes; cover raw edges with a buttonhole stitch (G). For machine-worked eyelets, follow your manual instructions.

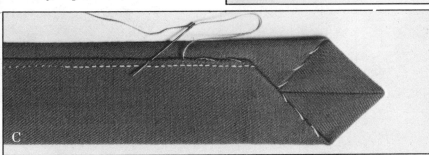

7

sewing today: basting, belts

101

Tie Belt

Stitched and turned belt: With right sides together, fold the belt in half lengthwise. Stitch along the seamline, leaving an opening at the center of the belt for turning; backstitch at both ends of the opening and at corners. Trim the seams and corners (A); then press them open to set the edge. Turn the belt right side out. Do this by using a ruler to push one end through the belt and out the opening, pushing the rest of the belt over this end. Repeat for the other end. Slipstitch the opening.

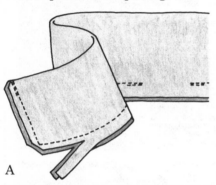

A

Quick tie belt: Press all seam allowances under. On heavy fabric, trim corners to eliminate bulk (B). With wrong sides together, fold

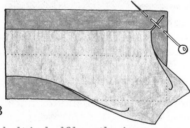

B

belt in half lengthwise; press. Edgestitch all around; topstitch ¼"-½" (6 mm-1.3 cm) from edges, if desired (C).

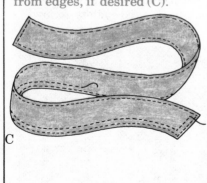

C

Elastic Cinch Belt

Use heavy, wide decorative elastic long enough to stretch comfortably around your waist, plus 2" (5 cm). Buy a clasp buckle with an opening the same width.

Slip the ends of the elastic through each half of the buckle and fold back 1" (2.5 cm). Pink the ends to prevent raveling. Pin and stitch the edges in place, backstitching to secure (D).

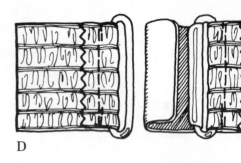

D

Belt Loops or Carriers

Fabric or thread loops are used to hold a belt in place. A pattern that calls for fabric loops will include a pattern piece and markings for placement. If you add loops to a garment that doesn't have them, center them over the waistline.

Fabric loop: Follow your pattern directions, or cut a strip of fabric along the selvage, three times the desired finished loop width. The length of the strip should equal the belt width plus ¾" (2 cm). Fold strip in thirds

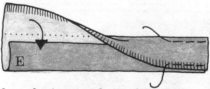

E

lengthwise so selvage is on top; press. Topstitch to secure the edges (E). To attach to garment, fold each end under ¼" (6 mm), and sew by hand or machine (F).

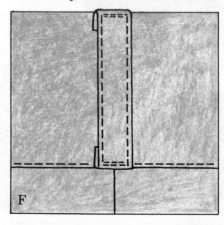

F

Hand thread loop: Use buttonhole twist or a double strand of regular thread. Fasten thread on the inside and bring the needle up at the side seam. Make three or four stitches ¼" (6 mm) longer than the belt width, centering them over the waistline. Then, work buttonhole stitches over the long stitches (G). Fasten the thread on the inside.

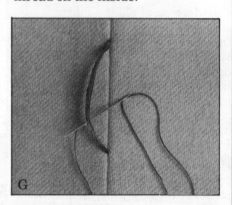

G

Machine thread loop: Zigzag-stitch over fine cord twice (H). Apply by catching the ends in a seam.

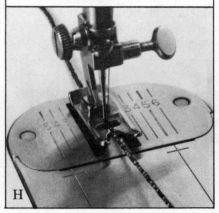

H

Bindings

Bindings are used to trim and finish a raw edge at the same time. Make your own bias binding or use purchased double-fold bias tape or foldover braid. These will work well on both curved and straight edges.

Making Bias Binding

Marking and cutting: Fold the fabric on the true bias. Use a strip of cardboard four times the desired finished width of the binding as a template and pencil-mark lines parallel to the fold. Then cut

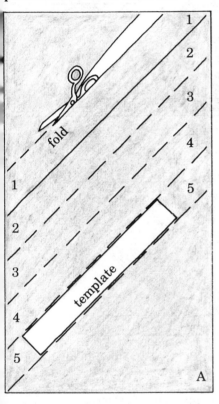

along each of the lines (A). Most patterns are designed with ¼″ (6 mm) or ½″ (1.3 cm) finished binding width, so your fabric strips will usually be 1″ (2.5 cm) or 2″ (5 cm) wide.

Joining two ends: With right sides together, pin ends of the strips at right angles to each other, as shown. Stitch a ¼″ (6 mm) seam (B). Press the seam open and trim away the extending points.

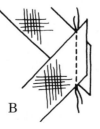

Joining several ends:
Instead of joining many strips individually, make one continuous strip to save time. Mark a rectangle of fabric as described opposite, but don't cut it. Trim off the excess unmarked fabric and be sure all fabric edges are grain perfect. With right sides together, form a tube by folding the marked fabric so that the ends of the drawn lines meet and one strip width extends beyond the edge at each end. Pin the edges together and stitch a ¼″ (6 mm) seam. Press the seam open. Start to cut on line 1, continuing to cut around the tube on the marked lines (C).

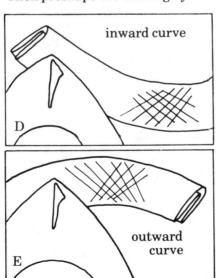

Application Tips

Follow these tips; then see pages 104-105 for specific directions.
• Trim off the garment seam allowance on the edge to be bound. Use the finished width of the binding as the new seam allowance width.
• For a curved edge, press binding edges as directed by the instructions for each method. Then preshape the binding by stretching and steam-pressing it to match the garment edge (D, E).

• Begin and end at an inconspicuous seam, such as the center back neck or underarm. Press under one binding end. For the two-step method, lap the *unpressed* end over the *pressed* end (F); for the one-step method, lap the *pressed* end over the *unpressed* one (G).

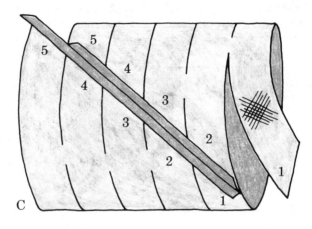

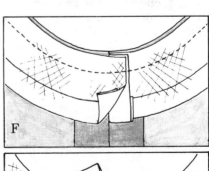

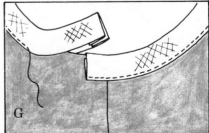

Two-step Binding

You can apply bias binding that you've made yourself, or purchased double-fold bias tape, in two easy machine-stitching steps. If you're using your own binding, press under one-fourth the binding width on one long edge (A).

Step 1: Open out one fold of purchased bias tape or use the unfolded edge of your binding.

Outside corner: Stitch binding to one fabric edge as described in Step 1 left, stopping where the seamlines meet at the corner (C). Raise the presser foot and cut the thread. Make a fold in the binding to turn the corner, forming a diagonal crease. Lower the needle into the corner and stitch along the next seamline (D). Then, follow Step 2, making another diagonal fold at the corner (E). Edgestitch or slipstitch the corner folds.

Inside corner: First, reinforce the corner with small stitches along the seamline. Clip the corner just to the stitches (F). Stitch binding to one fabric edge as described in Step 1, stopping at the corner. Keep the needle in the fabric and raise the presser foot. Spread the fabric at the clip to straighten the edge and line it up with the binding. Lower the

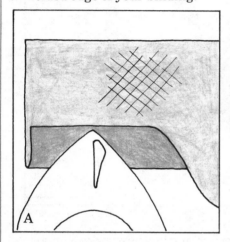

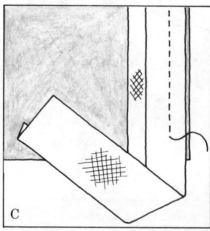

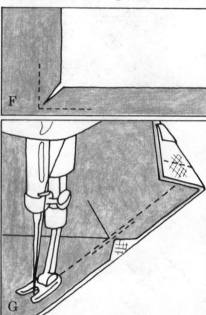

With raw edges even, place the *right* side of the binding against the *wrong* side of the garment. Turn the ends under. Stitch, using the finished binding width as your seam width. Press the seam toward the binding

Step 2: Turn the folded edge of the binding to the right side of the garment, enclosing the raw edge and covering the seam; press. Stitch close to the fold (B).

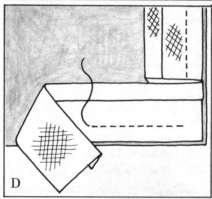

presser foot and resume stitching (G). Press the seam toward the binding—a diagonal fold will form at the corner (H). Then follow Step 2, forming another diagonal fold at the corner (I). Edgestitch or slipstitch the corner.

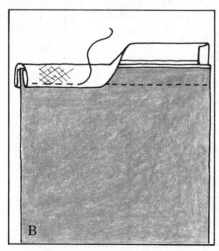

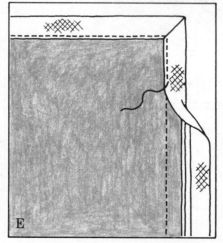

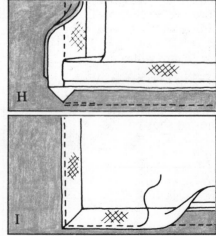

One-step Binding

This quick application works with purchased double-fold bias tape or foldover braid. Both types of binding come pre-pressed so one edge is wider than the other.

To apply: Slip the binding over the raw garment edge so the wider binding edge is on the inside of the garment. On the outside, edgestitch the binding in place, catching both binding edges in the stitching (A).

Outside corner: Bind one edge all the way to the raw edge of the fabric (A). Raise the presser foot and cut the thread. Turn the binding around the corner and pin it in place (B). Fold binding diagonally on both sides of the corner. Lower the needle into the diagonal fold and stitch the remaining side; backstitch (C). Edgestitch or slipstitch the folds.

Inside corner: Reinforce the corner with small machine stitches and clip just to the stitching (shown opposite, F). Then, stitch the binding to one edge of the garment, stopping at the corner. Keep the needle in the fabric and raise the presser foot (D).

Spread the fabric at the clip to straighten the garment edge and slip the binding over it. Lower the presser foot and continue stitching (E).

Make diagonal folds in the binding at the corner on both sides of the garment (F). Edgestitch or slipstitch the corner folds to keep them in place.

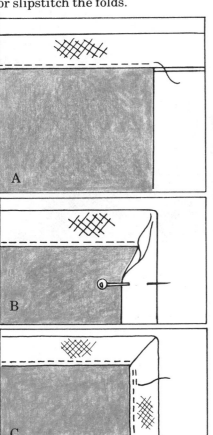

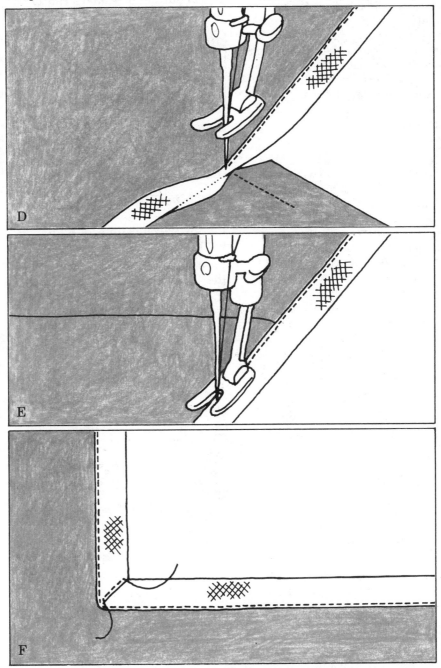

Buttonholes

A neat, even appearance is top priority with buttonholes. Before you begin, it's important to stabilize buttonhole areas with interfacing. For sheers or fabrics not suitable for interfacing, make a corded buttonhole instead.

Machine-Worked Buttonholes

Marking: Mark buttonhole placement just before you're ready to stitch, after the facing and interfacing have been attached. If you've chosen a button size different from that suggested by the pattern, adjust the length of the markings on the pattern, measuring from the end near the center front line.

To mark, place the pattern tissue on top of the garment, aligning the pattern seamline with the garment opening edge. Stick pins straight through the tissue and the fabric at both ends of each marking; then carefully remove the pattern without disturbing the pins (A). Secure the pins. Use pins as your final markings or use sewing tape, cellophane tape or machine-basting instead.

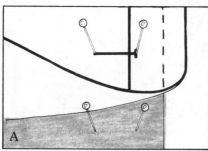

If you use *pins* to mark the ends of the buttonhole, lower needle into the fabric at the first pin, then remove pin. Stitch to the second pin, removing it just before you reach it.

If you use *tape, test it first* on a fabric scrap, because tape mars some fabrics. Cut tape ½″ (1.3 cm) longer than the buttonhole marking. Place tape on garment ⅛″ (3 mm) above the pin markers. With a pencil, mark buttonhole

length on the tape. Stitch next to the tape, being careful not to stitch through it (B).

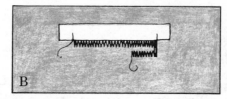

To *machine-baste,* make a ladder-style marking between the pins with your longest machine stitch. This will indicate buttonhole placement and length. For horizontal buttonholes, mark center front with different color thread (C).

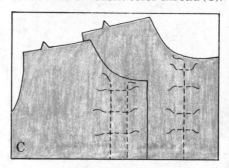

Stitching: Buttonhole attachments are shown on page 43. Follow your machine manual to make buttonholes.

First make a trial buttonhole on the same number of fabric layers as the garment, to check the size and stitch settings. You should be able to slash an opening without cutting the stitches.

If napped or glossy fabric doesn't feed evenly, stitch over plastic wrap, tissue paper or wax paper.

Corded buttonhole: Stitch over a fine cord for reinforcement (D), using a cording attachment (page 43) or guiding cord by hand.

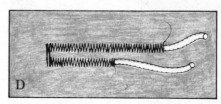

Cutting: Use a single-edged razor blade, seam ripper or buttonhole scissors to slash the buttonhole open neatly, taking care not to cut the stitches.

Hand-Worked Buttonholes

Marking and cutting: Mark placement with pins the same as for machine-worked buttonholes; draw a line between pins with chalk or pencil. Then, machine stitch ⅛″ (3 mm) above and below this line and across ends. Slash on line (E).

Sewing: Use a single strand of heavy-duty thread or buttonhole twist. Overcast the raw edges; then make the buttonhole stitch.

Working counter-clockwise from bottom right, with the needle

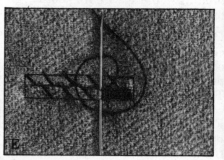

aimed toward you, insert needle into slit and bring it out below machine stitching. Loop thread under needle as shown and pull needle up so that a knot forms on the slit edge. Make successive stitches the same way, keeping them close together (E).

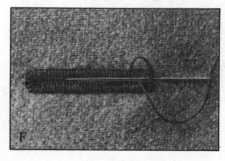

To turn the corner, fan the stitches, keeping the stitch depth even. Make a bar tack at the other end by covering several long straight stitches with blanket stitches as shown (F).

Bound Buttonholes

Marking: First, interface your garment as directed by the pattern. Then, mark the buttonhole positions *before* the facing is stitched on. Pin-mark and machine-baste as described for machine-worked buttonholes, through fabric and interfacing.

Lips: You need to make two lips for every buttonhole. Each lip should be cut 1" (2.5 cm) longer than the buttonhole.

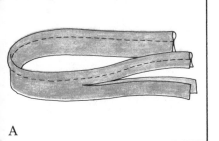

A

On the straight grain, cut a fabric strip 1" (2.5 cm) wide and long enough for all the lips. For instance, if you're making four 1" (2.5 cm) buttonholes, you'll need eight lips, each 2" (5 cm) long. So the fabric strip must be 8 x 2" or 16" (40.5 cm) long.

Fold the strip in half lengthwise, with *wrong* sides together, and stitch ⅛" (3 mm) from the fold. Trim the raw edges ⅛" (3 mm) away from the stitching (A). Then, cut the strip into individual lips.

Stitching: Pin pairs of strips to right side of the garment with the raw edges meeting at the buttonhole markings and ends extending ½" (1.3 cm) on either side of markings. Stitch strips in place along previous stitching, using a small machine stitch (B).

Pull thread ends to wrong side and tie. If you happen to sew a couple of extra stitches past the ends, the ones not needed can always be picked out with a pin. Open the buttonhole at the marking by cutting *only the garment*. From the wrong side, start at the center and slash the garment to within ¼" (6 mm) of the ends of the stitching. Carefully clip diagonally into the corners all the way to the stitching, forming little triangles (C).

Turn the strips and triangles through opening to the wrong side and press (D). With the garment right side up, fold it back out of the way so the strip ends and the triangular piece can be stitched together. Using your shortest stitch length, stitch across the base of the triangle, catching strips, too (E).

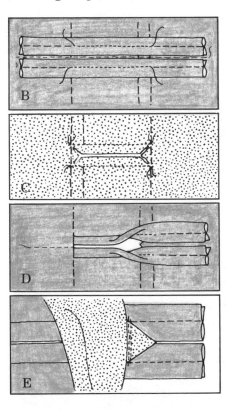

B

C

D

E

Finishing: After the facing has been attached, pin it to the garment in the buttonhole area to keep it from shifting. From the garment side, insert pins at the ends of the buttonhole through to the facing. Slit facing between these pin markers, clipping the slit a little at the center (F). Turn the raw edges under, forming an oval; whipstitch them to lips (G).

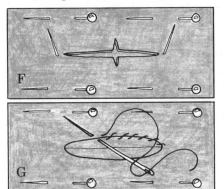

F

G

Quick-finish: On ravel-free fabrics, such as knits or suede-likes, pin the facing to the garment in the buttonhole area. Working on the outside, stitch in the ditch created by the buttonhole rectangle (H). On the inside, cut away the facing rectangle outlined by the stitches (I).

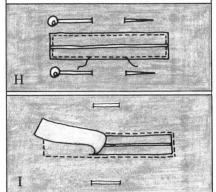

H

I

Buttons

Buttons come in all shapes and sizes, but actually, there are only two basic types—sew-through and shank. Whichever type you use, you can sew them on so they stay put. Or if you're in a real hurry, there are ways to anchor buttons without taking a stitch!

General Tips

Selecting size: Buy the button size suggested on the pattern. Otherwise, you'll have to adjust the pattern buttonhole length, as described on page 106.

Determining buttonhole size: Wrap seam binding or twill tape around widest part of button; pin. Half this measurement is button width (A). For buttonhole length, add ⅛" (3 mm) to button width for a flat button and slightly more for a thick button.

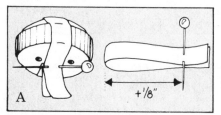

Button placement: After making buttonholes, lap garment edges, matching centers. Stick a pin through a horizontal buttonhole at center front or back, ⅛" (3 mm) in from buttonhole end (B). Stick pin through a vertical buttonhole ⅛" (3 mm) below buttonhole top.

Hand Sewing

Use a double strand of thread; run it through beeswax for extra strength (see page 45).

Sew-through button: Take a small stitch through fabric at button location. Place toothpick or wooden match on top of button; sew through holes of button, sewing over pick (C). Remove

toothpick. Wrap thread tightly around the thread under button, creating a shank (D). Without a shank, stress from the second fabric layer might cause the button to pop off. Anchor thread with a few little stitches.

Sew reinforcement button under fashion button on fragile fabric or

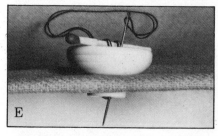

areas that take a lot of stress. Use a small, flat button with the same number of holes. Place it inside the garment and sew through both buttons at the same time (E).

Shank button: Take a small stitch under the shank to anchor thread. Sew shank to fabric with several small stitches (F). Secure thread as for sew-through button.

Machine Sewing

Most zigzag machines can handle sew-through buttons, so check your manual for directions. If tape won't mar your fabric, use it to keep button in place for stitching. To create a thread shank, sew over a darning needle held on top of the button (G).

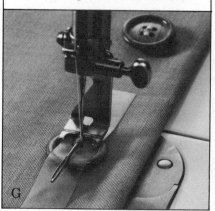

No-sew Methods

Plastic button fastener: Stick fastener through fabric and button's holes or shank; snap closed on underside (H).

Shank fastener: Make an eyelet in the fabric (see page 101); insert shank. Use the metal fastener from the button card to hold button (I).

Casings

A casing is a tunnel of fabric for inserting a drawstring or length of elastic. It's a quick way to ruffle, gather or control fullness in a garment.

General Tips

Marking: The easiest and by far the quickest way to mark the foldline for a casing is to make a small clip or snip in the seam allowance(A). Be sure to mark both ends of the foldline.

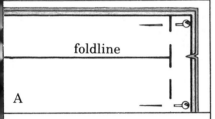

foldline

A

Anchor seam allowances: To save time when inserting the elastic or drawstring, machine-baste the seam allowances to the garment

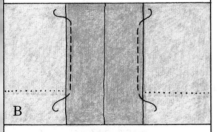

B

in the casing area (B) so that the elastic or drawstring won't get caught under them. Remove the basting when the casing is completed.

Elastic: Buy elastic ⅛''-¼'' (3 mm-6 mm) narrower than the casing. Use flat, braided elastic,

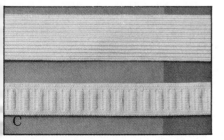

C

which is slightly ribbed and lightweight, or non-roll elastic which is extra firm and has heavy ribs to prevent it from twisting or rolling once inserted (C). Both types come in several widths. If you are planning to use elastic in swimwear, be sure the label indicates swimwear since regular elastic stretches when wet.

Cut elastic 1'' (2.5 cm) larger than body measurement, or according to pattern guide.

Drawstring opening: If the casing will carry a drawstring, make an opening for it with two machine-worked buttonholes (D).

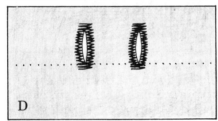

D

Or, if the opening falls at a seam-line, leave a section of the seam unstitched. Reinforce ends of stitching by including small squares of seam binding in the backstitching (E).

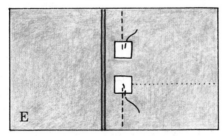

E

Folded Casing

At the waist or wrist edge, a folded casing is often used to gather the fabric. To make this casing, press the raw edge under ¼'' (6 mm) unless you are using knits or firmly woven fabrics which do not ravel. Press casing under on foldline. Stitch close to both edges of casing,

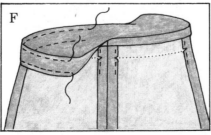

F

leaving an opening in the lower edge for inserting elastic (F). Insert the elastic. Stitch the opening closed.

Bias Tape Casing

Use single-fold bias tape when a casing away from an edge is needed—for example, at the waist of a one-piece dress. You can also use it at an edge when the fabric is too bulky for a self-fabric casing, for curves, or when there's not enough fabric to fold over for a conventional casing.

Away from an edge: Mark the casing line on the wrong side of the garment (see pages 86-88). Machine-baste across the seam allowances at casing area. Then place the lower edge of the bias tape along the casing line; fold ends under where they meet. Stitch along both edges (G).

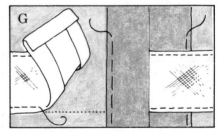

G

At an edge: Press the seam allowance or casing foldline under and trim to ¼'' (6 mm). Machine-baste across the seam allowances at casing area. Pin tape to garment to cover the raw edge, folding tape ends under where they meet. Stitch close to both edges of tape (H).

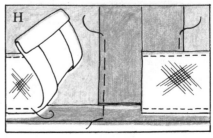

H

Inserting Elastic

Fasten a safety pin to one end of the elastic and insert it through the opening in the casing. Push the pin through, sliding the fabric over the pin. Try on the garment and pin the elastic to fit snugly. Trim elastic if needed, so ends will overlap ½″ (1.3 cm). Hold the ends together with pins and machine-stitch securely with parallel rows of stitches or a square (A).

Securing elastic: Try on the garment and distribute the fullness as desired. To keep elastic from twisting in the casing, pin the garment to the elastic at the seams. Remove the garment and stitch in the ditch, or groove, formed by each seam (B).

Casing with zipper: Insert a centered zipper (see page 172), stitching to upper edge of garment (C). Press under ¼″ (6 mm) on upper edge for wovens, not for knits. Turn casing to inside; stitch close to edges. Insert elastic and adjust to fit. Stitch across ends of casing to secure elastic (C); trim off elastic. Sew fasteners at top of zipper and casing.

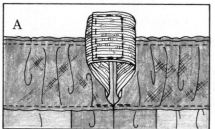

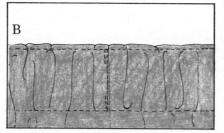

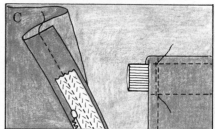

No-roll Elastic Casing

Here's a method that produces a totally twistproof elastic casing which looks just like the regular application. It's recommended especially for knits, although it can also be used for woven fabrics.

Cut elastic 3″ (7.5 cm) less than body measurement since elastic stitched to fabric will be longer than its original length.

If you are working with a woven fabric, finish the raw edge by turning it under ¼″ (6 mm) and stitching.

You can leave one garment seam open so the elastic can be stitched in place while your garment is still *flat*. Or, stitch the garment seams; then stitch the ends of elastic together, forming a circle. For both ways, divide the elastic and garment edge into four or eight equal parts, marking both with pins (D).

Matching all markings, pin the elastic to the wrong side so that the lower edge is on the casing foldline (E). Stitch along the lower edge of the elastic, stretching it to fit the fabric as you sew (F).

If you attached the elastic using the *flat* method, stitch the last garment seam, including the elastic. Turn the casing to the inside along the foldline; pin it at the seams (G). Stitch ¼″ (6 mm) from the lower edge, stretching as you sew. As you stitch, insert a folded strip of seam tape in the seam at center back to help you tell the front from the back at a glance (H).

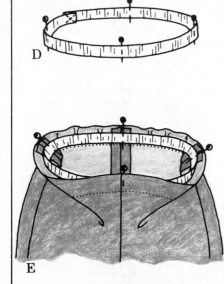

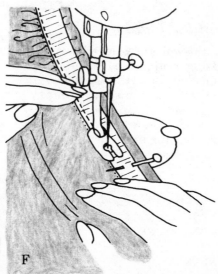

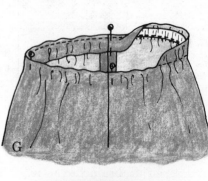

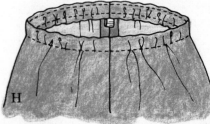

*C*ollars

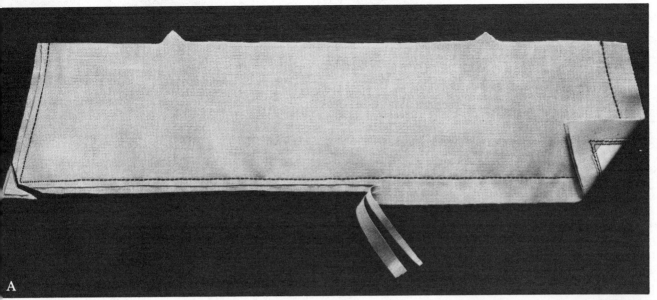

A

A collar is an important focal point on a garment because it frames your face. Thanks to quick interfacing, machine-stitching and pressing techniques, collars are easier than ever to make. You'll get a professional-looking collar every time, with a minimum of fuss.

Collar Basics

A collar is made of two fabric layers and is usually interfaced. The top layer is called the collar or upper collar, while the bottom layer is referred to as the facing or undercollar. Whatever style you're making, the procedures here will ensure a good-looking collar with well-defined edges.

Interfacing: Cut the collar and interfacing as shown in pattern. To reduce bulk, trim the corners of the interfacing diagonally just inside the seamline (A). For most garments, machine-baste the interfacing to the *upper collar* ½" (1.3 cm) from the raw edge and trim the interfacing close to the stitching. Or, trim ½"(1.3 cm) from fusible interfacing edges first; then fuse it in place.

Stitching: To keep the facing edge from curling up after the collar is applied, trim the facing a scant ⅛" (3 mm) along the outside edge. Then, with the outer edges even, pin the facing to the collar. Stitch, easing the collar to the facing as you sew (A).

To reinforce lightweight or loosely woven fabrics at corners or sharp curves, use a smaller stitch for about 1" (2.5 cm) on either side; take a diagonal stitch or two across each corner to make it easier to turn (B). Trim the seam allowances and corners . On thick fabrics, also trim the facing seam allowance to ⅛" (3 mm), grading the layers (A).

Pressing and turning: To preset the edge, press the seam open so that one seam allowance is toward the collar, as shown on page 194. After turning the collar right side out, coax the points out *gently* from the inside with the eraser end of a pencil or the points of scissors, or from the outside with a pin (C). Then press the collar, rolling the seam slightly to the facing side.

Preparing the garment: First, staystitch the neck edge. Then, clip up to the stitching (D) to release the fabric and help it lie flat as you pin the collar in place.

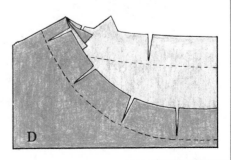

B

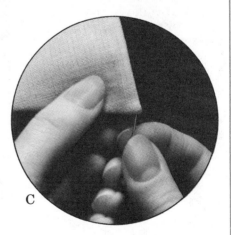

C

D

111

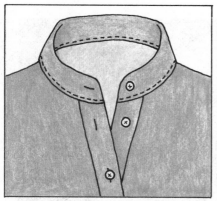

Band Collar

There are two ways to apply stand-up collars—by machine and hand stitching or by machine stitching entirely.

Machine and hand-stitched: Interface one collar section. On facing, press under and trim neckline seam allowance. Pin and stitch facing to collar, leaving neckline edge unstitched. Pin and stitch interfaced section to *outside* of neckline, matching notches and markings, keeping facing free (A). Trim seam; press toward collar. Pin pressed edge to neckline seam; slipstitch (B).

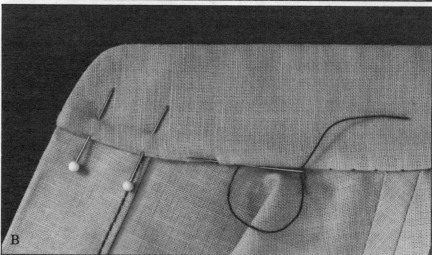

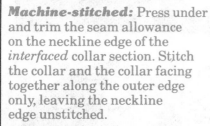

Machine-stitched: Press under and trim the seam allowance on the neckline edge of the *interfaced* collar section. Stitch the collar and the collar facing together along the outer edge only, leaving the neckline edge unstitched.

Pin the collar facing to the *inside* of the garment neckline, matching notches and markings and keeping the pressed edge of the collar free; stitch (C).

Trim and clip the seam; press the collar away from the garment with the seam toward the facing. Then, pin or fuse-baste the pressed edge along the neckline seam on the *outside* and edgestitch it in place (D).

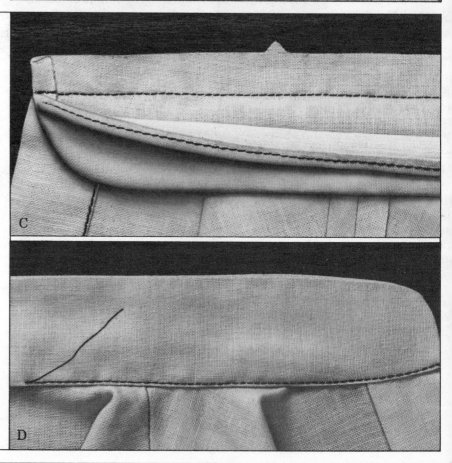

Convertible Collar

You can apply a convertible collar almost entirely by machine, with a little hand-finishing. Follow your pattern directions and page 111 to interface and assemble it.

If there's no back neck facing: Pin the collar section without interfacing to the outside of the garment neckline, leaving the upper collar free between the markings at the shoulders (A).

Clip the upper collar to the markings. Turn the front facings to the outside over the collar, matching notches and markings, and pin in place at the neckline. Stitch the entire neck seam, keeping the upper collar free between the clips. Clip through the remaining fabric layers at the markings; trim and clip the seam (B).

Turn the front facings to the inside. Turn under the loose collar seam allowance. Pin the collar edge to the neck seam; pin the shoulder edge of the facing along the shoulder seam. Slipstitch the collar edge to the neck seam (C). Tack the facing to the shoulder seam allowances.

If your pattern includes a back neck facing: Stitch the back neck facing to the front facing as your pattern shows. Finish the outer facing edge. Baste the collar to the outside of the garment neckline; then pin the neck facing on top, matching notches and markings. Stitch the neckline seam.

Trim and clip the seam (D). Turn the facing to the inside; press. Tack the facings to the shoulder seam allowances.

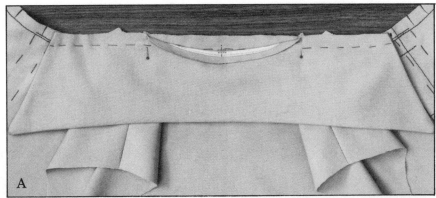

A

B

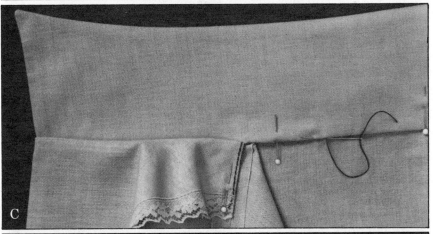

C

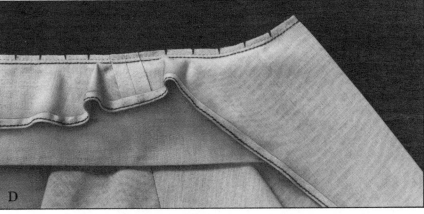

D

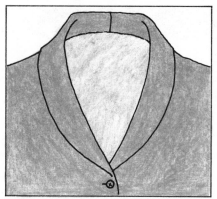

Shawl Collar

This collar has no separate pattern piece. The undercollar is an extension of the front and the upper collar is part of the facing.

Prepare the front: Reinforce the inner corners of the neckline with small machine stitches on the seamline. Clip to the stitches at the corner. Stitch the darts. Then, form the undercollar by stitching the front extensions together at the center back seam; trim. Press the seam open (A).

Stitch the neck and shoulder seams: First, prepare the garment back by staystitching and clipping the neckline and stitching any darts. Then, pin the front and undercollar extension to the back at shoulders and neckline, matching notches and markings and spreading the undercollar at the clips to fit the back neckline. Stitch shoulder and neckline seams (B). Trim the neck seam. Press the shoulder seams open and the neck seam toward the collar.

Prepare front facing: Interface the facing and upper collar. Reinforce and clip inner corners as for Prepare the Front, above. Finish the unnotched edge. Next, stitch the center back seam on the facing; trim and press open. Press under and trim facing shoulder and neck seam allowances. Pin to garment, matching notches and markings.

Attach facing to garment: Stitch the facing to the garment. Trim the seam and notch the curve (C). Turn the facing to the inside; press. Slipstitch the facing edges along the seams (D).

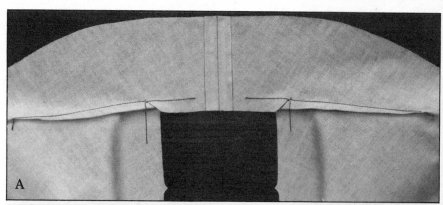

A

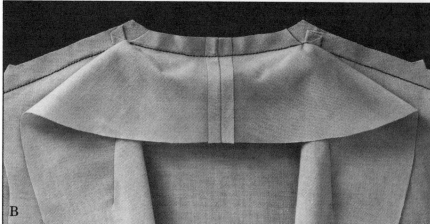

B

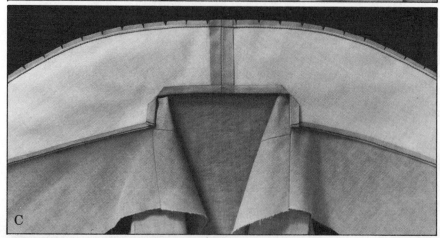

C

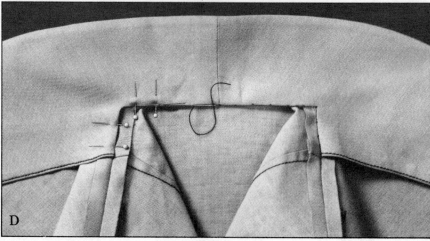

D

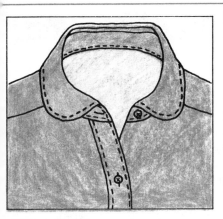

Shirt Collar

Here's an all-machine method for applying the popular shirt collar. This classic style includes a neckband which usually has a separate pattern piece. Follow your pattern instructions and the directions on page 111 to cut, interface and assemble the collar.

Attach neckband: Pin the interfaced neckband section to the outside of the garment neckline, matching notches and markings; stitch. Trim the seam and press the neckband and seam up (A).

Attach collar: Then, pin and machine-baste the un-interfaced side of the collar to the neckband, matching notches and markings (B).

Attach neckband facing: Press under and trim the seam allowance on the lower edge of the neckband facing. Pin the neckband facing to the collar and neckband, matching notches and markings; stitch. Trim and notch the curved seam allowances as shown (C).

Complete collar: Turn the neckband facing to the inside; press. Pin or fuse-baste the facing edge along the neckline seam and edgestitch it in place (D).

A

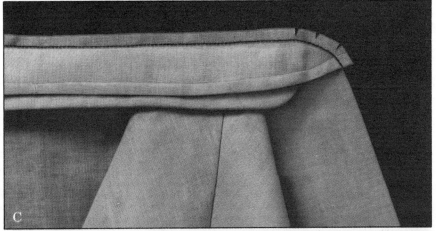

B

C

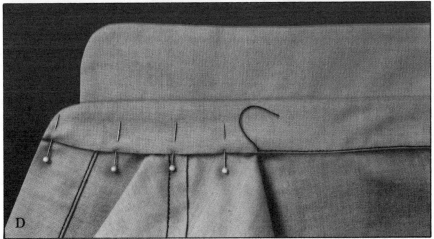

D

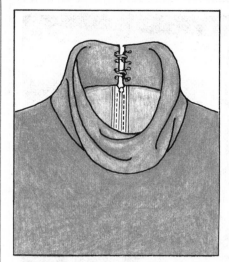

Turtleneck or Cowl Collar

A turtleneck or cowl collar is not interfaced so it drapes gracefully.

For woven fabric: Press under and trim the seam allowance on the long unnotched edge of the collar. Fold and stitch the collar as your pattern instructs. To maintain a soft edge, don't press the fold. Pin the collar to the garment neckline, matching notches and markings; leave the pressed edge free. Stitch, then trim seam (A). On the *inside*, pin the pressed edge over the seam; slipstitch (B).

A

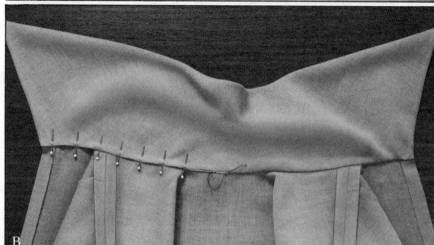

B

For knit fabric: You can apply the collar entirely by machine. First, stitch the center back seam of the collar and press it open. Turn the collar right side out, and place the raw edges together, matching seams, notches and markings. *Don't* press the fold. Pin the collar to the outside of the garment neckline, matching the raw edges, markings and seams (C). Stitch on the seamline and again ¼″ (6 mm) away (D). Raise the collar and press the seam toward the *garment.* Then, on the *outside,* topstitch through all thicknesses, close to the seam, catching in the collar seam allowances. Trim seam close to stitching.

C

D

Cuffs

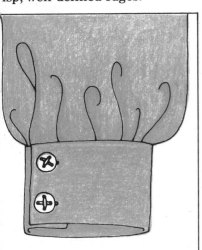

...ttoned and snug or turned up ...d loose, cuffs are popular de-...ils on sleeves and pants. Sewing ...cuff is similar to making a col-...r. Like a collar, a cuff is made of ...vo fabric layers and is usually ...terfaced. The top layer is called ...e cuff, while the underneath ...yer is referred to as the facing. ...elow are the details for sewing ...e most often used cuffs. What-...ver style you're making, these ...ethods ensure a neat cuff with ...isp, well-defined edges.

...uff With Opening

...his cuff is a buttoned band, used ...ainly on shirt, blouse and dress ...eeves. First, prepare the sleeve ...ening (see Sleeves, page 165). ...hen assemble and apply the cuff, ...sing either the Machine and ...and-stitched method below, or ...e Machine-stitched method on ...ge 118.

...achine and hand-stitched:
...terface the cuff section after ...imming off the interfacing cor-...ers to reduce bulk (see page 143).

...ress under the notched seam al-...wance on the cuff facing section ...nd trim it to 1/4″ (6 mm). To as-...mble the cuff, with right sides ...gether, stitch the facing to the ...uff on the unnotched edges. For ...osely woven or lightweight fab-...cs, reinforce corners or sharp ...rves by using a smaller stitch ...r about 1″ (2.5 cm) on either ...de. Trim the seam as shown (A).

To pre-set the edge, press seams open so one seam allowance is toward the cuff.

Turn the cuff right side out and coax corners out gently with scissor tips or a pin as shown for Collars, page 111. Press the cuff, rolling seams slightly to the facing side as you press.

Stitch two rows of gathering stitches on the lower edge of the sleeve as directed by your pattern. Then pin the cuff to the outside of the sleeve, matching notches and markings; place the sleeve open-ing edges at the ends of the cuff.

Gather the sleeve to fit the cuff by pulling up the thread ends and adjusting the fullness. Wrap the thread ends around a pin and pin or baste the seam (B).

With the sleeve on top, stitch the seam. Trim the seam and press it toward the cuff. On the inside, pin and slipstitch the pressed facing edge along the seam (C).

Apply buttons and make buttonholes.

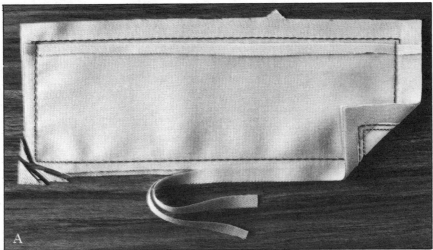

A

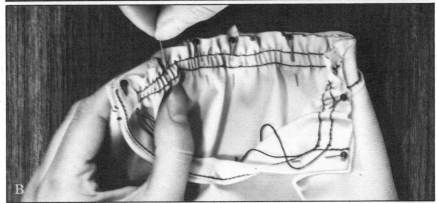

B

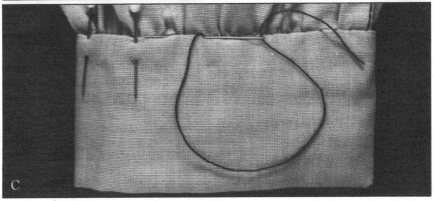

C

7

sewing today: collars, cuffs

Machine-stitched: Interface and assemble the cuff as shown in the Machine and Handstitched method on page 117, but press under the seam allowance of the *cuff* instead of the cuff facing. To apply the cuff, pin the right side of the cuff facing to the wrong side of the sleeve, matching notches and markings, and placing the sleeve opening at the ends of the cuff.

Gather the sleeve to fit the facing and pin or baste the seam. With the sleeve on top, stitch the seam. Trim the seam and press it toward the cuff (A). Pin or fuse-baste the outer cuff over the stitched seam. On the outside, edgestitch along the seam and stitch again ¼″ (6 mm) away on all the cuff edges, if desired (B). Apply the buttons and make buttonholes.

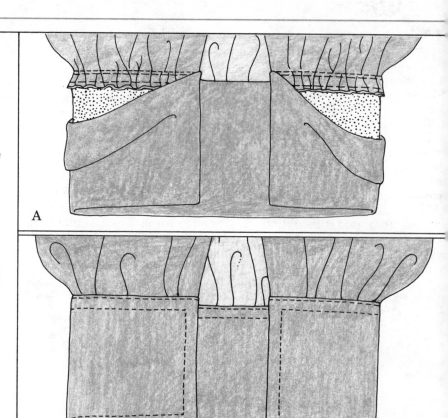

A

B

Rib-knit Cuff

These cuffs are a good way to finish sleeves or legs on a sporty garment. If you purchase knit cuffs, follow the manufacturer's instructions for applying them. Here's how to make your own cuffs from rib-knit trim which is available by the yard.

Prepare the cuff: Since it's easiest to apply rib-knit trim while the garment is still flat, leave the sleeve or one leg seam unstitched. To determine the cuff length, pin the edges of the trim together and try the cuff on.

Adjust the trim so that it slides comfortably over the widest part of your hand or foot, but will hug your wrist or ankle snugly when the cuff is relaxed. Add 1¼″ (3.2 cm) to allow enough for a ⅝″ (1.5 cm) seam.

Fold the trim in half lengthwise with wrong sides together. Baste the long edges together.

Apply the cuff: Divide the garment edge and the cuff into four equal parts with pin markers. Pin the cuff to the right side of the garment, matching markers (C). Stitch, stretching the cuff to fit the garment. Stitch again ¼″ (6 mm) away with a straight or zig-zag stitch; trim close to stitching. If your machine has an over-edge stitch, you can stitch the seam and finish the edge at the same time. Stitch the sleeve or leg seam and press it open. Finish cuff seam allowances by turning the ends under diagonally and machine-tacking them to the seam allowances (D).

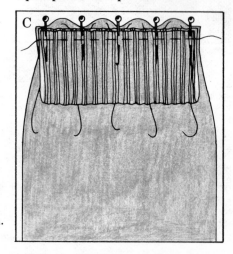

C

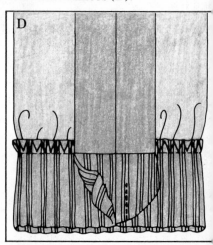

D

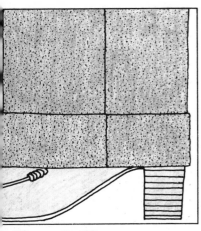

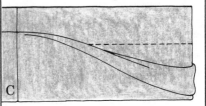

old-up Cuff

ou'll find this type of cuff on ants or short sleeves. Patterns yled this way have enough ngth built in, so you don't need add any for the cuffs. Mark the em and cuff foldlines. Turn the g or sleeve inside out and press e hem up (A). Finish the raw dges and sew the hem in place. urn the garment right side out. old the lower edge up along the ff foldline and press.

To hold the cuff in place, make a French tack between the cuff and the leg or sleeve at both seams. Take two or three loose stitches between layers. Work blanket stitches over the threads (B).

Shortcut fold-up cuff:

You can save time by machine-stitching the hem in place; the stitches won't show on the outside of the finished cuff (C). It's even easier if your machine has a free-arm feature. Then, turn the leg or sleeve right side out. Fold the lower edge up along the cuff foldline and press.

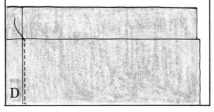

To keep the cuff in place, stitch in the ditch at the seams, through all layers (D).

Mock Fold-up Cuff

You can get the look of a cuff by making a quick tuck on straight, untapered sleeves or legs. Cut the pattern apart on the hemline. Spread it ½″ (1.3 cm) and pin or tape to paper (E). After stitching the seam, press the edge under at the hemline (F) and again the same amount. Stitch ¼″ (6 mm) from the lower fold to form the tuck and encase the raw edge of the hem (G). Press the tuck up, the cuff down.

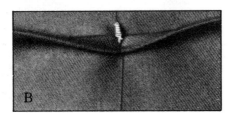

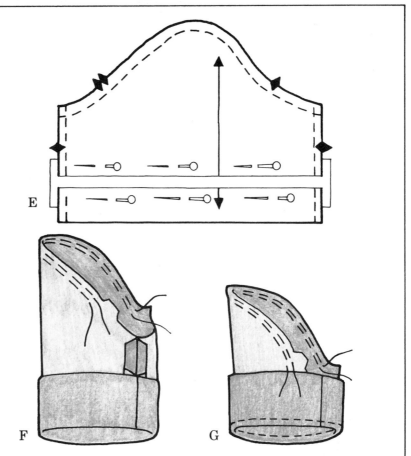

Darts

Darts shape flat fabric into a three-dimensional form that fits the body. They shape the bustline and shoulder on a dress or blouse, define the waist and shape the hipline on a skirt or pants, and form a bend at the elbow on a narrow sleeve.

Types of Darts

Straight: The most common dart is straight. It may be used at the bust (A), the back shoulder, on the skirt or pants back, and at elbows.

Curved: Curved darts may be used on a fitted dress bodice to shape the fabric above the waist. Curved darts can also make a skirt or pants front or a raglan sleeve conform to body curves (B).

Double-pointed: Straight or curved, this type of dart shapes the fabric at the waistline on one-piece dresses or closely-fitted shirts, blouses or jackets. The widest part falls at the waist (C).

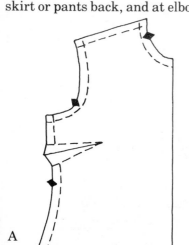

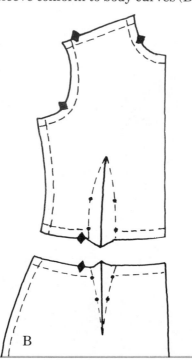

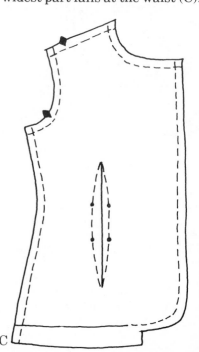

A

B

C

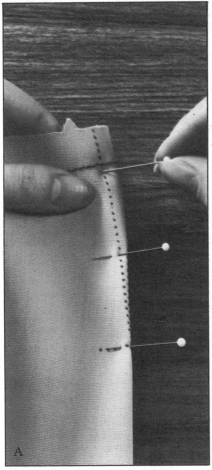

A

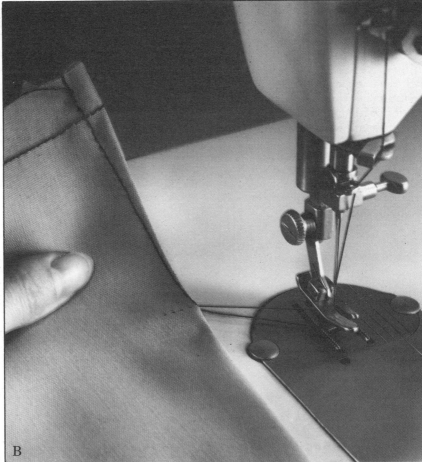

B

Dart How-to's

Stitching: With right sides
together, fold the fabric on the
center dart line, matching the
markings on the dart and stitching lines. Pin at right angles to
the stitching line (A). Stitch
the dart from the wide end to the
point, backstitching at the
beginning to secure the stitches.
To prevent a bubble at the point,
make the last few stitches right
on the fold and leave thread ends
long enough to tie a knot (B).
Don't backstitch.

Clip a *double-pointed* dart at the
widest part so it lies flat (C).

Pressing: Your pattern will tell
you which way to press the darts.
As a rule, vertical darts are
pressed toward the center of the
garment and horizontal ones are
pressed downward (C).

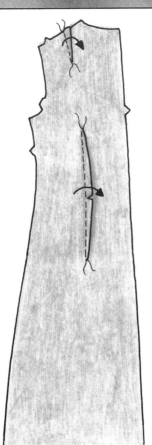

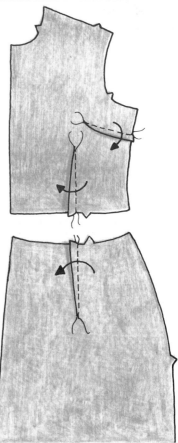

C

Easing

When one garment section is slightly larger than an adjoining one, it must be eased to fit the smaller piece. For example, you may have to ease a skirt waistline edge to fit the waistband, or a back shoulder to fit the front. Always stitch the seam with the eased side up. Smooth the fabric with your fingers as you stitch to prevent puckers.

Pin-easing

To ease a small amount, pin the sections together at notches and markings, with the eased layer on top. Distribute the fullness with more pins (A). Stitch.

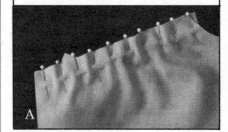

A

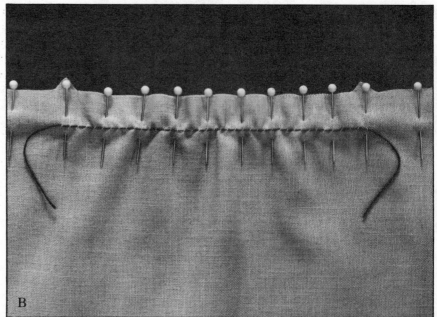

B

Ease Stitching

To control larger amounts of fullness, ease-stitch. Loosen the upper tension slightly. Use 8-10 stitches per inch (2.5 cm); if your dial is numbered 0-4, set it on 3. Stitch on the seamline of the area to be eased (B). On a sleeve cap, also stitch ¼″ (6 mm) away on the seam allowance (C).

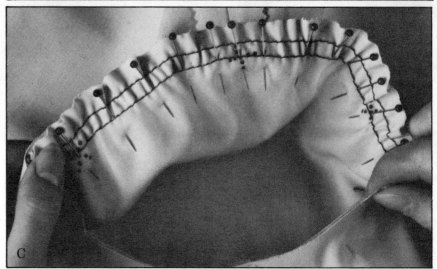

C

Pin the ease-stitched section to the adjoining section, matching notches and markings. Draw the fabric up along the bobbin thread and distribute the fullness evenly between markings, using closely-spaced pins (B, C). Stitch.

Ease-plus Stitching

You can ease moderate fullness—for example, on a back shoulder edge or a slightly flared hem—with a regulation stitch length. Press your index finger against the back of the presser foot. Stitch for several inches (centimeters), letting the fabric pile up against your finger (D). Release the fabric and repeat. This crowds the fabric, distributing the fullness.

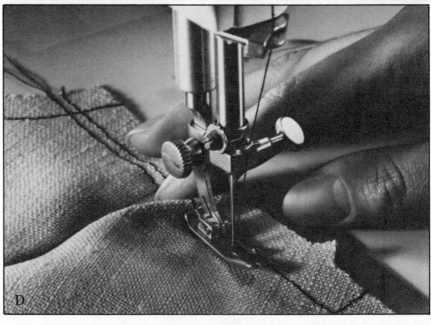

D

Edge finishes

Raw edges of seams, hems and facings on unlined garments should be finished to prevent raveling and add durability. You can skip this step if your garment will be lined. Finish each seam allowance if the seam is pressed open; finish edges together if the seam is pressed to one side. Always finish a seam before it's crossed with another seam. Otherwise, you won't be able to finish the entire seam. Suitable finishes for many fabrics are given below. The chart on pages 124 and 125 also tells which finishes to use for several common fabrics.

Straight-stitched
For knits that may curl, including swimwear fabrics, jersey and stretch terry, stitch ¼" (6 mm) from all edges *before* stitching the seams to minimize the curling (C).

Hong Kong Finish
Suitable for most fabrics, this luxurious finish is especially good for heavyweights. Use 1" (2.5 cm) wide bias strips of lining fabric. With right sides together, stitch the strip to the garment in a ¼" (6 mm) seam; trim to ⅛" (3 mm). Turn the strip to the inside, over the raw edge. Secure it by stitching in the ditch (over the seamline) on the outside (F).

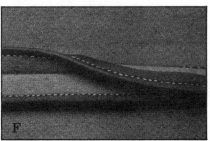

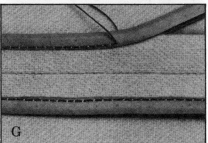

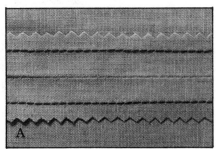

Stitched and Pinked
This is the quickest method for finishing a pressed-open seam or raw edge on fabrics that do not ravel easily. First, stitch ¼" (6 mm) from each seam allowance edge; then trim close to the stitching with pinking shears (A).

Clean-finished
This is a quick, casual-looking finish for light and medium weight fabrics. It's not suitable for bulky types. Stitch ⅛" (3 mm) from the raw edge. Turn the edge under on the stitching line and stitch again, close to the edge (D).

Bound
For a custom finish on any fabric, encase the edges in double-fold bias tape, with the wider side of the tape underneath. Stitch close to the tape edge through all layers (G). For curves, pre-shape the tape (see page 103).

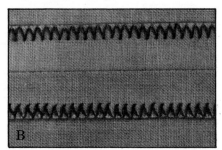

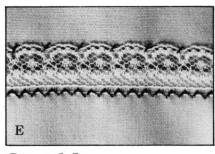

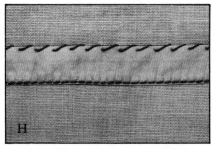

Zigzagged
This method is the best choice for heavyweight fabrics that ravel, but is suitable for other weights as well. Zigzag over the raw edge (B), or as close to the edge as possible, using a smaller stitch width for lightweight fabrics and a larger one for heavyweights.

Stretch Lace
Apply this product to finish raw edges on hems or facings, especially on knits and curved edges. To apply, lap lace ¼" (6 mm) over edge. Edgestitch in place with a straight or zigzag stitch (E).

Seam Binding
To finish raw edges on straight hems, use seam binding. Apply it with straight stitching (H), the same as for Stretch Lace.

Bias Tape
For curved hems, use single fold bias tape like Seam Binding; but first steam press it to match the curve of the raw edge.

Fabrics

Fabric	Thread	Machine Needle Size	Stitch Length Per Inch (2.5 cm)	Seam Type	Edge Finish	Special Information
Batiste		11		plain, French, mock French, double-stitched	clean-finished, seam binding	hold taut while stitching
Broadcloth	cotton/polyester, mercerized cotton	11 or 14	12-15	plain, topstitched welt, flat-felled	stitched and pinked, zigzagged, clean-finished, seam binding	
Brocade		14	10-12	plain	stitched and pinked, zigzagged, bound, seam binding	
Challis		11		plain	stitched and pinked, clean-finished, zigzagged, seam binding	
Chambray		11 or 14	12-15	topstitched, welt, plain, flat-felled		
Chiffon	extra-fine for lightweight fabric	9 or 11 all-purpose ball-point		French, mock French, double-stitched	none	use small-hole throat plate, hold thread ends to start, hold fabric taut while stitching, use tissue paper under seams if needed
Chino		14		plain, flat-felled, welt, topstitched	stitched and pinked, zigzagged, seam binding	
Corduroy	cotton/polyester, mercerized cotton	14 or 16	10-12	plain, welt, top-stitched, flat-felled	stitched and pinked, zigzagged, bound, seam binding	pin or baste closely or use even-feed foot
Crepe		11		plain, French, mock French, double-stitched	clean-finished, zigzagged	hold taut while stitching
Crepe de chine	extra-fine for lightweight fabric	9 or 11	12-15			use small-hole throat plate
Denim	cotton/polyester, mercerized cotton	14 or 16	10-12	plain, flat-felled, welt, topstitched, overedged	stitched and pinked, zigzagged, seam binding	
Double knit	cotton/polyester, polyester	11 or 14 ball-point	10-15	plain, topstitched, zigzagged, or stretch-stitched, double-stitched	none on most, straight-stitched if edges curl	stretch as you sew for straight stitching
Eyelet	cotton/polyester, mercerized cotton	11	12-15	plain, French, mock French	clean-finished, zigzagged, stitched and pinked	
Fake fur	heavy-duty cotton cotton/polyester, polyester	14 or 16	6-10	plain, overedged	none	stitch in direction of pile; use even feed foot
Felt	cotton/polyester mercerized cotton			plain, lapped		
Flannel and Gabardine		14	10-12	plain, topstitched, welt, flat-felled	stitched and pinked, zigzagged, bound, seam binding	
Gauze	cotton/polyester, mercerized cotton	11		plain, French, mock French, double-stitched	clean-finished	use small-hole throat plate, hold thread ends to start stitching
Georgette	extra-fine for lightweight fabrics	9 or 11				
Gingham	cotton/polyester, mercerized cotton	11 or 14	12-15	plain, flat-felled, topstitched	stitched and pinked, zigzagged, clean-finished, seam binding	
Jersey	cotton/polyester, polyester, extra-fine for light-weight fabrics	9 or 11 ball-point		plain, zigzagged or stretch-stitched, double-stitched, overedged	straight-stitched if edges curl	for straight stitching, stretch as you sew; tape shoulder and waistline seams

How to Sew Fabrics

Fabric	Thread	Machine Needle Size	Stitch Length Per Inch (2.5 cm)	Seam Type	Edge Finish	Special Information
Linen	cotton/polyester, mercerized cotton	11 or 14	10-12	plain, topstitched	clean-finished, stitched and pinked, seam binding	
Melton		16	8-10	plain, topstitched, welt	none or bound	test-stitch to see if pressure and tension should be decreased, pin or baste closely
Organdy and Organza	extra-fine for lightweight fabrics	9 or 11	12-15	plain, French, mock French, double-stitched	stitched and pinked, clean-finished	use small-hole throat plate, hold thread ends to start stitching
Piqué	cotton/polyester, mercerized cotton	11 or 14	10-12	plain	stitched and pinked, zigzagged, seam binding	
Poplin				plain, topstitched, overedged		
Quilted Fabric		14 or 16			zigzagged, bound	pin or baste closely, test-stitch to see if pressure and tension must be decreased
Satin		11 or 14	12-15	plain	bound, zigzagged, seam binding	pin only in seam allowance to avoid marring
Seersucker				plain, topstitched	stitched and pinked, clean-finished, zigzagged, seam binding	
Silk and Silk-like Blend	silk, cotton/polyester, extra-fine for lightweight fabrics	9 or 11		plain, French, mock French	clean-finished, seam binding	use small-hole throat plate, test-stitch to see if tension should be decreased
Single Knit	cotton/polyester, polyester, extra-fine for lightweight fabrics	9 or 11 ball-point		plain, zigzagged or stretch-stitched, double-stitched, overedged	zigzagged, straight-stitched if edges curl	for straight stitching, stretch as you sew; tape shoulder and waistline seams
Stretch Terry and Velour	cotton/polyester, polyester	14 ball-point	10-12			
Suede and Suede type	cotton/polyester, mercerized cotton	14 wedge-point for suede, all-purpose ball-point		plain, lapped, topstitched	none	paper-clip suede edges, use double-faced basting tape or fuse basting for suede types, or pin in seam allowance only
Sweater Knit		14 ball-point		plain, topstitched, zigzagged or stretch-stitched, overedged, double-stitched	straight-stitched if edges curl, zigzagged	for straight stitching, stretch as you sew, tape shoulder and waistline seams
Swimwear Knit	cotton/polyester, polyester	11 or 14 ball-point			zigzagged	for straight stitching stretch as you sew
Taffeta	cotton/polyester, mercerized cotton	11 or 14	12-15	plain	stitched and pinked, clean-finished, zigzagged	
Tricot	extra-fine for lightweight fabrics	9 ball-point		plain, topstitched, zigzagged, overedged, double-stitched		hold thread ends to start stitching; for straight stitching, stretch as you sew
Velvet, Velveteen and Velour (woven)	cotton/polyester, mercerized cotton	11 or 14		plain	zigzagged or bound	pin or baste closely or use even-feed foot
Vinyl	heavy-duty polyester, heavy-duty mercerized cotton	14 or 16 wedge-point	6-8	plain, lapped, topstitched	none	use roller foot for stitching on right side, pin in seam allowance only, or paper-clip

7

sewing today: fabrics

125

Facings

A facing is the piece of fabric that finishes a raw garment edge. Facings are used at necklines, armholes, front or back openings, and sometimes at waistlines.

Facing Tips

To make a facing that looks good and lies flat, follow these tips.

Preparing: Staystitch the garment neck and facing edges. Apply interfacing to the facing or to the garment, following your pattern instructions. Stitch the facing sections together at shoulders or underarms and finish the outer edge. Stitch the facing to the garment (see pages 128-129).

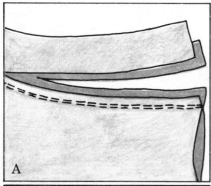

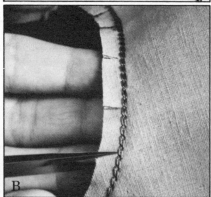

Trimming and grading: To prevent ridges from showing on the outside, remove bulk from the seams by trimming the seam allowances to ¼″ (6 mm). On thick fabrics, also trim the facing seam allowance to ⅛″ (3 mm), grading the layers (A). Clip or notch curved seam allowances to insure a smooth edge when the facing is turned to the inside (B).

Quick trimming tips: If you're using a lightweight fabric, try these shortcuts:
• Instead of clipping and notching curves, use pinking shears to trim the seam (C).

• Grade both seam allowances at the same time by holding the scissors at an angle as you cut. Each seam allowance will be trimmed to a different width.

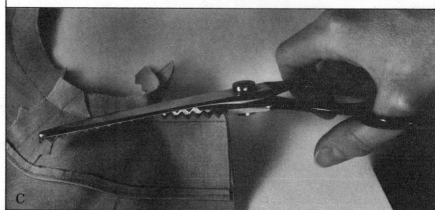

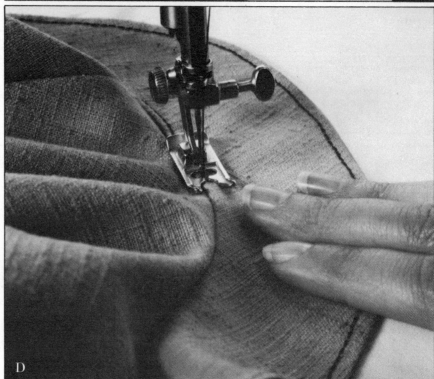

Understitching: To keep a facing from showing on the outside, it's a good idea to understitch. First, press the seam allowances open, then toward the facing. With the facing on top, stitch through the facing *and* both seam allowances very close to the seam (D). Turn the facing to the inside and press, first from the wrong side, then from the right side. This keeps the facing from rolling to the outside of the garment.

Tacking: To anchor a facing at a seam, hand tack it to the seam allowances (A), or try one of the following shortcuts:

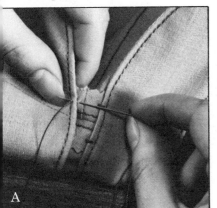

A

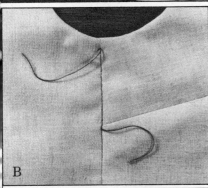

B

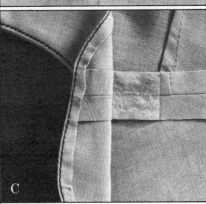

C

• On the side or shoulder seam, machine stitch through the garment *and* facing in the ditch formed by the seam (B). Draw the thread ends to the inside and fasten.
• Fuse instead of stitching. Place a small piece of fusible web between the facing and the garment at the seam (C); follow the manufacturer's instructions.

Neckline Facings

A neckline facing may be used, either with or without a collar, to finish off the neck edge smoothly and to conceal seam allowances.

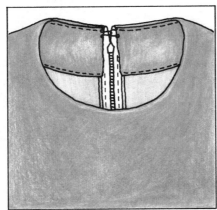

Preparing: First staystitch the garment neckline edges and the facing neckline edges. If you're using fusible interfacing, apply it to the facing sections, following the manufacturer's instructions. Then, stitch the facing shoulder seams and press them open. For medium to heavyweight fabrics, trim the seam allowances to ¼" (6 mm) to reduce bulk. Finish the outer edge of the facing (D).

If you're using regular interfacing, apply it to the garment neck edges before stitching the shoulder seams (E). Then baste the collar, if any, to the outside of the garment neck edge and apply a facing (see page 128).

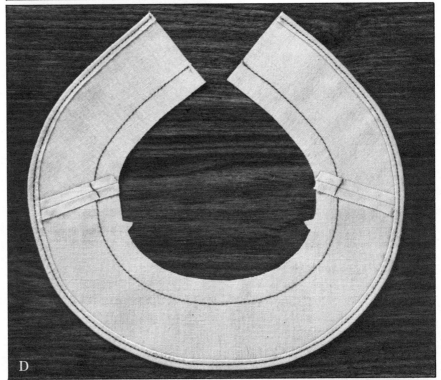

D

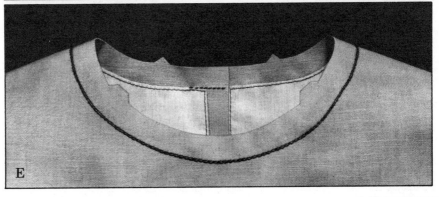

E

Applying the facing: *For a centered zipper,* insert the zipper; then pin the facing to the neck edge, matching seams, notches and markings. The ends of the facing will extend ⅝″ (1.5 cm) beyond the opening edges. Stitch seam (A). Trim, clip, press and understitch as on page 126.

Turn the facing to the inside, turning the ends under enough to clear the zipper teeth; pin. Slip-stitch the facing to the zipper tape (B). Apply a hook and eye to the top edge. Tack the facing to the shoulder seams.

For a lapped zipper, apply the facing before the zipper. Press under the left end of the facing 1⅛″ (2.8 cm) and the right end ½″ (1.3 cm). Pin the facing to the neck edge, matching seamlines, notches and markings; stitch. Trim, ending 1½″ (3.8 cm) from the left end and 1″ (2.5 cm) from the right end (C).

Press the seam open, then toward the facing; understitch. Insert the zipper. Then, trim the zipper tape even with the neck seam. Turn the facing to the inside and slipstitch the ends to the zipper tape (D). Apply a hook and eye and tack the facing to the shoulder seams.

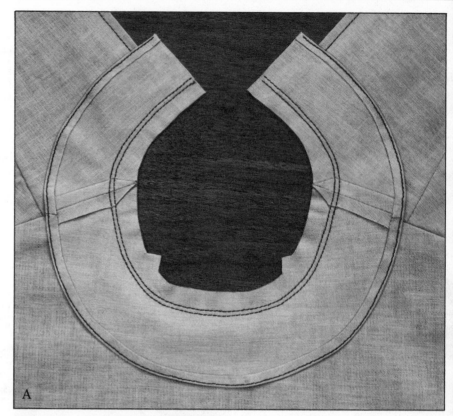

A

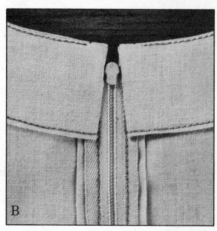

B

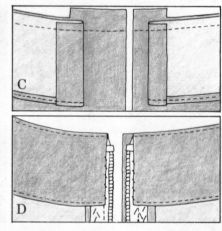

C

D

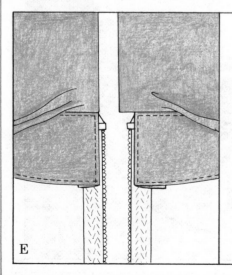

E

Facing shortcut: Apply facing, following directions for centered or lapped zippers above. Press facing and seam away from the garment. Trim zipper tape ends to ⅜″ (1 cm) above the top stop. Pin the facing to wrong side of the zipper, near the teeth; edgestitch (E). Pin facing and zipper to the garment; from the right side, stitch zipper in place through the facing (F). Apply a hook and eye. Fuse facing to shoulder seams or stitch in the ditch (page 127).

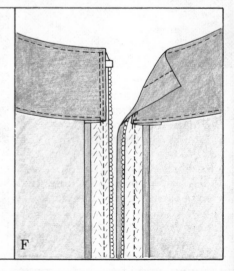

F

For an invisible zipper, insert the zipper. Trim ⅝" (1.5 cm) from the facing center back edges (A). With right sides together, pin the facing ends to the garment center back edges, over zipper. With a zipper foot, stitch a ⅜" (1 cm) seam (B).

Pin the facing to the garment neck edge, matching seams, markings and notches; a fold will form at the zipper. Stitch the seam, catching the fold (C). Trim, clip, press and understitch as on page 126. Turn the facing right side out (D); tack shoulder seams.

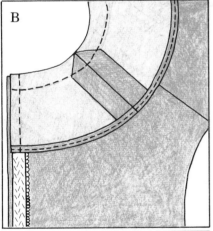

A

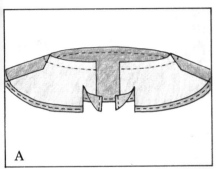

B

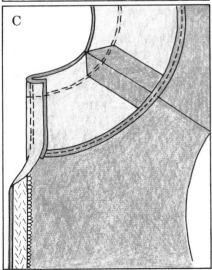

C

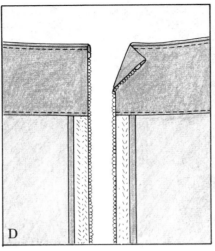

D

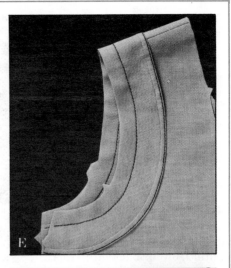

E

Armhole Facings

Armhole facings are used to finish the edges of sleeveless garments and may be applied either before or after the side seam is stitched.

Before stitching side seam:
Finish the outer edge of the facing. Then, pin the facing to the

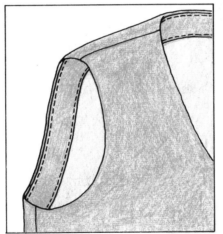

garment, matching notches and markings; stitch (E). Trim, clip, press and understitch as on page 126. Then, stitch the side seam of the garment and the underarm seam of the facing continuously (F) and press the seam open. Turn the facing down and tack it to the side seam (G).

After stitching side seam:
Finish the outer edge of the facing. Then stitch the facing underarm seam and press it open. Pin the facing to the garment, matching notches, markings and seams; stitch. Trim, clip, press, understitch and tack as on pages 126-127.

F

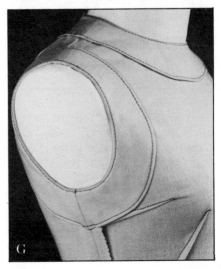

G

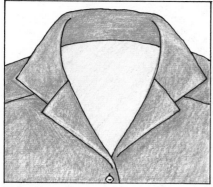

Front (or Back) Self-facing

A garment that opens at the center front or back often has a facing extension that is cut in one piece with the garment (A). When folded back, this extension becomes the facing for the opening edge and, usually, part of the neckline (B). Follow your pattern directions to cut, mark, interface and staystitch the garment and facing. Finish the outer edge of the facing extension and shoulder seam allowances. Stitch and press

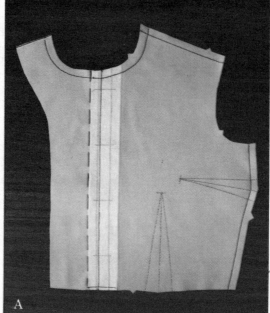

A

B

the garment shoulder seams, then see page 113 to apply a facing over a collar. To apply a facing to a neckline edge without a collar, stitch the facing extension to the back neck facing at the shoulder

seams; press. Turn the facing extension to the outside along the foldline, and pin the facing to the neck edge. Stitch and complete according to the Facing Tips on pages 126-127.

Bias Tape Facing

As an alternative to a regular facing, you can use purchased single-fold bias tape. Either the ½″ (1.3 cm) or the ⅞″ (2.2 cm) width works well. It's a time-saver because you don't have to cut out and prepare separate facing pieces, and the tape

To apply the tape, trim the garment seam allowance to ¼″ (6 mm). Open out one tape fold. If you're facing a curved edge, steam-press the tape and pre-shape it to follow the garment curve (C). With right sides together and raw edges even, pin the tape to the garment (D).

For a circular edge, turn under ½″ (1.3 cm) on the first tape end; lap the other end over it (D). Stitch a ¼″ (6 mm) seam (E). Turn the tape to the inside; press. On the outside, topstitch the tape in place close to the edge and again about ⅜″-¾″ (1-2 cm) away (F).

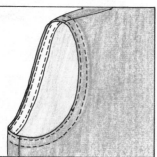

comes with the raw edges already pressed under for finishing. Since the bias grain shapes smoothly to fit curves, this type of facing is often used for necklines and sleeveless armholes, especially on children's clothing.

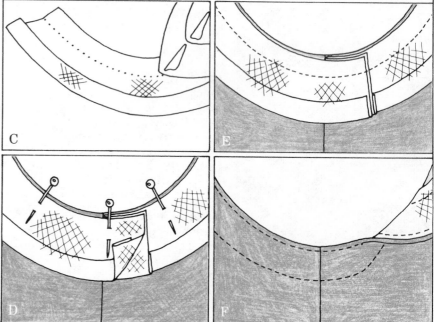

C

E

D

F

Fasteners

Wherever two garment edges meet, a fastener is needed to hold the edges together. Besides buttons and buttonholes, the most common type, there are many other choices. Here's a useful array of fasteners, conventional and otherwise. Some are sewn in place, while others are attached with simple tools.

To mark the fastener placement on your garment, line up the garment edges evenly and use pins to mark the placement.

Hooks and Eyes
These metal fasteners are used to hold edges very securely where there may be some strain. They range in size from 0 to 4, for light to heavyweight fabrics and many fastening needs. The hooks come with loop and straight eyes.

For edges that meet: Use a hook and *loop* eye. On the inside, sew the hook ⅛" (3 mm) from the right-hand edge, making a few tacking stitches through the holes. Also sew across the end, under the hook, to hold it flat. Don't let the stitches show on the outside of the garment. Sew the eye opposite the hook, letting it

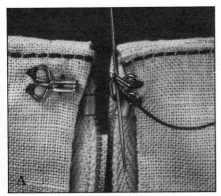

extend slightly beyond the garment edge. Take a few stitches along the sides of the loop to hold it flat (A).

For edges that lap: Use a hook and *straight* eye. For a waistband, sew on two sets. Sew the hook(s) to the inside of the garment on the overlapping side, ⅛" (3 mm) from

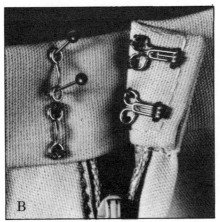

the edge, making a few tacking stitches through the holes. Also sew across the end(s), under the hook(s), to hold it flat. Don't let stitches for the hook show on the outside of the garment. Close the zipper or other closure to mark the eye position(s) with pins. Sew the eye(s) to the outside of the underlap (B).

Heavy Duty Waistband Hook and Eye
A large, flat metal hook and eye is a great fastener for most skirt and pants waistbands. It's large

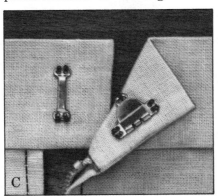

enough for you to use only one set, thin enough to be inconspicuous, yet sturdy enough to take almost any strain (C). Apply it like the regular hook and eye, above.

No-sew type: This waistband hook and eye hammers or clamps on—stitch-free. Apply it before you finish the waistband, following the manufacturer's instructions (D)

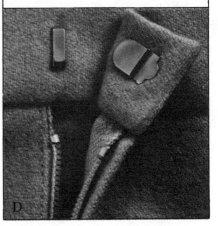

Snaps
These fasteners should be used only where there will be very little strain. They come in many sizes for light to heavyweight fabrics and different fastening needs, and are used where edges lap.

Sew-on types: Sew the ball half of the snap to the overlapping section on the inside of the garment, about ⅛" (3 mm) from the edge. Make several tacking stitches through each hole, carrying the thread under the snap to the next hole without letting stitches show

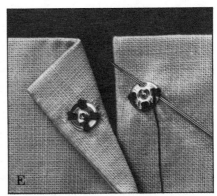

on the outside. To mark the position of the socket half of the snap on the outside of the underlapping section, close the garment and use a pin stuck through the socket. Sew the socket in place the same way you did the ball half (E).

No-sew snaps: Sturdy, hammer-on snaps are a fast substitute for buttons and buttonholes (A). They're available in different sizes and are a favorite for children's clothes and sportswear. Follow the package instructions to hammer the snaps in place. Or, apply them with a plier-like tool you can buy (B). It's easier to use and also comes with instructions.

Frogs

Purchased frogs are fast alternatives to buttons and buttonholes. Position them the same as for Toggles, below. Tack them in place (E).

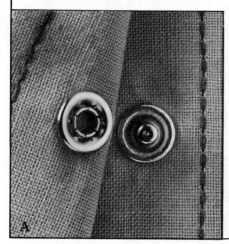

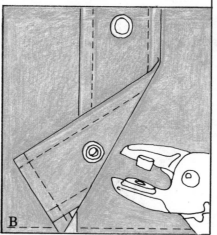

Snap tape: Another time-saver, snap tape consists of two strips of grip-tight snaps. Machine-stitch the ball strip to the garment underlap and the socket strip to the overlap, stitching along all tape edges and turning the ends under (C).

Self-gripping Fasteners

These flexible, two-part fasteners are quick to apply and use. They have tiny, stiff hooks and soft loops which interlock when you press them together. To open, gently pull them apart. Position each part at least ¼″ (6 mm) from the edge. Machine-stitch or hand-sew the loop part to the facing on the overlap; stitch the hook part to the outside of the underlap (F).

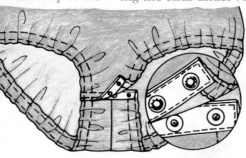

Toggles

Decorative toggles and loops come in many styles to be used on jackets and vests instead of buttons and buttonholes.

To mark toggle and loop positions, lap the garment edges so that center fronts match or the edges meet.

Position the toggles on the left garment edge and the loops on the right (do the opposite for men's clothes), so that they close directly over the center front. Hold them in place with pins or with double-faced basting tape. Then machine-stitch to the garment as shown (D).

Loops

For an attractive closure that can be used in place of buttonholes, try loops. When you apply them to the garment, use the center front as the seamline. First, cut out and mark your garment as usual. Then, cut the right front section along the facing foldline. This will give you separate front and facing sections. Apply the loops before attaching the facing. If your pattern has a collar that extends beyond the center front, trim the collar front edges so that they end at the center front. To position buttons, lap the edges, matching centers; pin. Mark for buttons.

For continuous loops: Form a continuous length of cord into loops on a paper guide. On the paper, draw a vertical line the same distance from the edge as

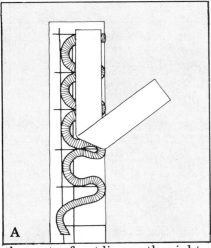

the center front line on the right garment section. Draw a second line, spacing it the width desired for the finished loops. Each loop should be long enough for the button to pass through, plus enough extra to be caught in the seam allowance with loops and garment edges even. Draw horizontal lines across the vertical lines to indicate the placement of each loop. Tape the loops to the paper (A). Test loop size by inserting a button through it.

Then, position the paper and loops on the garment, with the taped edge even with the garment edge. Machine-baste next to the seamline. Remove the tape and tear the paper away from the stitching. Apply the facing.

For single loops: Cut each loop long enough for the button to pass through, plus seam allowances. To make self-fabric loops, cut a bias strip (see page 103) four times the desired finished width and long

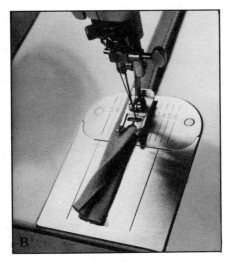

enough for all loops. Fold the raw edges to the center of the strip; then, fold the strip in half lengthwise; edgestitch (B). Cut the strip into equal sections.

On the outside, position the raw loop edges even with the garment edge. Make narrow loops curved, wide loops pointed. Tape loops to hold them in place (C).

Machine-baste the loops next to the seamline (C). Remove the tape and trim ends of the loops to reduce bulk. Apply the facing.

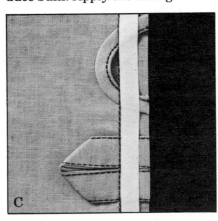

For super-fast loops: Use purchased cord, ribbon, fine braid, etc. to form loops (D). Then, to apply, follow the directions given for Single Loops, above.

Ties

Self-fabric ties are ideal for overlapping closures. First, use a measuring tape to determine the length. Then, cut a bias strip for each tie four times the desired width and the length of the tie plus 1¼" (3.2 cm). Fold the raw edges to the center of the strip, turning one end in ⅝" (1.5 cm). Then, fold the strip in half lengthwise and stitch close to all three folded edges.

On the garment, mark the position of each tie 1" (2.5 cm) inside the center front. Pin the tie to the garment with the raw edge ⅜" (1 cm) over the mark. Stitch ⅜" (1 cm) from the edge; trim (E). Press the tie over the raw edge. Stitch through all layers ¼" (6 mm) from the turned edge and backstitch (F).

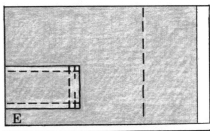

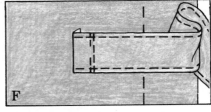

Ribbon ties are speedy substitutes for self-fabric ties. After stitching them to the garment, notch or cut the ends diagonally to prevent raveling (G).

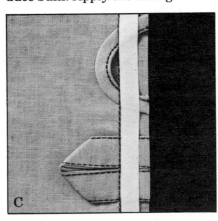

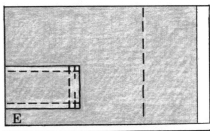

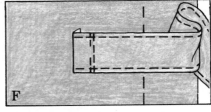

Fusibles

These revolutionary aids—tapes, interfacings, webs, etc.—not only save time; they're also easy to use. Fusibles are sensitive to heat so pressing can replace hand and machine stitching. For most applications, all you need is a press cloth, a steam iron and firm pressure. Always read the manufacturer's directions first, since they may vary from one brand to another.

Most fusibles work on a large variety of fabric types, but there are occasional exceptions. Check the product package to be sure your fabric is suitable, and always make a test sample first.

EASY GUIDE TO FUSIBLES

Types	Uses	Availability	Application
Hem Tape	Secures hems.	Packaged in a variety of colors.	Position tape over hem edge, adhesive side down. Press.
Interfacing	Gives body, shape and support to collars, cuffs, waistbands, necklines, front edges, pockets and flaps.	By the yard or in pre-packaged amounts; in woven, knitted, non-woven and stretchable nonwoven types; from very lightweight to heavyweight versions.	Trim across corners; cut ½″ (1.3 cm) from interfacing seam allowances. Fuse with steam and a damp press cloth. Also see Interfacing, page 143.
Mending Fabric	Decorates or repairs tears in fabrics that can take a hot iron.	Packaged in patches, strips or rolls; in an assortment of colors; embroidered, printed, knitted, etc.	Cut to size, rounding corners. Place shiny side down on fabric and press, using a press cloth. Let cool before handling.
Waistband Interfacing	Adds firmness and prevents rolling.	Pre-packaged perforated strips 1¼-2″ (3.2-5 cm) wide.	Cut interfacing the length of the finished waistband. Place it on the wrong side of the waistband with the perforations along the waistband foldline. Fuse with a steam iron and a damp press cloth.
Webbing	Secures two layers of fabric together for basting, hemming, appliqué, mending, trim application, crafts, etc.	By the yard or in pre-packaged strips of varying narrow widths.	Sandwich webbing between two layers of fabric. Fuse with a steam iron, using a damp press cloth.

Gathering

Gathering can control the fullness at the waistline, a yoke seam, the cuff of a full sleeve or the cap of a puffed sleeve. It can also create ruffles. Here's how to gather fabric easily.

Machine Gathering

Loosen the needle thread tension slightly to make it easier to pull the bobbin thread later. Set the stitch length for a long stitch—the heavier the fabric, the longer the stitch. On the right side of

shorter one, matching notches, seams and markings; pin (A).

Gently pull the bobbin threads at each end, sliding the fabric along the threads until it fits the shorter section. At both ends, wrap the excess bobbin thread around the pins in figure eights. Distribute gathers evenly and pin (A).

Stitch with the gathered side up (B); be careful not to let tucks form on the seamline.

Gathering over a cord:

Here's a fast method for gathering a long area. Cut strong, thin cord a little longer than the edge to be gathered. Place it on the seam allowance next to the seamline. Set your machine for a zigzag stitch wide enough to stitch over the cord without catching it in the stitches (D); the stitches should fall just short of the seamline. Wrap one end of

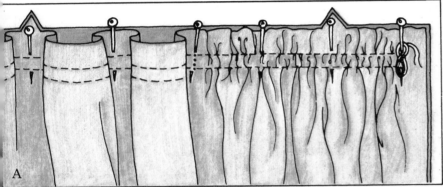

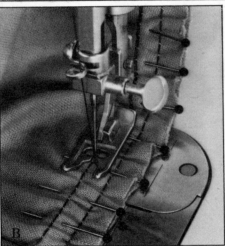

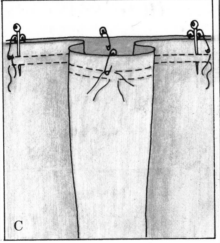

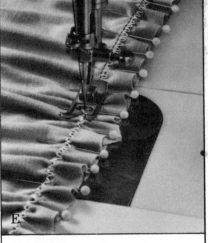

your fabric, stitch on the seamline of the area to be gathered. Then stitch again ¼" (6 mm) away on the seam allowance. Leave long thread ends; do not backstitch.

If gathering will cross a previous seam, diagonally trim the ends of the seam allowances before stitching (page 158). On bulkier fabrics, stitch up to the seams, keeping the seam allowances out of the way. With right sides together, pin the section to be gathered to the

Long-distance Gathering

To gather long areas, divide both edges into four or eight equal parts and mark with safety or straight pins (C). On the edge to be gathered, make separate rows of gathering stitches for each section. Then if the thread breaks when you pull up the gathers later on, you won't have to re-stitch the entire edge. Pin the edges together, distribute the fullness and stitch, following Machine Gathering directions.

the cord around a pin in a figure eight to secure it (see Machine Gathering).

Pin the corded piece to the adjoining piece, matching notches, seams and markings. Pull the free end of the cord to gather the fabric to fit. With the gathered side up, stitch along the seamline, being careful not to catch the cord (E). Remove the pins from the fabric and gently pull out the cord.

Hand sewing

Although your sewing machine can handle most sewing jobs, there are still times when hand sewing is a must. Check page 44 for a description of the various hand sewing tools you'll need. There's also a chart to help you choose the right size needle for hand sewing all types of fabrics.

Hand Sewing Hints

Even if you're used to sewing by hand, these often overlooked tips can help make the job a lot easier and quicker.

For tangle-free sewing:
• Cut the thread in lengths no longer than 18" (46 cm).
• Draw the thread through beeswax.

For easy needle-threading:
• Choose a needle with an eye large enough for fast threading, but not so large that the thread keeps slipping out or the eye makes holes which can damage your fabric.

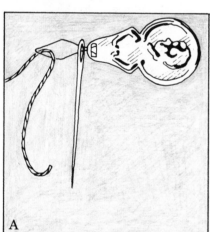

A

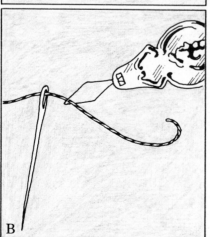

B

• Cut the thread diagonally by holding your scissors on a slant.
• Hold the needle up against a light background so you can see the eye clearly.
• Use a needle threader. Push the wire through the needle eye and slip the thread through the wire (A). Then, pull the wire back out of the needle, drawing the thread through the eye (B).
• Use a calyx-eyed needle, which is open at the top (see page 44).

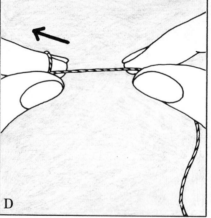

C

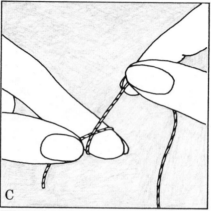

D

To knot the thread:
• Knot the end you just cut.
• Hold the thread end between your thumb and index finger and wrap the thread around your index finger (C).
• Hold the thread taut and slide your index finger back along your thumb until the thread end twists into the loop (D).

• Continue sliding your index finger back until the loop slides off your finger (E).

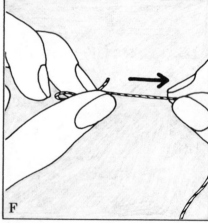

E

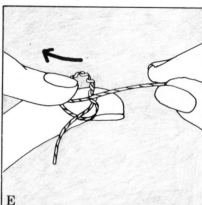

F

• Bring your middle finger down to hold the open loop; pull on the thread to form the knot (F).

Hand Stitches

Here are nine hand stitches that you are likely to use at one time or another. In most cases, you should use a single strand of thread for best results and take two or three stitches on the needle at a time, keeping the stitches fairly loose.

Backstitch: This stitch looks like machine stitching. Use it to mend a minor popped seam, or

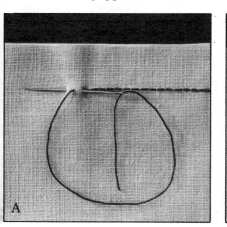

any small area where very secure stitching is needed and you don't feel like setting up your machine. Fasten the thread on one side. Insert the needle ⅛″ (3 mm) to the right and bring it up again ⅛″ (3 mm) to the left of where the thread first emerged. Insert the needle back into the spot where the thread first emerged and bring it up again ⅛″ (3 mm) to the left. Continue (A).

Basting: Use this stitch whenever you need to hold fabric together temporarily. Don't knot the thread. Instead, backstitch once at the beginning and end so that the thread will be easy to remove later. Take several long stitches by weaving the point of a long, fine needle in and out of the fabric (B). Slide the stitches back on the needle without removing it from the fabric. Repeat several times; then pull the needle out and draw the thread through the fabric.

Even basting, with stitches ¼″ (6 mm) long and ¼″ (6 mm) apart is fairly strong. Use it for seams, darts, waistbands, and pleats to prepare a garment for a try-on fitting (see page 100).

Uneven basting, with stitches ¼″ (6 mm) long and ½-¾″ (1.3-2 cm) apart (B), is used to mark or hold areas that will not receive stress, such as a hem or a foldline.

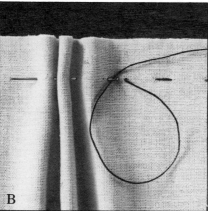

Blindstitch: Because they are sewn between a hem and the garment, blindstitches prevent the hem from forming ridges on the right side of a bulky or knit fabric. Fold the hem edge back slightly and hold it with your thumb. Fasten the thread inside the hem. Working from right to left, take a tiny stitch about ¼″ (6 mm) to the left in the garment. Then, take the next stitch ¼″ (6 mm) away in the hem. Continue alternating from the garment to the hem, keeping the stitches evenly spaced (C).

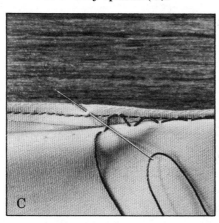

Catchstitch: A flexible stitch that is good for knits, the catchstitch holds edges, such as hems, facings, etc., in place. Work from left to right, with the needle pointing to the left. Fasten the thread on the wrong side of the hem or facing. Take a tiny stitch in the garment ¼″ (6 mm) to the right, close to the hem or facing edge. Take the next stitch ¼″ (6 mm) to the right in the hem or facing so that the stitches crisscross (D). Repeat, keeping the stitches fairly loose.

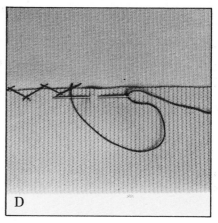

Hemming stitch: A clean-finished hem, or one finished with regular or lace seam binding, can be sewn with hemming stitches. Begin at a seam, fastening the thread in the seam allowance. Take a tiny stitch through the garment, picking up a single thread. Insert the needle diagonally under the hem edge about ¼″ (6 mm) away and take another stitch in the garment. Continue in this manner along the entire hem, taking several stitches on the needle before drawing the thread through the fabric (E).

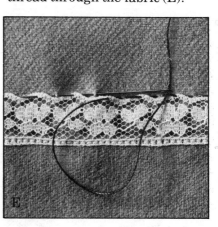

Overcast or whipstitch: You can overcast a single fabric layer to prevent raw edges from raveling or whipstitch two or more layers together. For either stitch, fasten the thread on the wrong side of the fabric. Working from

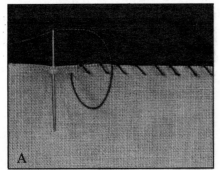

either direction, make slanted stitches about ⅛″ (3 mm) from the edge and ¼″ (6 mm) apart (A).

Hand picking: This is a half-backstitch used as a decorative stitch on collars, cuffs, pockets, etc. instead of machine top-stitching. It's also used to insert zippers in special garments or fabrics where a luxurious touch is desirable (B).

To assure a straight line of hand picking, make a row of basting stitches as a guideline. Using a single strand of heavy-duty thread or buttonhole twist, secure the thread on the underside of the fabric. Bring the needle up through all fabric layers at the basting line. Insert the needle a bit behind the point where the

thread first came out, covering only two or three fabric threads. Then, bring the needle up again about ¼″ (6 mm) ahead of the previous stitch (B). Continue this way, following the basted line.

To avoid puckering the fabric, don't pull up the thread too tightly. When the hand picking is complete, remove the basting stitches.

Running stitch: Used for fine seaming, mending or hand gathering, the running stitch is like even basting, only smaller,

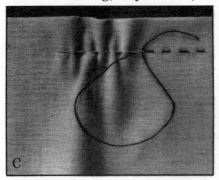

and the stitches are permanent. Working from right to left, take several even stitches on a long, fine needle by weaving the point in and out of the fabric. Slide some of the stitches back onto the thread without taking the needle out of the fabric. Repeat several times before you draw the thread through the fabric (C).

Blanket stitch: See page 229.

Buttonhole stitch: See page 106.

Padstitching: See page 242.

Slipstitch: Wherever you want a stitch that's invisible from both sides—for example, on hems or other turned edges—use a slip-stitch. Working from right to left, pick up a single fabric thread just below the folded edge. Directly above this, slip the needle inside the fold for about ¼″ (6 mm) (D). Then bring it out and pick up another single thread below the fold. Continue in this manner.

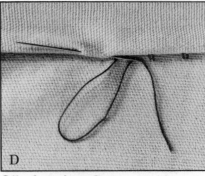

Slip basting: See page 100.

Hand tacking: This stitch helps keep facings in place at seams. Hold the edge of the facing and the seam allowance together and take three or four short stitches in one place through both layers. Do not sew through the garment fabric. Repeat on the other seam allowance (E).

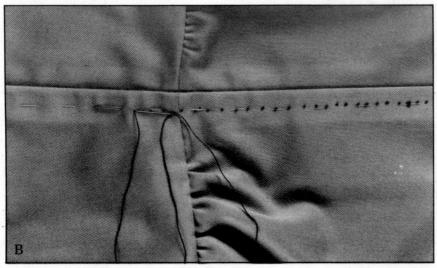

Hems

A hem, whether narrow or wide, should be barely visible from the right side of the garment. This can be easily accomplished by hand-sewing, machine-stitching or fusing the hem in place. When you are hand-sewing, pick up only one or two threads of fabric. And be sure to use thread the same shade as, or one shade darker than, your fabric. To eliminate guesswork, Simplicity patterns include a hem allowance that's right for the garment style.

Hem Basics

Whatever method you use, there are two basic steps that apply to all hems: 1) measuring and marking the hemline, and 2) trimming the hem allowance. Easing is another step that's needed only on curved hems to eliminate or control fullness.

Marking: To get a true picture of how the finished garment will look, try it on, wearing any undergarments, shoes and belt that you plan to wear with it. If there's a drawstring, pull it up and adjust the gathers evenly.

Mark the distance from the floor to the desired finished hem length, placing pins parallel to the floor about 2-3″ (5-7.5 cm) apart. Have a friend do this, using a yardstick (A) or a pin-type skirt marker. If you mark the hem yourself, use a bulb-type marker that works with powdered chalk.

Pinning: Turn the garment wrong side out and place it over an ironing board or table. Turn the hem to the wrong side along the pin-marked line. Match the seamlines first and insert pins through both layers at right angles to the hemline (B).

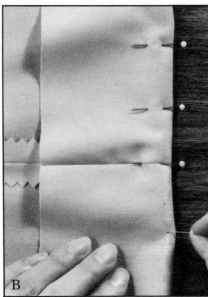

On slippery fabrics, baste about ¼″ (6 mm) from the folded edge, removing the pins as you baste.

Trimming: Measure and mark the desired hem depth plus ¼″ (6 mm) extra for finishing; then trim away the excess (C).

To minimize bulk at the hem, trim the seam allowances to half their width, starting at the raw edge of the hem and continuing up to the hemline as shown (D).

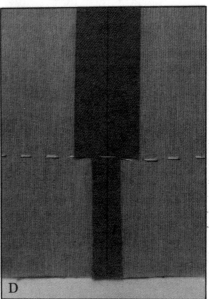

Easing: Curved hems have extra fullness which forms ripples when the lower edge is turned up. This fullness must be eased so that the hem lies flat against the garment. Except for a clean-finished edge, ease the hem *before* you finish the edge. Ease-stitch ¼″ (6 mm) from the edge. Working on a flat surface, use a pin to draw up the bobbin thread wherever the fabric ripples and distribute the fullness evenly (E). Steam-press to shrink out some of the fullness.

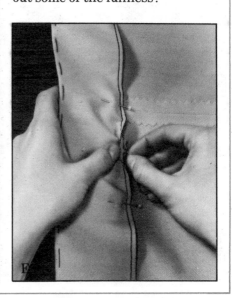

Hand-sewn Hems

Plain hem: This basic hem can range from 2″ to 3″ (5-7.5 cm) wide finished, depending on your pattern. After measuring, marking and trimming the hem, choose the appropriate finish for the raw edge of your fabric (see Edge Finishes, page 123).

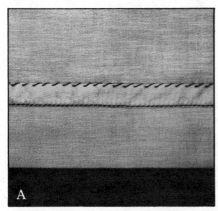

If your fabric does not ravel, no edge finish is necessary. After finishing the edge, sew it in place, using a hemming stitch (A), blindstitch (B), or catchstitch (C). Note: Ease in the fullness on a curved hem after clean-finishing.

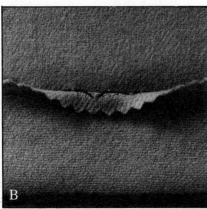

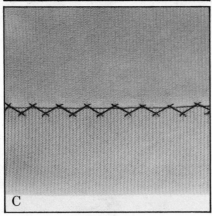

Faced: Apply bias or stretch lace hem facing to a garment edge without a deep enough hem allowance for a plain hem, or to fabric that is very bulky.

Trim the hem allowance to ½″ (1.3 cm). Open out one folded edge of the hem facing and press under ½″ (1.3 cm) on one end. With right

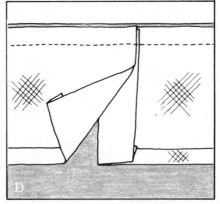

sides together and raw edges even, pin the facing to the garment, lapping the remaining end over the pressed end.

Stitch a ¼″ (6 mm) seam (D). To eliminate bulk, press the seam toward the facing and the facing

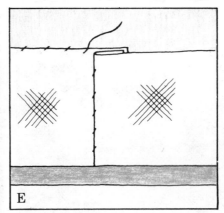

away from the garment. Turn the hem up along the hemline, ¼″ (6 mm) below the facing seam. Sew the hem in place. Slipstitch the overlapping ends of the facing closed (E).

Lockstitched: This method is especially good for pants because it's secure and resists being pulled out when the pants are pulled on over shoes. Hold the garment with the hem fold toward you. Fasten the thread in the hem, then lay the thread to the left and

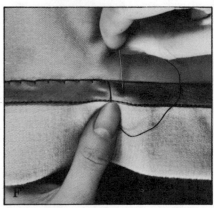

put your left thumb over it. Take a tiny stitch through the garment; then take a stitch through the top edge of the hem ¼″ (6 mm) to the right of the fastened thread. Draw the needle through. Holding the thread with your left thumb, take another stitch ¼″ (6 mm) to the right of the first and continue around the entire hem (F).

Rolled: A fine hand-rolled hem is a good choice on sheers or delicate fabrics. Staystitch ⅛″ (3 mm) outside the hemline, then trim any excess ⅛″ (3 mm) from this stitching. Turn in the raw edge along the stitching. Make tiny, loose blindstitches through the fold and the garment, taking several stitches at a time. Then pull up the stitches to roll the hem (G).

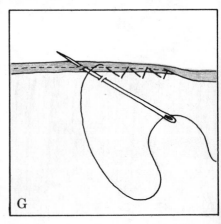

Machine-stitched Hems

Stitching hems by machine can really save you time. Just choose a method that's right for your fabric and style.

Lettuce edge: Use this method to create a decorative, rippled effect on lightweight, stretchy knits. Trim the hem allowance

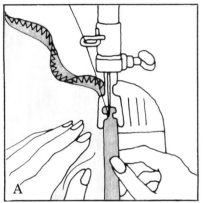

to 3⁄8″ (1 cm) and press it under. Stitch with a medium zigzag stitch, stretching the fabric gently to form ripples (A). Test it first on a scrap; do not use if your knit runs from the hem.

Machine blindstitched: Many machines have this built-in stitch, which can be used for straight or nearly straight hems on medium weight wovens or stable knits. A special guide or foot is available to make stitching easier. The garment is folded back 1⁄4″ (6 mm) from the hem edge. The machine makes a few stitches on the hem allowance, then takes one zigzag stitch into the garment (B). Follow your manual for details.

Narrow topstitched: Suitable for sheer, lightweight or medium weight fabrics, this hem is often used for shirt hems and ruffles.

On woven fabrics, trim the hem allowance to 5⁄8″ (1.5 cm). Stitch 5⁄8″ (1.5 cm) from the raw edge. Press the raw edge under so it *meets* the stitching; then press the folded edge under *along* the stitching. Edgestitch in place (C).

If you have a hemming foot, your machine can turn and stitch the hem all in one step (D). Check your machine manual for directions.

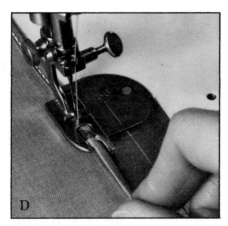

On knits, trim the hem allowance to 5⁄8″ (1.5 cm). Press under along the hemline, easing fullness on curves. Then, from the right side, stitch along the pressed edge and again 1⁄4″ (6 mm) away (E).

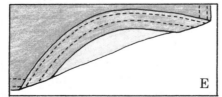

Wide topstitched: Most fabrics and styles, except those with very curved hems, can be topstitched. The hem allowance should be 1½-2″ (3.8-5 cm) wide for the most attractive proportion.

On woven fabrics, press the raw edge under ½″ (1.3 cm); then turn up the entire hem and

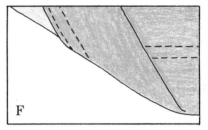

press. Ease in the fullness on curves. Then, stitch from the wrong side, catching the folded edge. Stitch again 1⁄4″ (6 mm) below the fold (F).

For knits, press the hem to the wrong side. Stitch close to the raw edge and again 1⁄4″ (6 mm) below the edge.

Fused: This fast and easy hemming method suits all but very sheer or lightweight fabrics. Use packaged precut strips of fusible web, or cut your own. Place a strip of web that's narrower than your hem just below the finished edge of the hem and fuse, following the manufacturer's instructions (G). To be sure that no ridges show through on the right side, test the fusible web on scraps first. If ridges show, pink the edges of the web and fabric before applying, and try not to rest the iron on the raw edge of the hem.

GUIDE TO HEM TYPES

Garment or Fabric Type	Finished Hem Depth	Hem Type
Casual or children's garments	⅜-2″ (1-5 cm)	Plain, faced, machine-blind-stitched, topstitched, fused
Coats, tailored jackets	1½-2″ (3.8-5 cm)	Plain, faced, fused
Knits	⅝-2″ (1.5-5 cm)	Plain, lettuce edge, top-stitched, fused
Pants	1½-2″ (3.8-5 cm)	Plain, faced, fused, lock-stitched, machine-blindstitched
Sheers	Plain: 2-6″ (5-15 cm) Rolled: ⅛″ (3 mm)	Plain, rolled, topstitched, double (page 213)
Shirts, blouses	⅜-⅝″ (1-1.5 cm)	Topstitched
Skirts, dresses	Plain: 2-3″ (5-7.5 cm) Narrow: ⅜″ (1 cm)	Plain, faced, fused, topstitched, machine-blindstitched
Suede-likes	⅝-2″ (1.5-5 cm)	Topstitched, fused, glued (page 210)

Changing a Hem

Fashions change and so do hemlines. While it's easier to shorten a hem than to lengthen one, both jobs can be done simply. Try on the garment to see how much the hem needs changing and, if necessary, remove the original stitching.

Lengthening: When you let down a hem, the new hem allowance will be narrower than the old one. If there's not enough fabric left for a new hem allowance, you can use purchased bias or stretch lace hem facing as a substitute (see Faced Hem, page 140). After you've lengthened the hem, you'll need to remove the crease at the old hemline. On some fabrics, steam-pressing will remove the crease. If this doesn't work, use a brush or eye-dropper to apply white vinegar diluted with water; then press. *Test first* on an inside seam allowance to be sure the vinegar doesn't harm the fabric by changing the color. If the crease still remains or leaves a fade mark, conceal it by covering it with trim such as lace, rickrack or embroidered braid. Add the same trim elsewhere on the garment to make the overall effect appear planned (A).

A

To lengthen cuffed pants when creases are removable, put in the hem by machine, since the cuff will cover the hem completely. If pants need to be only slightly longer and the cuff is deep enough, leave the hem intact. Remove any tacks at side seams and press a new bottom foldline, making the cuff shallower and the pants longer. Retack the cuffs.

Shortening: Pin up the garment along the new hemline. Then, trim and finish it as described on pages 138-141.

There are also two very quick ways to shorten hems on casual clothes or children's wear.

On a very lightweight garment with a straight hem, leave the old hem in and turn up the lower edge the depth of the hem or more. Then hand-sew or machine-stitch the new hem in place.

For another fast way to raise a straight hemline, machine-baste a tuck within the hem allowance. Make the tuck depth half of the amount to be shortened, but be sure the hem allowance is deep enough to conceal the tuck (B). You can shorten cuffed pants the same way, but make the tuck just above the top of the hem (C). Remove any thread tacks and replace them after stitching the tuck.

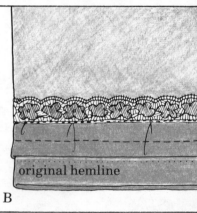

original hemline

B

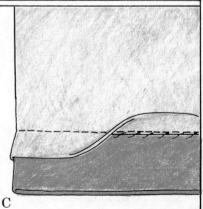

C

Interfacing

The right interfacing in the right place is very important for a professional-looking garment. Although you can't actually see the interfacing on a finished garment, the built-in benefits are certainly visible. Interfacing gives edges and details the shape and support they need and helps keep them from wilting. Here are some tips that will help you use your interfacing correctly.

Interfacing Types

The two basic types of interfacing are *sew-in* and *fusible*. Both are available in woven, knit or nonwoven versions, and in a variety of weights, ranging from heavyweight to featherweight. Use the chart on page 34 as a guide to interfacing selection. Be sure to check labels or wrappers for use and care information.

Where to Interface

In general, detail areas such as collars, cuffs, pockets and flaps, waistbands, necklines and opening edges need the support of interfacing. Your pattern will tell you which pieces require interfacing. If you want to add interfacing where it's not specified, use the pattern piece or its corresponding facing piece to cut the interfacing.

Interfacing is usually applied to the wrong side of the outermost part of the garment—for example, to the upper collar or cuff rather than to the collar or cuff facing. Since there are exceptions, be sure to follow your pattern instructions.

Cutting and Marking

If interfacing is required by your pattern, the directions will include the necessary cutting layout. For woven interfacing, pay attention to lengthwise, crosswise and bias grainlines when you lay out and cut your pattern pieces.

Mark the interfacing pieces rather than the fabric (pages 86-88), except when you're making buttonholes. Mark buttonholes as described on pages 106-107.

Non-woven interfacing often has no grain. It's a time-saver because pattern pieces may be laid out in any direction unless the manufacturer recommends otherwise.

Application

Sew-in type: Trim the outside corners of the interfacing diagonally, just inside the point where the seamlines meet to minimize bulk. Then pin and machine-baste the interfacing to the wrong side of the garment piece, ½″ (1.3 cm) from the edges. Trim away the interfacing close to the stitching (A). Also trim interfacing from the hem allowance area.

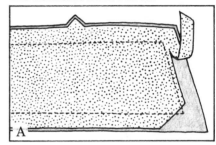

Fusible type: Apply fusible interfacing to the outermost fabric layer if the interfacing will cover the entire area from seamline to seamline—for example, on an upper collar or patch pocket section (B).

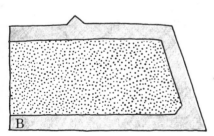

On an area where the interfacing will not go from seamline to seamline—for example, the front edge of a jacket—test it on a fabric scrap first to be sure the interfacing edge won't form a ridge that shows through on the outside. If a ridge forms, try pinking the interfacing edge and making another test (C). If this doesn't help, interface the facing instead of the outer garment section (D).

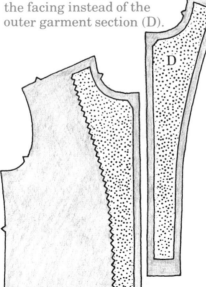

To apply fusible interfacing, trim the corners as for Sew-in Type, above. Then trim ½″ (1.3 cm) from all interfacing seam allowances, trim the interfacing from the hem allowance area, and fuse the interfacing to the fabric, following the manufacturer's directions (C,D).

Fusible interfacing is now available as precut strips in assorted widths and weights. So that you can stitch an even waistband or placket band, some interfacings are perforated to indicate seamlines and foldlines (E).

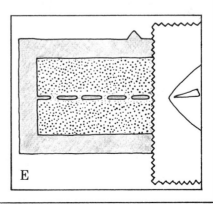

Machine stitching

Your sewing machine will work very well if the stitch length, thread tension and presser foot are all suited to the particular fabric you're sewing. These three variables can be adjusted as explained below. Consult your machine manual for specific details. For extra assurance, test-stitch on the same number of fabric layers you'll be sewing.

Stitch Length

Most machines have either a lever or a dial for setting the stitch length. If your lever is numbered from 6 to 20 (A), it means 6 to 20 stitches per inch (2.5 cm). The *larger* the number, the *smaller* each stitch will be. Most new machines have a dial numbered 0-1-2-3-4; each number represents millimeters. For example, when the dial is on 2, each stitch will be 2 mm long (B). For this kind of dial, the *larger*

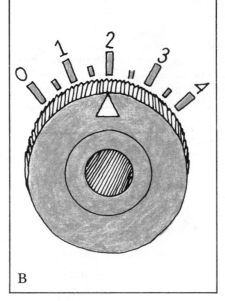

B

the number, the *larger* each stitch will be.

The basic stitch lengths and their uses are listed below. Within each category, the length to use depends on your fabric weight— a lightweight fabric requires a shorter stitch length than a heavyweight fabric. The How to Sew Fabrics chart on pages 124-125 gives additional information on stitch lengths for specific fabric types.

Regulation: 10 to 15 stitches per inch (2.5 cm) or 2½ to 2 mm long. These stitch sizes are normally used for stitching seams.

Basting: The longest stitch on your machine, usually 6 to 8 stitches per inch (2.5 cm) or 4 to 3 mm long. This stitch length is used as temporary stitching because it is easy to remove.

Reinforcing: The shortest stitch length—18 to 20 per inch (2.5 cm) or 1½ to 1 mm long. Use this stitch size to add strength at points of strain or to prevent fraying when fabric must be clipped.

Easing or gathering: 8 to 10 stitches per inch (2.5 cm) or 3 to 2½ mm long. Use this length to ease in fullness or to gather.

Thread Tension

The tension setting on the machine determines how the needle thread and bobbin thread interlock to form a stitch. When the tension is correctly set, you will get a perfectly balanced stitch that interlocks in the center of the fabric and looks the same on both sides (C).

If the *needle thread* tension is too tight, the thread lies on top of the fabric, pulling the bobbin thread up (D). The reverse happens if the *bobbin thread* is too tight; the bobbin thread lies in a straight line under the fabric, pulling the needle thread down (E).

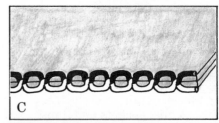

C

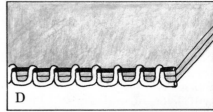

D

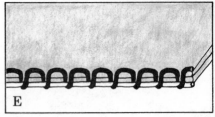

E

Most machines have a numbered dial for adjusting needle thread tension. The *larger* the numbers on this dial, the *tighter* the needle thread tension will be. Although a screw on the bobbin case controls the bobbin tension, most machine manuals do not recommend adjusting this screw. Check your machine manual for details.

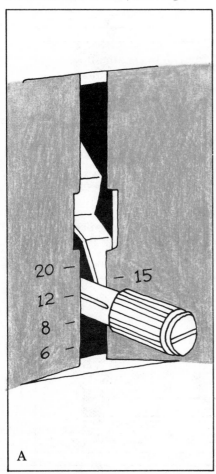

A

A

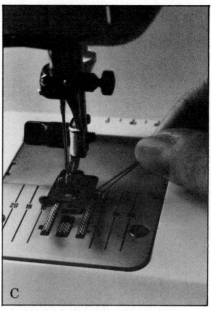

C

Testing tension: Cut a square of on-grain fabric. Fold it in half diagonally and cut along the fold, making two triangles. Thread the machine with cotton thread since it breaks more easily than synthetic thread. Stitch along the bias edge. Then, pull the fabric at both ends of the stitching until a thread breaks (A). If the bobbin thread breaks, *tighten* the needle tension. If the needle thread breaks, *loosen* the needle tension. Generally, it's not a good idea to change the bobbin tension unless you can't get a balanced stitch by changing the needle tension.

Presser Foot Pressure

The force of the presser foot on the fabric is called pressure. The correct pressure allows both layers of fabric to move at the same rate without being damaged by the feed dog. The amount of pressure needed varies with the weight, bulk, texture and finish of the fabric. Pressure on most machines can be regulated by a knob or a dial as instructed in your sewing machine manual.

Testing pressure: Cut two lengthwise strips of fabric, each 8″ (20.5 cm) long. Match all edges; then pin the ends together. Stitch a seam. The two strips should come out even. If a ripple forms in the top layer (B), *decrease* the pressure. If the bottom strip

B

comes out longer than the top strip, *increase* the pressure.

Stitching

Now that your stitch length, tension and pressure are all in tune, you're ready to start your sewing machine humming. Here's how to stitch a seam from start to finish.

Starting and ending: Before threading the machine, turn the hand wheel until the needle is at its highest point so the thread won't slip out of the needle,

and raise the presser foot. Draw the needle and bobbin threads under and behind the presser foot, leaving 4″ (10 cm) long tails (C).

Place the fabric under the presser foot with the seam edge on the right and the bulk of the fabric on the left of the presser foot.

Turn the wheel to lower the needle into the fabric near the beginning of the seamline. Hold the thread tails and lower the presser foot. Set your machine to stitch in reverse; backstitch for ½″ (1.3 cm). Change the setting to forward and stitch exactly over the backstitching (D). Stitch the seam. Support the fabric so it doesn't drag. Slow down near the end of the seam and backstitch (E).

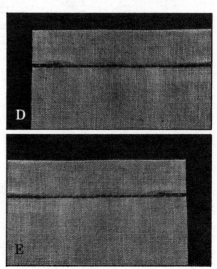

D

E

Removing the fabric: Raise the needle, lift the presser foot and pull the fabric toward the back of the machine until the needle and bobbin threads are 3″ (7.5 cm) long (A). Cut the threads close to the fabric.

A

C

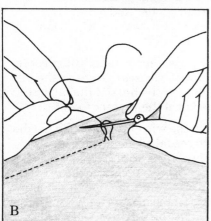

B

If you can't backstitch because your machine doesn't stitch in reverse, knot the threads instead. Also knot thread ends at dart points or the ends of released tucks. Cut the threads, leaving 3″ (7.5 cm) tails. Pull the bobbin thread tail up until a loop of needle thread is visible. Insert a pin through the loop and draw the needle thread through to the same side as the bobbin thread (B). Tie the threads in a knot.

Guiding the fabric: Most sewing involves stitching two layers of fabric together. It's advisable to pin or baste complicated seams or those on slippery fabrics, but you can stitch many straight seams without even pinning. Line up the two layers at seam edges, markings and notches. As you stitch, hold the layers together with one hand in front of the presser foot and place the other hand flat in back of the presser foot (C).

If you're using pin, machine or hand basting (page 100), guide fabrics by placing both hands lightly on top of the fabric in front and to the side or back of the presser foot (D).

Once your fabric is under the presser foot and you have started stitching, it feeds through the machine automatically. It is not necessary to push or pull the fabric to get it to move, but you must guide it in order to keep your line of stitching straight.

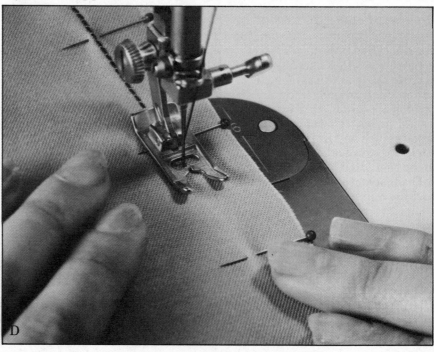

D

A

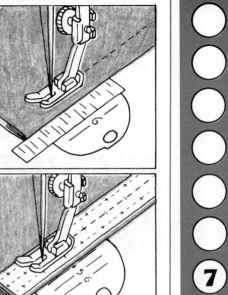

E

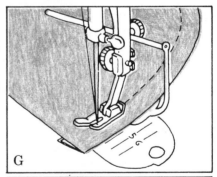

F

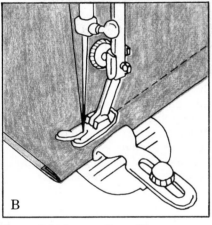

B

Some fabrics, such as filmy sheers, lightweight silky types and some knits, need a little extra help to keep them from puckering. With one hand, hold these fabrics taut *behind* the presser foot, as you guide them with the other hand in front (A). To add more "give" to seams on knits, stretch the fabric *slightly* as you stitch. Hold both fabric layers firmly in front and in back of the presser foot while the machine feeds the fabric.

Stitching accurately: Straight stitching is easy to achieve with a little practice. Just line the fabric edges up with a stitching guide.

There are lots of handy stitching guides for your machine:
• Screw-on or magnetic seam guides placed the desired distance from the needle hole, parallel to the presser foot for straight edges (B) or at an angle for curves (C).
• Guidelines on the throat plate at ⅛" (3 mm) intervals (D).
• Tape placed on the throat plate the desired distance from the needle hole (E).
• Adhesive sewing tape, printed or perforated with guidelines, and placed on the fabric for guiding topstitching (F). You can stitch through some tapes and only alongside others; consult the manufacturer's directions.
• Quilting foot attachment for guiding stitching on curves (G) and edges up to 2" (5 cm) away from the needle; good for topstitching seams that are not near the edges of a garment.
• Toe of the presser foot for stitching close to an edge or ¼" (6 mm) away from it (H).

C

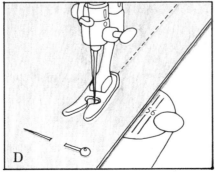

D

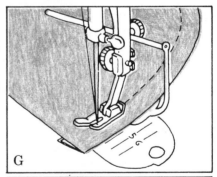

G

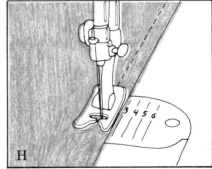

H

Corners

Stitch slowly as you approach the corner. Use the hand wheel to take the last few stitches before the corner so that you don't stitch past it. Lower the needle exactly

at the point. Raise the presser foot, and pivot the fabric to bring it into the correct position for stitching the seam on the second side of the corner or point (A). For more information about stitching corners, see page 159.

Topstitching

A row of stitching on the outside of the garment along or near the finished edge is called topstitching. It is usually decorative, but can be functional as well—for example, topstitching a patch pocket to a jacket (B). Use topstitching to accent details such as collars, lapels and pockets, and to keep seams on edges flat (B). Test-stitch your fabric first, using the same number of layers as your garment will have.

To make each stitch more pronounced, slightly loosen the needle thread tension.

Thread: Use a matching or contrasting color, depending on how much you want the topstitching to stand out. Use regular thread and a size 11 needle for lightweight

fabrics. On medium or heavy-weight fabrics, use buttonhole twist, heavy duty thread, top-stitching thread or two strands of regular thread in a size 16 needle; or make two rows of stitching on top of each other for emphasis. Generally, it's best to use regular thread in the bobbin.

B

Stitching guides: To guide topstitching accurately close to an edge, use the guides shown on page 147—the edge of the presser foot, lines or tape on the throat plate, or seam guides.

When topstitching away from an edge, use adhesive sewing tape or, if you have one, a quilting foot attachment (see page 147) on your machine. The quilting foot is adjustable for stitching lines up to 2″ (5 cm) apart and is especially good when you're topstitching along curved seamlines away from edges.

Zigzag Stitching

One of the most useful and versatile stitches is the zigzag. Your machine manual will tell you how to set the machine for zigzag stitching. Usually this stitch requires a looser tension than a straight stitch does. Stitch length can be adjusted with the same lever or dial as for straight stitching. Stitch width is adjusted with a lever or dial usually numbered from 1 to 5 (C), from narrowest to widest. When zigzag-stitching, be sure to use the general purpose zigzag foot and wide hole throat plate (see page 43).

You can use the zigzag stitch to seam knits, finish edges, topstitch and decorate. And, you can zigzag elastic directly to a garment waistline for controlling fullness without making a casing first. Divide the elastic and garment waistline into four or eight equal parts, marking them with pins. Matching all markings, pin the elastic to the wrong side of the garment, with one edge on the casing placement line. Stitch, stretching the elastic to fit the garment area as you sew. Use one or two rows of stitching, depending on the elastic width (D,E).

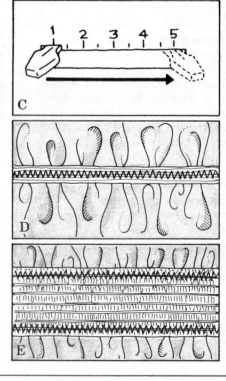

Zigzag stitching is also handy for fabric crafts, such as machine patchwork and appliqué (see pages 232 and 233). For patchwork, cut out random shapes of fabric and arrange them on a background fabric, like the pieces of a puzzle. Pin or fuse them in place and zigzag over the edges (A).

Decorative Stitching

Many interesting effects are possible with the special stitches on many zigzag machines, such as scalloped edges on collars (B) and cuffs, borders of fagoting and appliquéd designs.

The satin stitch, often used to appliqué, is a very close zigzag stitch. Rows of satin stitch done in different color threads will resemble decorative braid.

Embroidery, floral designs, script lettering and monogramming (C) can be done by free-motion stitching without a presser foot; a hoop is used to control the fabric movement. Monogramming can also be done with a special attachment. Whichever you use, monograms are a nice touch for the lining of a coat or cape, or for children's outerwear. You can also use them to create letters for whimsical slogans to frame or to decorate pillow tops.

For detailed stitching directions, see the chapter on Personal Touches and consult your sewing machine instruction book.

Removing Stitches

Use a seam ripper or small scissors to cut stitches at ½" (1.3 cm)

intervals on one side (D). Pull out the thread on the other side; then remove any threads that remain on the first side.

Special Attachments

Most machines have some special built-in features, such as a buttonhole stitch or decorative stitch patterns. In addition, many machines have a wide variety of attachments available for special-purpose stitching, such as binding, blindstitching, edge-stitching, etc. (see page 43). Here are two convenient examples.

Even-feed foot: It's important in stitching that both fabric layers feed through the machine at the same rate. Some fabrics, such as vinyl, fake fur and other pile or napped textures, need the help of an even-feed foot or attachment, which is available for many machines. This foot helps, too,

when stitching striped or plaid fabric, because it prevents the fabric layers from shifting after you've matched the design at one end of the seam (E).

Buttonholer: Most buttonhole attachments make only a few buttonhole sizes. But a buttonholer (on a few machines) automatically adjusts the buttonhole to the right length for your button size. Just mark the end of the buttonhole, insert the button into the back of the buttonholer, and stitch (F).

Mitering

A miter joins two edges diagonally to form a corner. There are different methods of mitering, depending on whether you're turning under a corner in a flat piece of fabric, applying a trim or binding an edge.

Garment Corners

Turning under seam allowances of patch pockets or facing the corners of skirt slits creates extra bulk. You can eliminate this unneeded fabric and create sharp angles by mitering the corners.

Stitched miter: Turn the seam allowances or the hem and facing to the inside and press. Open out the pressed edges. Fold the corner diagonally across the point so the pressed lines meet; press. Open the corner and trim it ¼″ (6 mm) from the crease (A). With right sides together, fold the corner, matching the trimmed edges; stitch on the diagonal crease (B). Trim the fold diagonally at the point and press the seam open (C). Turn the seam allowances or the hem and facing to the inside and press (D).

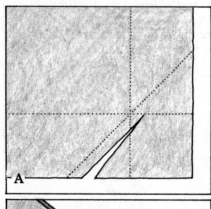

A

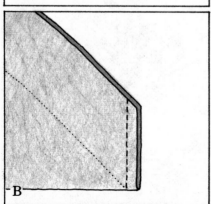

B

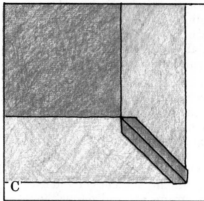

C

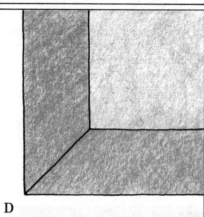

D

Folded Miter: This easy method works on patch pockets and slit hems. Stitch along the pocket seamlines; then press the seam allowances to the inside along the stitching. Open out the seam allowances at the corner. Press the corner up diagonally, and trim ¼″ (6 mm) from the diagonal crease, as shown. Turn the seam allowances to the inside again—the folded edges will just meet, forming a neat corner; slipstitch hem edges together (E).

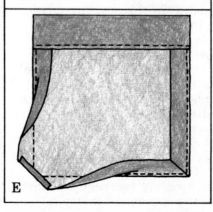

E

Band Trims

For trims with two straight edges: Pin the trim to one garment edge. Topstitch both trim edges to the corner. Fold the trim back on itself; press. Then fold it diagonally so it turns the corner; press again. Open out this fold and stitch along the diagonal crease through all layers (F). Refold the trim to turn the corner; continue topstitching along both trim edges (G).

F

G

For trims with one straight edge: Stitch the straight edge of the trim to one garment edge, all the way to the corner. Fold the trim back on itself, extending the fold slightly beyond the fabric edge; press. Turn the trim down diagonally so that it turns the corner; press again. Open out the trim and stitch along the diagonal crease through all layers (H). Turn the trim down and press. Continue stitching the trim to the garment (I).

Bindings

To miter corners of binding, see pages 104 and 105.

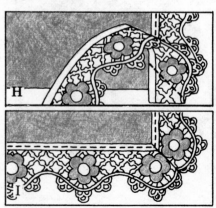

H

I

Pleats

straight pleats

inverted pleat

box pleats

Pleats are folds of fabric used to control fullness. They may be crisp or soft, depending on whether or not they're pressed.

Making Pleats

Your pattern will tell you whether to make pleats on the inside or outside of the garment. Mark the pleat lines on the wrong side of the fabric; then transfer them to the right side, if necessary.

Straight or knife pleats: Make all pleats in the same direction, following the arrows printed on the pattern. Fold your fabric on the solid line and bring the fold to the broken line. Baste or pin pleats along the folded edges; then baste across the top of all pleats (A). If pleats are to be pressed, do it now. Pleats can also be edgestitched in place from waist to hip (see above).

Box pleats: Each pleat consists of two straight pleats facing in opposite directions (see left). Follow the directions for straight pleats.

Inverted pleats: Often used at center front or back, an inverted pleat looks like two straight pleats facing each other, with their folds meeting at the center. It's usually made with a pleat underlay. Pin the front or back sections together along the center seamline, with right sides together. Baste along the pleat line from the lower edge to the medium dot; then stitch along the seamline above the medium dot. Press the seam open (C). Then, with right sides together, pin the underlay to the pleat extensions, matching notches and dots. Stitch one long edge, pivot at the dot and end at the center front or back dot. Stitch the other long edge the same way (D). Do not press the underlay seams open; press the pleat flat.

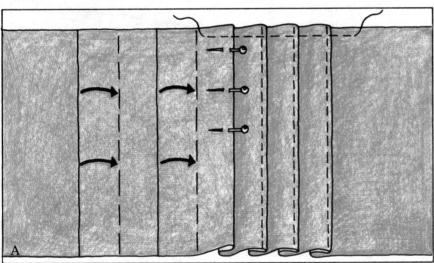

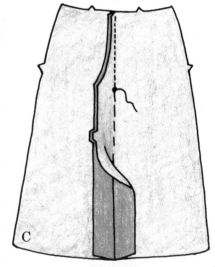

Straight pleat shortcut: This quick method eliminates most basting. Snip-mark ends of pleat lines at edges and pin-mark along the length of the pleat lines. Crease the fabric along the solid line and press it (B). Then, bring this pressed edge to meet the broken line and pin it in place. Machine-baste across the top of all pleats. Press the inside folds.

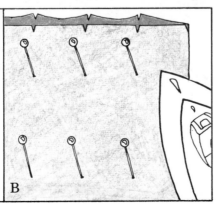

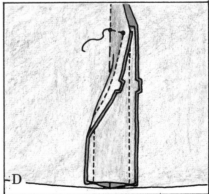

If your pattern doesn't have a pleat underlay, it will have either a solid line or a seam in the center of the pleat, with broken lines on each side of it. Stitch the seam if there is one. Then, with right sides together, fold the fabric on the solid line or the seam, matching broken lines. Baste or pin along the broken line from bottom to top (A). *Note:* Some pleats are permanently stitched (rather than basted) in the hip area; if so, your pattern will indicate this.

Press the pleat flat so the stitching meets the solid line or seam and baste across the top (B).

Topstitching: Pleats may be topstitched or edgestitched through all layers from the waist to the hip (C, D). You can also edgestitch below the hip, only through the pleat fold, to hold the crease (D).

Hemming: When the inside fold of a pleat is a seam, the hem requires special attention. Clip the seam allowances to the stitching at the top of the hem. Press the seam allowances open below the clip; trim them to ¼" (6 mm) (E). After hemming, edgestitch the pleat fold to keep it flat (F).

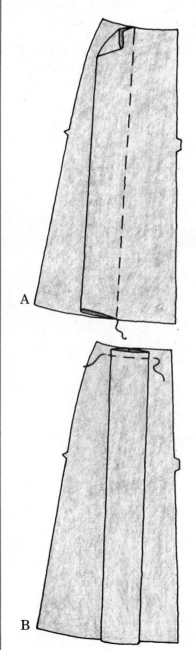

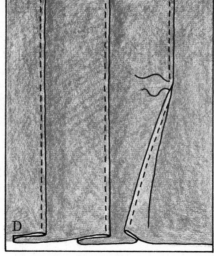

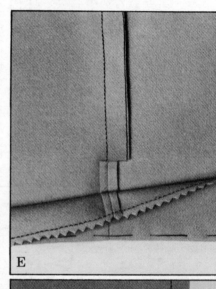

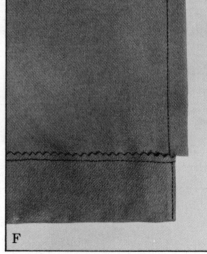

Pockets

Whatever their shape or size, pockets are simple to sew. The most popular styles are patch, front hip and in-seam pockets. Patch pockets are applied to the outside of a garment, front hip pockets are partially hidden from view at the hipline, and in-seam pockets are concealed in side seams.

Patch Pockets

Because they can be any size and shape, patch pockets are the most versatile. They are used to create design interest on all sorts of

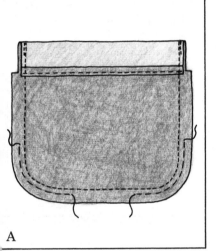

A

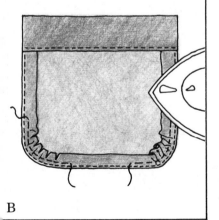

B

garments—skirts, blouses, pants and tailored jackets. There are three common types of patch pockets: unlined, lined and self-lined.

Unlined: For casual clothes and children's wear, unlined pockets are the easiest to make. On the top edge, press under ¼" (6 mm) and edgestitch. Then, turn the top edge to the right side of the pocket along the foldline to form a facing; press. Starting at the fold, stitch along the seamline at the edges, backstitching at the ends. Trim seam allowances in the facing area to ¼" (6 mm) (A).

For a curved pocket, make a row of machine gathering stitches ¼" (6 mm) away from first stitching on the seam allowance around the curved edges (A).

Turn the facing to the wrong side of the pocket, working out the upper corners with a pin. Pull up the gathering threads to shape the curve; then press under the seam allowance, rolling the stitching to the wrong side. To eliminate bulk, notch out the fullness in the seam allowance at the curves as far as the stitching (B). Press the facing seams and the fold. Edgestitch or topstitch the facing in place.

For square or rectangular pockets, miter the lower corners (see page 150).

Lined: When you're tailoring a jacket or suit, a pocket lining makes a nice finish. After cutting out the pocket, fold the pocket pattern piece along the foldline to omit the facing. Use this folded pocket pattern piece to cut the lining. Press under the upper lining edge half the depth of the pocket facing. With right sides together, pin or baste lining to the pocket, matching side and lower edges (C).

Turn the pocket facing down over the lining so that the raw edges match. Then, stitch around the raw edges, starting at the fold and backstitching at the ends. Trim the seam allowances and corners or notch any curves. Press the lining seam allowance toward lining to pre-set the edge (D).

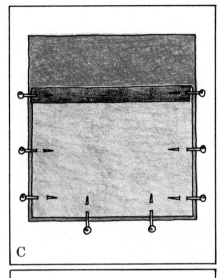

C

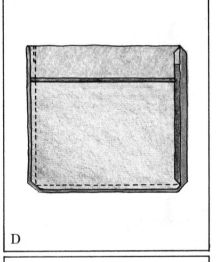

D

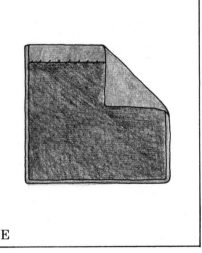

E

Turn the pocket right side out and press, rolling the seam slightly to the lining side. Slipstitch folded lining edge to the facing (E).

Self-lined: A pattern for this type of pocket tells you to cut the pocket and self-lining in one. Or, you can convert a conventional-style lined pocket to a self-lined one by laying out and cutting the pocket pattern with the foldline on a crosswise fold of fabric. The facing part of the pattern will extend beyond the fabric fold and won't be cut.

To make the pocket, fold it in half along the foldline, with right sides together. Stitch along the raw edges. Trim the seam and corners or notch curves. Press one seam allowance toward the pocket to pre-set the edge. Then, on the same side, cut a 1½" (3.8 cm) slash (A). Turn the pocket right side out through the slash. Press, rolling the seam toward the slashed side. Fuse a strip of interfacing or mending tape over the slash (B).

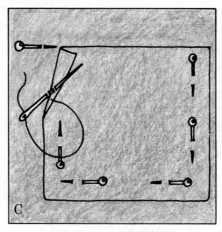

C

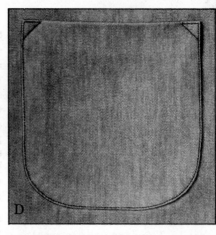

D

Invisible hand application: Baste or pin the pocket in place. Turn back the pocket edge slightly and slipstitch it to the garment (C), taking several small stitches at the beginning and end.

Topstitched application: Pin, baste or tape the pocket in place. Then edgestitch and/or topstitch ¼"-⅜" (6 mm-1 cm) from the edge. To reinforce the upper corners, stitch diagonally (D) or backstitch.

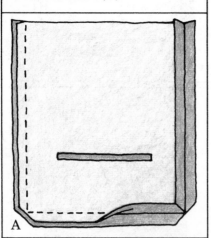

A

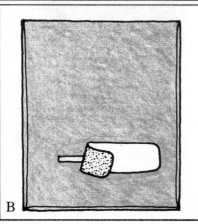

B

Invisible machine application: A fast way to attach an unlined patch pocket invisibly is by machine-stitching it in place. For this method, the pocket must be curved and fairly large. After finishing the raw facing edge, press under the facing and stitch or fuse it in place. On the right side, stitch around the pocket on the seamline. Notch curves; then press the seam allowance to the wrong side, rolling the stitching under (E). Pin the pocket in place and machine-baste it with a large zigzag stitch that barely catches the pocket edge.

Pulling the pocket out of the way, stitch halfway around the inside, following the original stitching on the seamline. Stop midway and stitch the other half of the pocket (F). Remove the zigzag stitches.

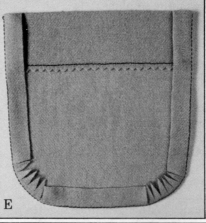

E

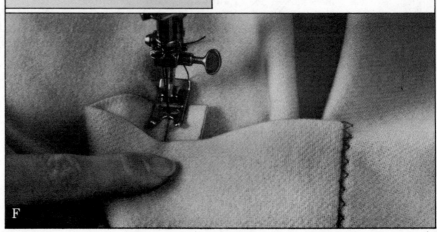

F

In-seam Pockets

Handy pockets can be sewn into the side seams of a garment in two ways. The method directly below uses a separate pocket pattern piece. It's especially good for heavy fabric because you can cut the pockets from less bulky lining fabric. Below, right, is a shortcut method which shows you how to cut in-seam pockets in one piece with the garment.

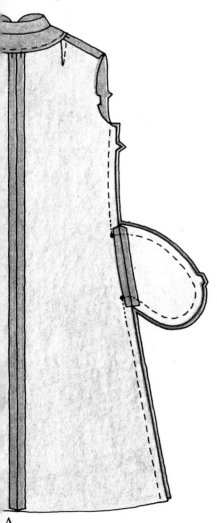

A

Separate: Before the side seams of the garment are stitched, attach the pocket sections to the garment front and back as follows. With right sides together, pin and stitch the front pocket to the front garment extension, matching the notches and markings; press the seam open. Stitch the back pocket to the garment back the same way. Pin the front to the back at the side seams, matching notches and markings; pin pocket edges together. Beginning at the lower edge of the garment, stitch one continuous seam, pivoting at the pocket markings. To reinforce the pivots, use a short stitch for about 1″ (2.5 cm) on both sides of each corner (A).

Above and below the pocket, clip only the back seam allowance to the reinforcement stitches. Press the garment seam open; press the pocket toward the front (B).

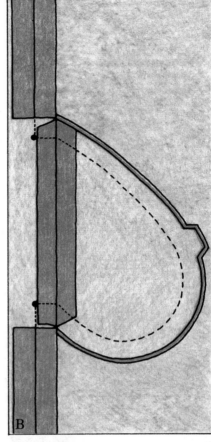

B

Built-in: Some Simplicity patterns have the pocket shape built into the front and back pattern pieces. This saves time because you don't have to cut out the pockets separately; there's also no need to stitch the pockets to the garment. You can use this method even if your pattern wasn't designed this way, as long as your fabric is wide enough. Just lap the pocket and garment pattern pieces at the seamline, matching markings; pin (C). Cut out the front and pocket as one section. Repeat the procedure for the back. Stitch the garment side and pocket seams continuously, pivoting at the markings to stitch around the pockets. To reinforce the pivoted corners, use a short stitch for about 1″ (2.5 cm) on both sides of each corner (D).

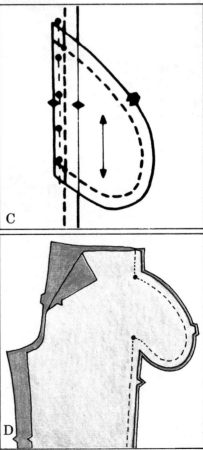

C

D

Front Hip Pockets

Many pants and skirts feature partially hidden hipline pockets. While the opening edge of the pocket may be straight or curved, the sewing method is the same for either shape.

If your fashion fabric is heavy or bulky, cut the *pocket facing* from lightweight lining fabric in a matching color. First, staystitch the waistline edges of the front section and the side front pocket section, as well as the pocket opening edges of the front and pocket facing sections, to keep them from stretching.

Stitching: With right sides together and notches and markings matching, pin the pocket facing to the garment front along the opening edge; stitch (A). Trim and clip this seam; then press the seam open (B). Turn the pocket facing to the inside and press again. On the outside, edgestitch close to the seam; you may also topstitch ¼"

(6 mm) away if desired (C). With right sides together, pin the side front pocket piece to the pocket facing along the double-notched edge, matching raw edges, notches and markings. Be careful not to catch the garment front when you pin. Stitch the double-notched edges together (D). On the outside, lap the garment front over the side front pocket; machine-baste them together at the side hip and waistline edges as shown (E).

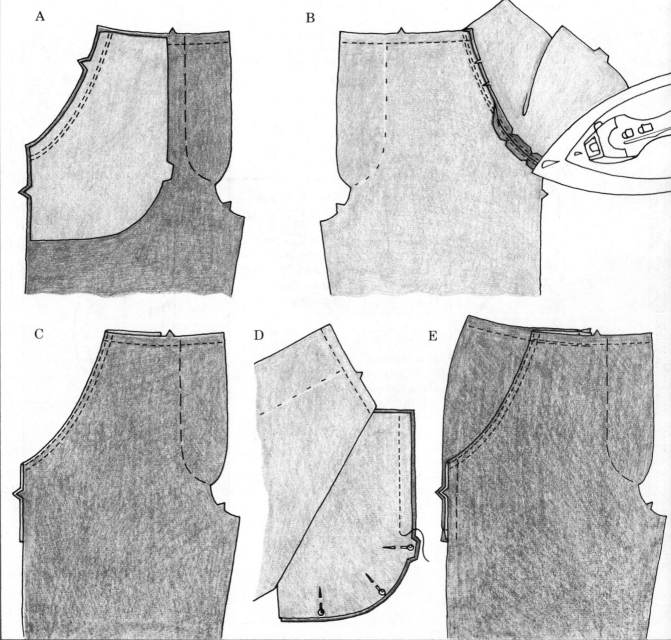

Ruffles

The techniques for sewing ruffles are the same as for gathers. There are two familiar types of ruffles — single and double.

Single Ruffles

Single ruffles have one hemmed edge and one edge sewn in a seam or applied to a garment edge.

Preparing: Ruffles may be cut on the straight grain or on the bias. If you don't have a pattern piece, cut a strip two to three times the desired finished length, depending on the ruffle depth and the fabric (very wide or sheer ruffles should be fuller). *For most*

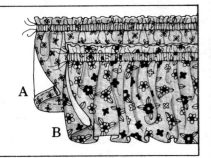

fabrics, cut the strip the desired depth plus 1¼ " (3.2 cm) for a hem and a seam allowance. Narrow-hem one edge and run gathering stitches on the other edge (A).

For lightweight fabrics, cut the strip twice the depth plus two seam allowances. Fold the strip in half lengthwise with wrong sides together, and gather the raw edges with two rows of stitches (B).

If your machine has a ruffler, use it to gather and attach ruffles in one step, following your manual (C).

In a seam: With right sides together, pin the ruffle to one garment edge; adjust the gathers and machine-baste in place. Pin the right side of the remaining garment section over the ruffle. Stitch the seam next to the basting (D).

At a hem edge: Trim the garment hem allowance to ⅝" (1.5 cm); press it under along the hemline. Then, with right sides

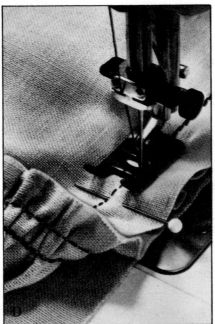

up, pin the pressed edge over the raw edge of the ruffle so that the raw edges match. Adjust gathers to fit, allowing extra fullness around corners; pin. If you like, include a trim, such as rickrack. Edgestitch through all layers (E). Then finish the raw edges.

Double Ruffles

A ruffle with two hemmed edges is topstitched in place.

Preparing: Cut a strip the same length as a single ruffle; the depth should include two ⅝" (1.5 cm) hem allowances. Narrow-hem both long edges. Run two lines of

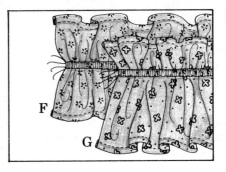

gathering stitches along the ruffle center (F) or near one edge (G).

Applying: Pin the wrong side of the ruffle to the right side of the garment. Adjust the gathers and pin them. Topstitch over the gathering stitches. To hide the stitches, you can include trim as you stitch. For a very narrow trim, gather the ruffle with *one* row of stitching (H).

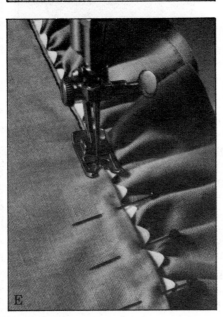

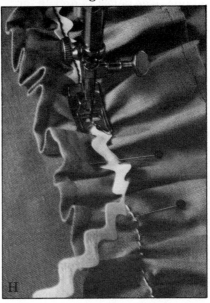

7

sewing today: pockets, ruffles

Seams

A *seam* is a line of stitching that joins two or more fabric layers. It is stitched along the *seamline* which is ⅝" (1.5 cm) from the cut edge, unless otherwise indicated on your pattern. The *seam allowance* is the fabric between the seamline and the cut edge (A).

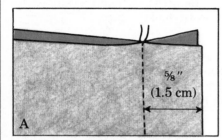

It's important to use the right equipment, techniques and seam type for your fabric—see the chart on pages 124 and 125. Remember to test-stitch seams on a double layer of fabric for the best stitch length, thread tension and presser foot pressure.

To sew smooth seams, line up the layers so that notches and markings match. Baste next to the seamline; then, stitch along it, backstitching at the beginning and end. Remove the basting.

Equipment

Besides the sewing machine, many gadgets and aids are available to help you stitch a fine seam. Here are some of the important ones (see pages 44 and 46 for more details).
• *Needles, pins and thread* are basic to any seam.
• *Seam guides, throat plate lines,* the *presser foot edge, seam tape* and a *quilting foot* are all used as guides for accurate stitching.
• *Tissue paper* and *tissue tape* help prevent puckering on lightweight fabric, keep presser foot toes from catching in lace or looped fabrics and help slippery or sheer fabrics slide under the presser foot.
• *Seam binding* and *twill tape* can reinforce stress points and prevent stretching; seam binding can also be used to finish raw edges.
• *Basting tape* and *double-faced tape* are used to hold fabric layers together at seams; double-faced

tape can hold a zipper in place for stitching. Test the tape on a scrap to be sure the tape doesn't mar your fabric when you remove it. Position the tape on the seam allowance next to the seamline so you won't stitch through the tape (B). Pull the tape off before pressing.

Seam Techniques

See Machine Stitching on pages 144-149 for basic how-to's, such as starting and ending a seam and guiding fabric. Then, read the following seam techniques.

Staystitching: To keep curved, crosswise or bias edges — necklines, shoulders and waistlines — from stretching out of shape, stitch ½" (1.3 cm) from the cut edge. Arrows printed on your pattern show you which direction to staystitch (C). This is especially helpful for beginners; once you become more expert at handling fabric, it won't be as essential.

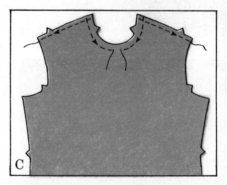

Directional stitching: Stitch the way arrows on the pattern point, in the direction of the grain —usually from a wide part of the garment to a narrow one. This helps keep fabrics, especially knits and napped fabric, from stretching out of shape or curling.

Trimming and grading: Most seams must be trimmed and graded to reduce bulk or thick-

ness. After stitching an enclosed seam (a collar, cuff, edge, etc.), or pressing a seam to one side, *trim* the seam allowances to ¼" (6 mm). On medium to heavy-weight fabrics, *grade* the seam allowances—trim the one closest to the inside of the garment to ⅛" (3 mm) and the outermost one to ¼" (6 mm) (D).

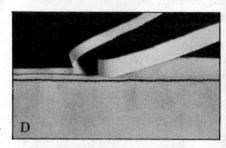

Grade thick seams quickly by holding your scissors at an angle; then trim all seam allowances at once.

Intersecting seams: When one seam or dart will be crossed by another—for example, side seams crossed by a waist seam—trim the ends of the seam allowances or dart diagonally to reduce bulk. Pin the sections together, aligning the seams exactly; pin through the seam and the seam allowances. Stitch the new seam (E, F).

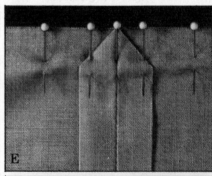

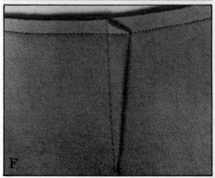

Corners: To strengthen seams at corners, reduce the stitch length to reinforcement-length stitches (see page 144) for 1″ (2.5 cm) on each side of the corner. This will prevent the corner from fraying after it is trimmed and turned right side out.

At sharp *outward* corners, as on a collar point, take one or two diagonal stitches across the point instead of stitching right up to the point. To reduce bulk, trim the corner diagonally as shown (A). Clip into an *inward* corner, almost to the stitching (B). These procedures will ensure smooth corners when they're turned right side out.

To join an *inward* corner to an *outward* corner—for example, on a yoke—first, reinforce the *inward* corner with small stitches and clip just to the stitching (C). Pin the two sections together along one edge, with the clipped section on top; stitch to the corner. Leave the needle in the fabric and raise the presser foot. Pivot by turning the fabric around the

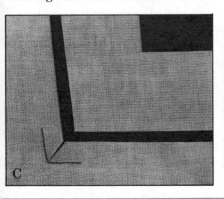

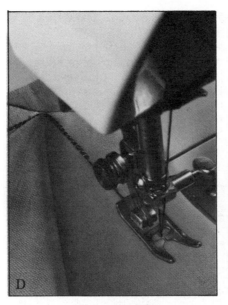

needle; then spread the clipped edges apart to match the next edge. Lower the presser foot and continue stitching (D).

Curves: To stitch a smooth, accurate seam at a curve, reduce the stitch length and use a seam guide, placed on an angle (see page 147). *Clip* the seam allowances of an *inward* curve so that they will lie flat when the seam is pressed open (E). Cut wedge-shaped *notches* from the seam allowances of *outward* curves to eliminate excess fullness when the seam is pressed open (F).

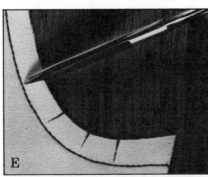

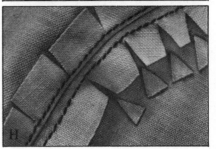

Sometimes an inward and outward curve are joined together, as in a *princess seam*. Staystitch both curves and clip the inward curve at even intervals (G). Pin the two sections together with raw edges even and spread the clips so the inward curve fits the outward curve. Stitch the seam and press it open. Notch the fullness ripples from the outward curve (H).

Gathered or eased seam: Stitch with the gathered or eased side up. Guide the fabric with your hands to prevent unwanted tucks or puckers from forming. For more gathering and easing techniques, see pages 135 and 122.

Bias seams: To join two bias edges—such as a side seam of a bias-cut skirt—hold the fabric in front and in back of the presser foot and stretch it as you stitch. This will allow the seam to "give" with the fabric, which will relax slightly after stitching.

When joining a bias edge to a straight-grain edge—for example, stitching a bias-cut yoke to a bodice—stitch with the bias edge facing the machine. *Don't* stretch the fabric as you sew.

Seam finishes: Most seams should be finished to prevent raveling or to create a neat appearance. See Edge Finishes, page 123, and the chart on pages 124 and 125.

Seam Types

Although you'll use a plain seam fairly often, you should know when other types of seams are required. To help you decide which seams are right for your fabric, check the chart on pages 124-125 and these seam types. If you are a beginner, read pages 158-159 first.

Flat-felled seam: Attractive and durable, the flat-felled seam is a good choice for sportswear, menswear and reversible garments. Stitch a plain seam. Press the seam to one side. Trim the underneath seam allowance to ⅛″ (3 mm). Turn under ¼″ (6 mm) of the top seam allowance and baste it over the trimmed edge. Topstitch close to fold (D).

Lapped seam: Commonly used for non-woven fabrics, such as suede and leather types (see page 209), the lapped seam may also be used for wovens or knits in small areas, such as yokes.

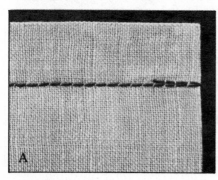

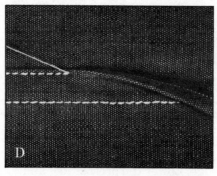

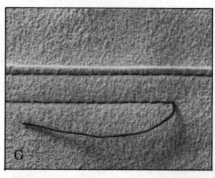

Plain seam: With right sides together, stitch along the seamline —usually ⅝″ (1.5 cm) from the cut edge—using a regulation stitch (A). For knits, stretch the fabric slightly as you sew. Press the seam open and finish the seam allowances with an appropriate edge finish for your fabric (see page 123).

French seam: For sheer fabrics, this seam is preferred because it is narrow and encloses the raw edges. With *wrong* sides together, stitch ⅜″ (1 cm) from the cut edge. Press the seam to one side. Trim it to a scant ⅛″ (3 mm). With *right* sides together, fold the fabric at the seam; press. Stitch ¼″ (6 mm) from the fold (E); press to one side.

For non-wovens, trim away the seam allowance on the upper section. Lap this edge over the underneath section, placing the trimmed edge along the seamline; hold it in place with double-faced basting tape or fabric glue. Edgestitch in place. Stitch again ¼″ (6 mm) away from the first stitching if desired (G).

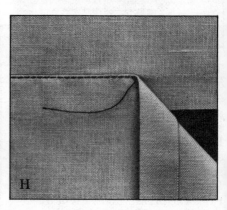

Double-stitched seam: A combination seam and edge finish, this seam is stitched twice to prevent raveling. It's a narrow seam, especially good for sheers and knits. Stitch a plain seam. Then stitch again ⅛″ (3 mm) away on the seam allowance, using a straight or zigzag stitch. Trim close to the second stitching (B, C). Press the seam to one side.

Mock French seam: This is a good choice for sheers and lightweight fabrics. Begin with a plain seam. Then turn in the seam allowances toward each other and match the folded edges. Stitch them together close to the fold (F).

For wovens or knits, press under the seam allowance on the upper section. Lap this over the seam allowance on the underneath section, placing the fold along the seamline. Topstitch close to the fold, through all layers (H) and again ¼″ (6 mm) away if desired.

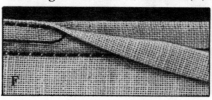

Topstitched seam: For a seam accent on sportswear and crease-resistant fabrics, stitch a plain seam and press it open. From the outside, topstitch ⅛″-¼″ (3-6 mm) on each side of the seam (A). Or, press the seam allowances to one side and topstitch ⅛″-¼″ (3-6 mm) from the seam through all layers (B).

Welt seam: When you want a flat seam, a welt seam is a good choice —especially for heavyweight fabrics. First, stitch a plain seam. Press the seam allowances to one side. Trim the underneath seam allowance to a scant ¼″ (6 mm). On the outside, topstitch ¼″ (6 mm) from the seam, catching the untrimmed seam allowance (C). For a *double welt seam,* also topstitch close to the seam.

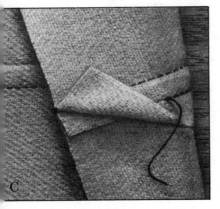

Knit seams: Stretch knits need seams that are supple enough to "give" with the fabric. You can sew them with straight or zigzag stitching. If you think you might have to reopen a seam after fitting the garment, remember that straight stitches will be easier to remove than zigzag stitches. When straight-stitching, hold the fabric in front and in back of the presser foot and stretch the fabric slightly as you sew. Here are several ways to stitch knit seams.

• For a plain seam, straight-stitch along the seamline and press the seam allowances open.
• For extra strength, straight-stitch along the seamline two or three times close together; stitch

again ¼″ (6 mm) away and trim close to the last stitching (D).
• Straight-stitch along the seamline. Then trim the seam allowances to ¼″ (6 mm) and zigzag the trimmed edges together (E).

• Use a narrow, medium-length zigzag stitch for the seam; trim the seam allowances to ¼″ (6 mm) and zigzag the edges together (F).

• Some machines have special stretch stitches that can only be used for seams. Others have an overlock or overedge stitch that lets you stitch the seam and overcast the edges in one step (G-J). For these stitches, the seam allowances must be trimmed before stitching; follow the instruc-

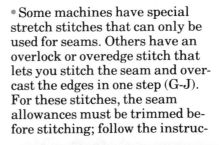

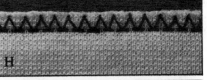

tions in your manual, as they vary from one machine to another.
• Seams at necklines, shoulders and waistlines should *not* stretch, or they will lose their shape. Stabilize them by stitching seam binding or twill tape into the seam (K). When trimming or clipping seams, be careful not to cut into the seam binding or tape.
• For more information on sewing knits, see pages 206-208.

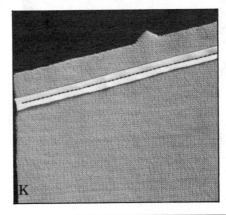

Sleeves

Most sleeve styles fall into three basic categories—set-in, kimono and raglan. The techniques given below and on the next pages will help you sew well-made sleeves.

Set-in Sleeves

The rounded area at the top of a set-in sleeve is called the *sleeve cap*. On the sleeve pattern piece, the cap is the curve between the notches, which is designed to fit the shape of your upper arm at the shoulder. When you sew the sleeve in, you ease the sleeve cap into the armhole, creating the rounded shape for your shoulder.

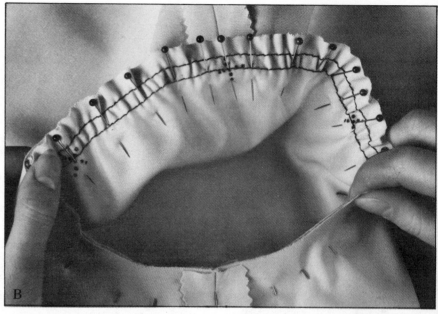

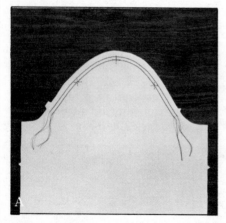

Stitch the sleeve seam and press it open. Then follow your pattern instructions and the information on page 165 to finish the lower edge of the sleeve; it's easier to do this before you sew the sleeve into the armhole.

Turn the sleeve right side out. To pin the sleeve to the armhole, hold the garment wrong side out, with the armhole facing you. Slip the sleeve inside the armhole. Match the sleeve and garment underarm seams, shoulder markings and notches; place pins at these points. Then match the re-maining markings on the sleeve and the armhole and pin these, too.

Now, pull the threads of the ease stitching at each end. Slide the fabric along the threads. Distribute the fullness evenly in the area between the notches until the sleeve fits the armhole. Pin closely all around the eased area, being careful not to create any puckers. Pin the underarm area between the notches as well (B). If your machine does not stitch over pins, hand-baste close to the seamline and remove the pins before stitching the seam.

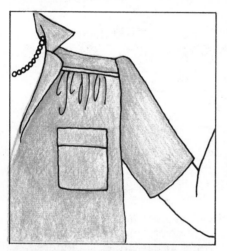

In woven fabric: Ease-stitch the sleeve cap twice on the right side of the fabric. First, ease-stitch along the seamline between the notches; then, stitch ¼″ (6 mm) away on the seam allowance. Leave thread ends long enough to pull for easing (A).

Ease a sleeve cap in a pliable woven fabric just by stitching along the seamline with a regular stitch. While stitching, place one forefinger on each side of the seamline in front of the needle. Pull the fabric horizontally so it is stretched off-grain. At the same time, push it forward under the presser foot for four or five stitches (C). Stop and move to the next section. Continue pulling horizontally, pushing the fabric under the presser foot, and stitching. The sleeve will automatically shape itself into a cap. Then stitch the sleeve to the armhole as described below.

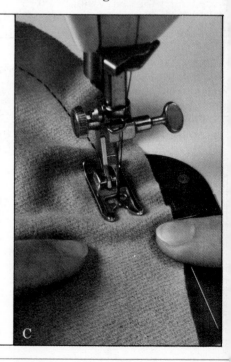

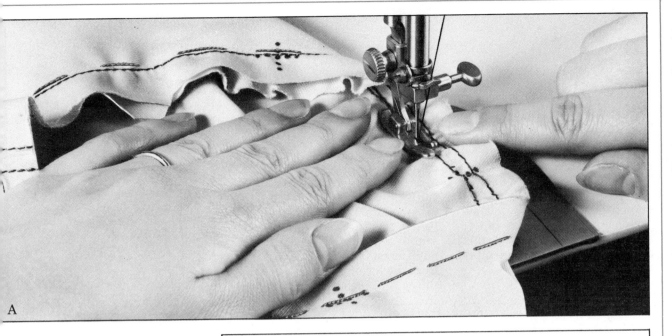

A

With the sleeve side up, begin at the underarm seam and stitch along the seamline just inside the first row of ease stitching. Use your fingertips to keep the eased area from puckering under the needle (A). Complete the seam by stitching over your first few stitches to secure them. Stitch a second row 1/8" (3 mm) away from the first row, on the seam allowance. In the underarm area between the notches, trim close to the stitching (B). Press the seam allowances, not the seam (see page 192).

Easy method: When the sleeve cap has only a moderate amount of ease—as on casual clothes, children's wear or men's shirts—you can stitch the sleeve to the garment while the sleeve is flat, before sewing the sleeve underarm seam and garment side seams.

Stitch the garment shoulder seams only. Ease-stitch the sleeve cap the same as for Set-in Sleeves, on the opposite page. However, don't stitch the sleeve seam.

With right sides together, pin the sleeve to the armhole. Pull up the ease-stitching threads and distribute the ease as for Set-in Sleeves, opposite. With the sleeve side up, stitch on the seamline and again 1/8" (3 mm) away on the seam allowance (C). Trim the seam close to the stitching and press it toward the sleeve. *Note:* On a man's shirt, use a flat-felled seam (see page 160). Stitch the garment side seam and sleeve seam in one continuous stitching.

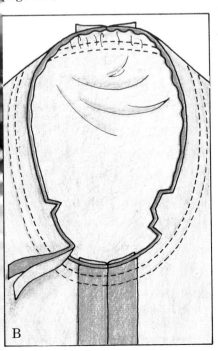

B

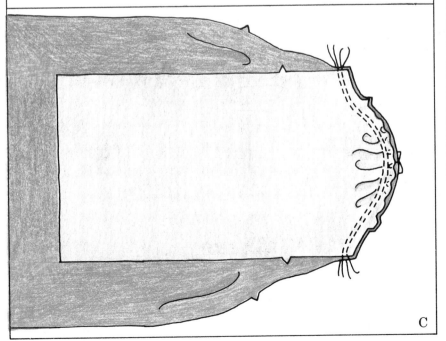

C

Set-in sleeve for knit fabric:

There's no need to ease-stitch the sleeve cap on knit fabric. Stitch the sleeve to the garment before the underarm and side seams are stitched. Pin the sleeve to the armhole edge, matching notches and markings. Then stitch the seam, with the garment side up. As you stitch, stretch the armhole to fit the sleeve so that the sleeve fullness is eased in (A). Stitch

Kimono Sleeves

Since kimono sleeves are cut as part of the garment front and back, they're the easiest style of sleeve to sew. Stitch the garment front to the back at the shoulder seams and press the seams open. Finish the neck edge as your pattern directs. Pin the front to the back at the side and underarm seams, matching raw edges, notches and markings. Stitch from the lower garment edge to the edge of the sleeves.

Raglan Sleeves

Raglan sleeves are joined to the garment front and back by diagonal seams running from the underarm to the neckline. These seams are usually stitched before the underarm and side seams.

Preparing: Stitch the sleeve shoulder dart or seam, if any, and press it open; slash the dart to within ½" (1.3 cm) of the point before pressing.

Stitching: With right sides together, pin the sleeve to the garment front and back, matching

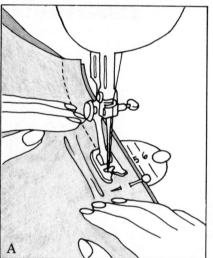

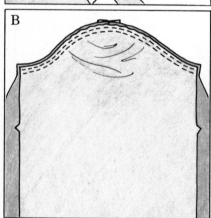

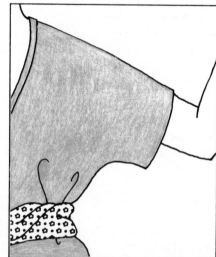

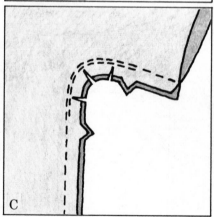

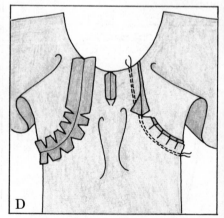

again ¼" (6 mm) away inside the seam allowance; trim close to the second stitching (B). Turn the seam toward the sleeve; press the seam allowances.

To reinforce the underarm, where there may be some strain, stitch over the first stitching at the curves. Clip the curves (C) and press the seams open. Then finish the sleeve hems as your pattern directs.

notches and any markings; stitch. To reinforce, stitch over the first stitching. Clip the curves and press the seams open (D). Then, stitch the underarm and side seams in one continuous stitching, the same as for Kimono Sleeves. Finish the lower sleeve edges as your pattern directs.

Sleeve Openings

Long sleeves with cuffs usually have openings at the cuffs to make it easy for you to slip your hands into the sleeves.

Continuous lap: For sleeves on a tailored shirt, the opening is usually bound with a straight fabric strip before the underarm seam is stitched. Your pattern will usually include a pattern piece for this strip.

To create an opening, mark the stitching lines on the lower edge of the sleeve. Stitch along these lines, using reinforcement-length stitches for 1″ (2.5 cm) on either side of the point; take one stitch

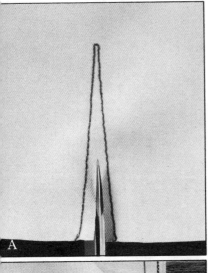

A

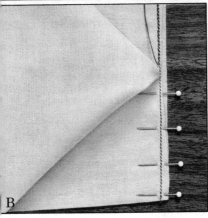

B

across the point. Slash between the stitching (A) right up to the point so that the opening will lie flat later. Spread the edges of the slash apart, forming an almost straight line. Pin the right side of the fabric strip to the wrong side of the slashed edge so that the sleeve stitching line is ¼″ (6 mm)

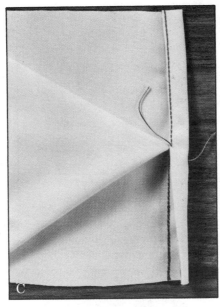

C

from the edge of the strip. With the sleeve right side up, fold the extra sleeve fabric out of the way and stitch ¼″ (6 mm) from the strip edge, on top of the previous stitching (B). To reinforce the seam, stitch again. Press the strip away from the sleeve and press the seam toward the strip. Then, press under ¼″ (6 mm) on the remaining long strip edge. Pin this edge over the seam on the outside of the sleeve; stitch close to the strip edge, through all layers (C). Press the front edge of the lap to the inside (D); baste.

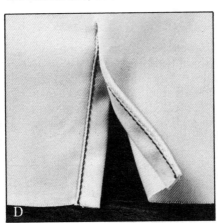

D

Faced opening: On casual clothes and blouses, the sleeve opening is usually faced. Your pattern will include a piece for the facing. Transfer the stitching lines and dots to the facing and to the lower edge of the sleeve. Finish the outer edges of the facing. Then, with right sides to-

gether, pin the facing to the sleeve. Stitch along the stitching line, taking one stitch across the point. To reinforce, stitch over the first stitching. Slash between the stitching up to the point (E). Press the seam toward the facing. Turn the facing to the inside of the sleeve and press. Slipstitch the finished edges in place (F).

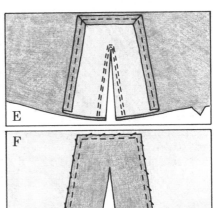

E

F

Hemmed opening: Some sleeve patterns have small hemmed openings which you can make entirely by machine. The opening is really a seam allowance that's turned and stitched. Reinforce the seamline by stitching for ½″ (1.3 cm) on each side of the markings. Clip to the stitching at the markings. Press the seam allowance under; then turn the raw edge under. Zigzag this edge and the ends (G).

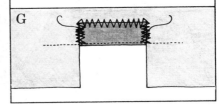

G

Finishing

After completing the sleeve openings, apply the cuffs as your pattern directs. Also see Cuffs, pages 117-118.

Tucks

A tuck is a stitched fold of fabric, made on the inside or outside of the garment. Groups of tucks are used to control fullness or add a decorative touch to shoulders, waistlines, yokes, pockets or cuffed sleeves.

Marking and Stitching

For tucks stitched on the inside of the garment, transfer the markings to the wrong side of the fabric, using any of the marking methods shown on pages 86-87. For tucks stitched outside, mark foldlines and any stitching lines with pins, snip or press marking, hand basting, or tailor's tacks.

To make tucks that are straight and parallel, press the folds before you stitch them. A sewing gauge can help you space the folds evenly. Stitch all tucks in the same direction. Then, press them in the direction indicated on the pattern instructions (usually away from the center front or back of the garment). Use brown paper strips underneath the tuck folds on fabrics that imprint.

Decorative tucks: If your sewing machine does decorative stitching, you can add pretty shell tucks or tucks with fancy stitches to lingerie, dainty blouses or children's dress-up clothes. Lightweight knits or sheer fabrics are suitable for shell tucks. Instead of making the tuck with a straight stitch, use a machine blindstitch over the edge (C). Or, to make decorative tucks, stitch the tuck with a machine embroidery stitch so that the design falls on the tuck (D).

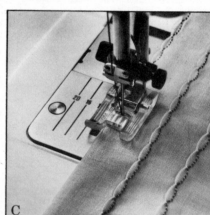

Very narrow tucks: Sometimes called pin tucks, these are usually indicated by a series of solid lines printed on the pattern piece. Fold the fabric on each line and stitch close to the fold (A).

Wider tucks: A pattern piece with wide or spaced tucks will usually have solid and broken lines printed on it. Fold the fabric on the solid line, matching the broken lines. Then, stitch along the broken lines.

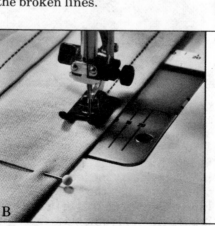

To save time when you're making wide tucks, you can transfer only the solid lines to the fabric, not the broken lines. When you stitch, use the markings on the throat plate, a strip of tape placed on the throat plate, or a seam guide to help you stitch the correct distance from the folded edge (B).

Waistbands

There are several methods for applying waistbands. Whichever one you choose, first interface the waistband as directed on page 43. If you use sew-in interfacing, baste it in place and trim close to the stitching as described. Then, to keep the interfacing from shifting, baste it to the facing side, near the foldline (A).

Machine and Hand-sewn Method

Press under 5⁄8″ (1.5 cm) along the long unnotched waistband edge and trim it to 1⁄4″ (6 mm). With right sides together, pin the waistband to the garment, matching notches, markings, centers front and back, and side seam markings. One end of the waistband will extend 5⁄8″ (1.5 cm) beyond the opening edge; the other will extend more (A).

Stitch the seam from the waistband side and trim it to 1⁄4″ (6 mm).

Press the seam toward the waistband and the waistband away from the garment (B). Fold the waistband in half with right sides

together; stitch across the ends and trim (C). Turn the waistband right side out and press. Pin the free edge along the waistband seam on the inside of the garment. Slipstitch the edge to the seam, catching a thread on the seam with each stitch (D). Slipstitch the underlap edges closed. Since the waistband is finished by hand sewing on the inside of the garment, no stitching will be seen on the outside.

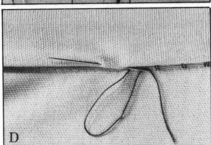

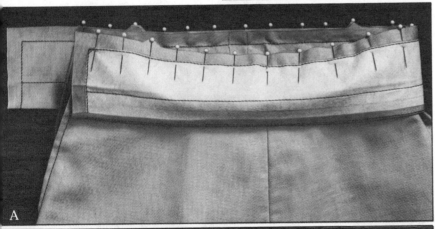

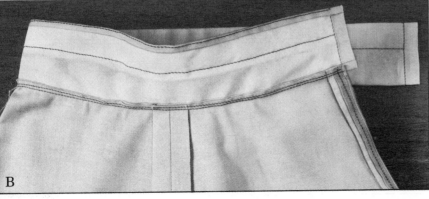

Machine-stitched Method

Often used on sportswear, this topstitched waistband is finished with stitching on the outside. If your pattern doesn't call for this method and you want to use it, place the waistband pattern piece face down when you cut.

Press under 5⁄8″ (1.5 cm) on the long unnotched waistband edge and trim it to 1⁄4″(6 mm). With the garment right side out, pin the *right* side of the waistband to the *wrong* side of the garment, matching notches, centers and markings. Stitch from the waistband side. Trim the seam; press it toward the

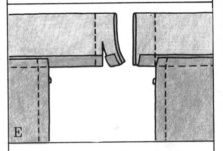

waistband and the waistband away from the garment. Fold the waistband in half with right sides together. Stitch across the ends and trim them (E).

Turn the waistband right side out and press. Pin or fuse the pressed-under edge over the seam on the outside and edgestitch it in place (F). If desired, topstitch around the other edges and again 1⁄4″ (6 mm) away.

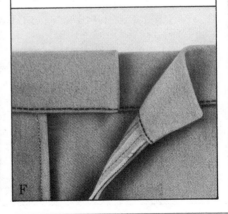

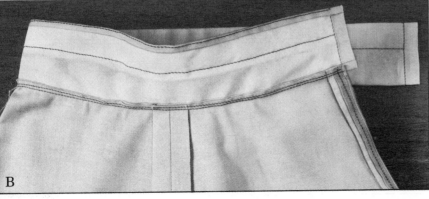

167

Overedged: An excellent choice for knits, the overedged method is a quick way to attach a waistband and finish the raw edges in one step. If your machine does not make an overedge stitch, use a double-stitched seam instead (see page 160).

With right sides together, fold the waistband in half lengthwise; stitch across the ends. At the underlap end, also stitch the lower edge, ending at the small dot. Clip to the seamline at the dot; trim the seams (A). Turn the waistband right side out and press the ends and the fold.

Pin both cut edges of the waistband to the outside of the garment, matching notches, centers and markings. Stitch the seam with an overedge stitch (see your machine manual) and trim the seam close to the stitching (B). Press the seam toward the garment and the waistband away from the garment; hand-tack the seam allowances to the zipper tape (C).

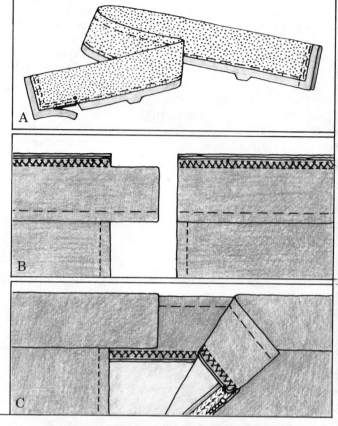

Stitched-in-the-ditch: Since the finished waist seam area is very flat, this machine method is good for heavyweight or bulky fabrics.

First, trim ¼″ (6 mm) from the unnotched edge of the interfaced waistband. If your fabric ravels, finish the raw edge. Or, for a built-in finish, cut the unnotched edge along a selvage, allowing a ⅜″ (1 cm) wide seam allowance.

With right sides together, pin and stitch the notched waistband edge to the garment, matching notches, centers and markings. Press the seam toward the waistband and the waistband away from the garment; trim the seam to ⅜″ (1 cm) (D).

With right sides together, fold the waistband along the foldline and stitch the overlap end. On the underlap, turn the waistband seam allowance down. Stitch the end to ⅜″ (1 cm) from the lower edge; then pivot and continue stitching to the small dot marking. Clip the seam allowances to the dot marking. Trim the seams (E).

Turn the waistband right side out; press. On the inside, fold the finished or selvage edge under diagonally at the zipper; pin. Lap the finished or selvage edge ⅜″ (1 cm) over the waistline seam and pin on the inside. Transfer the pins to the outside. Then, from the outside, stitch in the ditch, or groove, of the waistband seam, catching the finished edge and the diagonal turn-under (F).

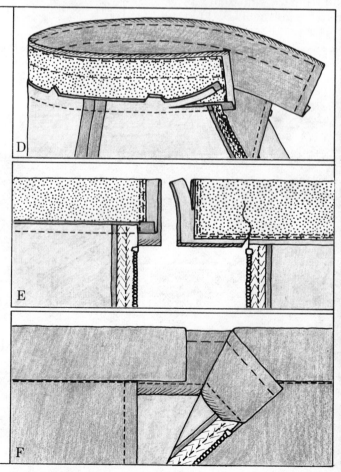

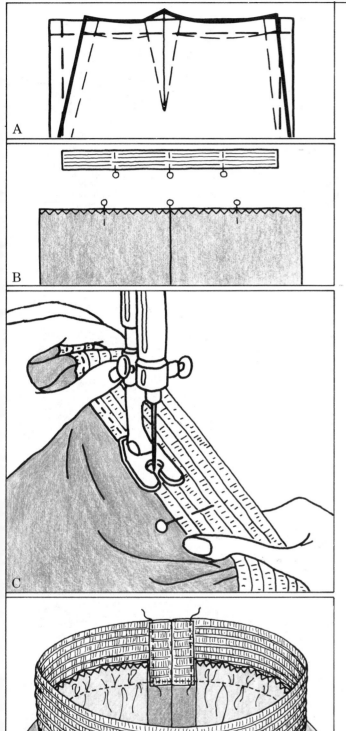

A

B

C

D

Elastic Waistbands

Instead of the standard waistband, try using wide decorative elastic. This elastic is available in many solid colors as well as stripes; you can choose one to match your skirt fabric or to contrast with it. Elastic waistbands work best on knits and on full skirts that are not closely fitted to the waist or hips. If your pattern is fitted to the waist and not to the hips, you can adapt it for elastic by drawing a straight line from the hipline to the waist; extend the waist seamline to meet it, as shown (A). Omit all darts in the waistline area; omit the zipper as well.

To determine the length of elastic you will need, hold the elastic around your waist so that it fits comfortably but is fairly snug. Add 1¼″ (3.2 cm) for seam allowances.

Stitch all the skirt seams except one, usually the center back seam. If your fabric ravels, finish the raw waistline edge. Divide both the elastic and the garment waistline into four equal parts (or eight parts, if the skirt is very full), using pins as markers (B).

On the outside, pin the lower edge of the elastic over the skirt seamline, matching the pin markers. Use a slightly loosened tension and 8-10 stitches per inch (2.5 cm). On the outside, stitch along the elastic edge, stretching the elastic to fit the skirt as you sew (C).

Stitch the remaining skirt seam, continuing across the elastic. Press the seam open and machine-tack the elastic ends flat (D).

Instead of regular decorative elastic, you might want to try a commercial elastic waistband, which can be purchased by the yard. This is a heavy, foldover elastic with stripes on the section that shows on the outside. To apply it, follow the manufacturer's instructions.

Zippers

Try the methods explained here—particularly the shortcuts—and you'll find that inserting a zipper is no trouble at all.

Basics

To use zippers successfully, check out the terms and tips below.

• A zipper has synthetic *coils* or metal *teeth* attached to woven or knitted *tapes. Guidelines,* woven or knitted into the tapes, show where to stitch. The *tab* allows you to open and close the zipper. The *top* and *bottom stops* prevent the tab from coming off the zipper.
• Common zipper types include *regular,* for dresses, skirts and pants; *invisible,* sewn into a seam without stitching on the outside; and *separating,* with a special bottom stop that allows jackets or coats to open all the way.
• To choose the right zipper type and length for your garment, check the pattern envelope back.
• If the zipper is for a washable garment, preshrink it.
• Press the tapes to remove folds, *using a press cloth.* Never touch the coil with a hot iron.
• Whenever possible, insert the zipper before the garment side seams are stitched.
• There are five basic zipper applications: centered, lapped, fly front, invisible and separating. Your pattern will tell you which zipper application to use.
• Close the zipper before laundering or dry-cleaning the garment.

Centered Zipper

Prepare the garment: Insert the zipper before attaching a waistband or facing. Stitch the seam, backstitching at the bottom of the opening and machine-basting the zipper-opening portion. To make the basting easy to remove later, clip every inch (2.5 cm) or so. Press seam open.

Insert the zipper: Open the zipper and place it *face down* along one seam allowance with the top stop 1″ (2.5 cm) below the upper garment edge and the coil or teeth along the seam. Using a zipper foot, machine-baste along the

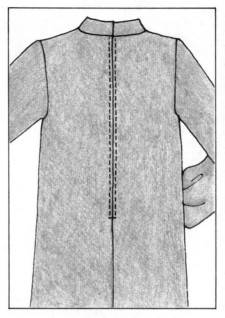

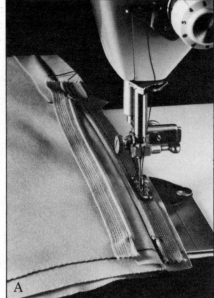

tape guideline (A). Close the zipper, turn the tab up and spread the garment flat, *right side up.*

To help you stitch accurately, center ½″ (1.3 cm) wide sewing tape over the seam; stitch close to the tape edge, not through it. Test tape first on a fabric scrap to be sure it won't leave a mark when removed. Or, use pins placed parallel to the seam, ¼″ (6 mm) away; remove pins as you stitch. Starting at the seam, stitch for ¼″ (6 mm) across the bottom of the zipper; then pivot and stitch to the top, ¼″ (6 mm) from the seam. Shift the zipper foot to the other side of the needle and stitch the other side the same way (B). Pull thread ends to the wrong side and knot them. Remove basting.

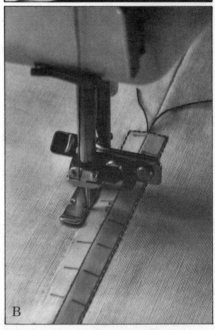

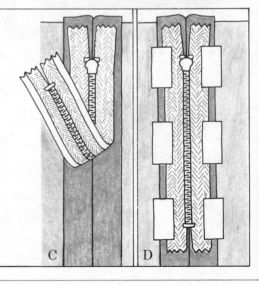

Quick centered zipper: Place double-faced basting tape on the right side of the zipper tapes, *close to the edges.* Turn the pull tab up and place the zipper face down on the seam allowances, with the coil or teeth along the seam and the top stop 1″ (2.5 cm) below the cut edge (C). Or use cellophane tape on the wrong side of the zipper tapes (D). Then, stitch as for the Centered Zipper, above. Remove all tape.

form. Starting at the bottom, stitch through the fold and the tape (B). Turn the pull tab up.

Spread the garment flat, *wrong side up*. Turn the zipper face down over the seam (C); tape the un-stitched side as for Quick Centered Zipper, or pin from the outside.

On the outside, place ⅜″ (1 cm) wide sewing tape alongside the seam as a stitching guide. Or use pins ⅜″ (1 cm) away, parallel to the seam; remove pins as you get to them. Start at the seam and stitch ⅜″ (1 cm) across the bottom of the zipper; pivot and stitch to the top (D). Pull threads to the underside; knot. Remove basting.

Lapped Zipper

First prepare the garment as for the Centered Zipper, opposite. If you have a facing, apply it as directed on page 128. For a lapped zipper on leather-like fabrics, see page 210.

Insert the zipper: Open the zipper and place it *face down* on the underlap seam allowance, keeping the garment out of the way. Place the top stop 1″ (2.5 cm) below the cut edge and the coil or teeth along the seam. Using a zipper foot, machine-baste close to the zipper coil (A).

Close the zipper and turn it face up, smoothing the fabric away from the zipper; a narrow fold will

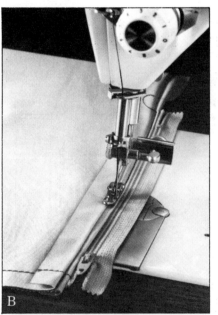

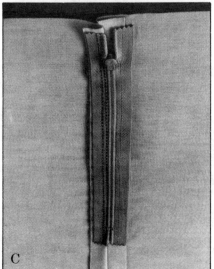

Quick lapped zipper: First stitch the seam up to the bottom of the zipper opening. Press the underlap edge under ½″ (1.3 cm), forming a tiny fold at the lower end; press the overlap edge under ⅝″ (1.5 cm). With the closed zipper face up, tape the underlap close to the zipper coil so the top stop is 1″ (2.5 cm) below the cut edge. Using a zipper foot, stitch close to the fold (E). Then position the overlap to cover the stitching on the underlap. Pin or tape in place and finish as for regular Lapped Zipper, above.

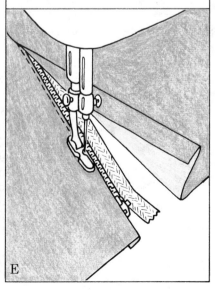

Prepare the front: Mark the zipper stitching line on the left pants front with speed hand basting (page 88). To reinforce the left front section, stitch along the center front seamline for about 1″ (2.5 cm) on each side of the small dot marking, stitching through the marking (A).

Fly Front Zipper/His

On men's and boys' pants, the left side, or overlap, of the fly is interfaced and the right side, or underlap, has an extra, lined piece called the fly shield.

With the following method, the fly is constructed before any of the pants seams have been stitched, so it's easy to insert the zipper.

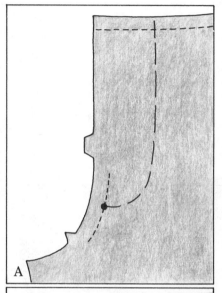

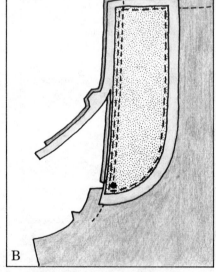

Left fly: Interface the left fly. If needed, finish the curved edge. Then, with right sides together, pin the fly to the left front edge, matching notches and small dot markings. Stitch above the small dot marking. Clip the left front as far as the dot; then trim the entire fly seam allowance and the front seam allowance above the clip (B). Press the seam toward the fly and the fly away from the pants.

Zipper: Place the closed zipper face down over the left fly, with the bottom stop of the zipper about ¼″ (6 mm) above the small dot marking on the fly seam and the zipper tape edge close to the fly seam. The top of the zipper will

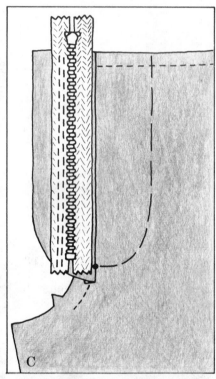

extend above the front; you'll shorten it later. Using a zipper foot, stitch close to the zipper coil as shown and again ¼″ (6 mm) from the first stitching (C).

Turn the fly to the inside and press. Baste or pin the fly in place, keeping the lower end of the unstitched zipper tape free (A).

Right fly: On the right front, make a ⅜″ (1 cm) deep clip at the small dot marking on the center front seamline. Above the clip, press under ⅜″ (1 cm) (C). Open the zipper. Pin the right front over the unstitched zipper tape, close to the coil, with the small dot marking about ¼″ (6 mm) below the bottom stop of the zipper; baste (D). When the zipper is closed, the left front will lap ¼″ (6 mm) over the right front and the dot markings at the lower end of the opening will match.

Fly shield: With right sides together, pin the fly lining section to the fly; stitch the curved edges together. Trim the seam and notch the curve (E). Turn the fly right side out and press.

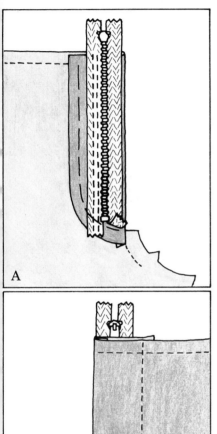

A

B

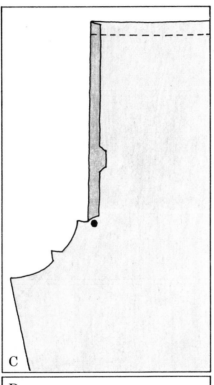

C

D

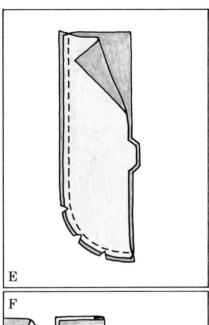

E

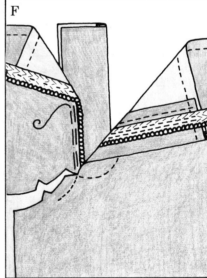

F

On the outside, topstitch close to the basted stitching line, still keeping the unstitched zipper tape free on the inside. Remove the basting (B).

Pin the right front ⅝″ (1.5 cm) over the unstitched fly edges, with upper edges even; baste (F). Using a zipper foot, topstitch close to the zipper coil through all layers. Remove the basting.

With the *zipper open*, stitch across *both* fly sections at the waistline edge, catching in the tops of the zipper tapes. Then cut off the excess zipper so that it's even with the waistline edge.

Fly Front Zipper/Hers

Many pants and skirts have a fly front zipper. Here's a simple way to make a fly zipper application on women's clothes.

Prepare the front: First, mark the zipper stitching line on the right garment front with speed hand basting (page 88). Stitch the center front seam, backstitching at the dot marking for reinforcement and machine-basting the fly extensions together along the center front line. Clip the seam allowances below the fly extension. Press the extensions open. If your fabric ravels, finish the extension edges.

Insert the zipper: Open the zipper. Place it face down on the *right* side of the *left* fly extension only, with the coil along the seam and the top stop 1″ (2.5 cm) below the waistline edge. Hold the zip-

per in place with pins or double-faced basting tape. Using a zipper foot, machine-baste along the zipper tape guideline (A).

Close the zipper and turn it face up, smoothing the fabric away from it. With a zipper foot, stitch close to the fabric fold through all layers as shown (B).

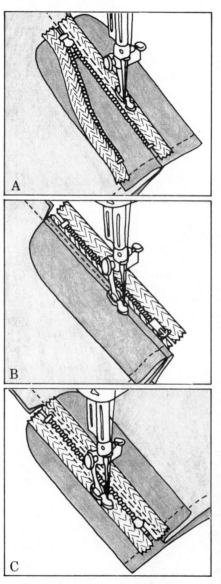

Turn the zipper face down over the *right* fly extension only, with the pull tab turned up. Keep the rest of the garment out of the way. With a zipper foot, stitch along the zipper tape guideline, through the tape and the fly extension (C).

Spread the garment flat, *wrong side up,* and pin the right fly extension to the garment front (D). Then repin it from the outside, removing pins from the inside so they won't get caught in the machine as you sew.

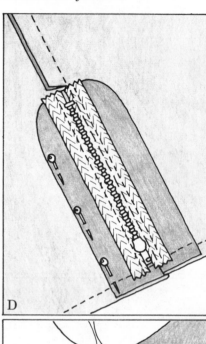

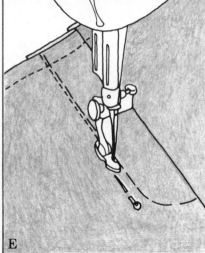

On the outside, stitch close to the baste-marked stitching line, removing the pins as you get to them (E). Remove the basting.

Invisible Zipper

To insert an invisible zipper, you'll need a special foot, preferably one intended for the brand of zipper you're using. Instead of stitching and basting the seam where the zipper will be inserted, leave the *entire seam unstitched* until after the zipper is applied.

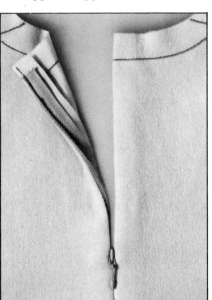

Open the zipper and unroll the zipper coil by pressing it or using your fingers (follow the manufacturer's directions). Position the zipper face down on the *right* side of the fabric, as shown, with the zipper tape on the seam allowance, the coil along the seamline and the top stop 1″ (2.5 cm) below the cut edge (A). Hold zipper in place with double-faced basting tape or pins placed parallel to the fabric edge. Lower the presser foot so the zipper coil is in the groove of the foot and stitch down the zipper tape (A). For bulky fabrics, position the needle farther away from the zipper coil, not centered in the zipper foot hole.

To position the second side, close the zipper. Place the unstitched zipper tape face down on the *right* side of the other garment section,

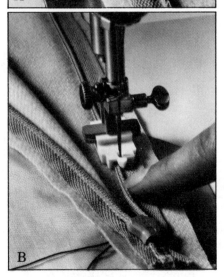

with the zipper tape on the seam allowance, the coil along the seamline and the top stop 1″ (2.5 cm) below the cut edge. Pin the zipper in place at the top or use double-faced basting tape to hold it in place. Now open the zipper and stitch the second side the same way you did the first (B). Close the zipper.

To stitch the seam below the zipper, slide the foot to the left of the needle. Place the right sides of the fabric together, aligning the raw edges. Insert the needle in the fabric three stitches above and slightly to the left of the last zipper stitching. Lower the foot and stitch to the end of the seam (C).

Pull the starting threads through to one side and knot them. Stitch the lower ends of the zipper tapes to the seam allowances *only* (D). Press the seam open.

Separating Zipper

The front of a jacket is the most common location for a separating zipper which opens completely at the bottom. These zippers may be inserted with the teeth covered or exposed. For an exposed applica-

Covered: Usually, the jacket front section has an extension that forms a self-facing. Follow your pattern instructions for finishing the inner edges of the front facing extensions and assembling the jacket. After you have turned the facings inside and attached the collar, pin the closed zipper, face up, under the opening edges, with the pull tab

Exposed: Whether or not your garment has self-facings, this application method is essentially the same for either style.

If there are self-facings, finish the raw edges as your pattern directs. Press the facings inside along the foldline. Pin the pressed edges over the closed zipper, close to the zipper teeth, so that the pull tab is ⅛″ (3 mm) below the neck seamline. If the zipper is inserted before a collar or hood is attached,

tion, choose a decorative zipper with plastic teeth and colorful tapes that match or contrast with the garment color.

⅛″ (3 mm) below the neck seamline. The opening edges should meet at the center of the zipper, covering the teeth. Baste or use double-faced basting tape to hold the zipper in place, turning the zipper tapes under at the upper end (A). On the outside, use a zipper foot to topstitch ⅜″ (1 cm) from each opening edge, sewing through the zipper tapes (A).

let the tape ends extend above the neck seamline (B). Otherwise, turn the tape ends under so they're even with the top stop. Baste or use double-faced basting tape to hold the zipper in place. Then, when your pattern directs, use a zipper foot to stitch close to the front edges (B). If desired, stitch again ¼″ (6 mm) away from the first stitching.

If there are no self-facings, press the front edges under on the seamlines. Then proceed as described for the style with self-facings.

Extra-sure sewing...

Sewing is becoming easier and surer all the time because the new methods are geared to today's fabrics and styles. On the following pages, there's a sampling of these extra-sure techniques.

(Right) An elegant, silky dress with piping detail inspired this clever way to make pre-measured piping with a minimum of fuss. Make a cardboard template to mark the bias strips (see page 103) the length needed for each garment section. Using a zipper foot, encase the cord, strip by strip, in one continuous step (A). When you're done, cut the cord apart between strips. It's so easy!

Dressing up

You can *never* have too many all-occasion dresses. And sewing these three beauties is sure to be smooth and easy when you follow our up-to-the minute techniques.

(Near Right) A neatly-finished collar tops off this simple classic perfectly. It's completely machine-stitched, too! Just apply the collar as shown on page 113, machine-stitching the back neck edge over the seam instead of hand-sewing it (A). You can finish the cuffs by machine, too; page 118 tells you how.

(Middle Right) Topstitch a crisp edge, even on slippery crepe that doesn't hold a pressed crease. Just use fine thread, looser top tension and 10 to 12 stitches per inch (2.5 cm). You'll find more easy topstitching tips on page 148.

(Far Right) Tucks galore! Now, thanks to snip, pin and press marking (pages 86-87), making even tucks doesn't have to be the chore it used to be (B). No more hand-basting! Another extra-sure tip: stick tape on your machine and use it as a guide to help you stitch extra-wide tucks evenly and accurately (C).

Tops are #1!

Some of the most popular items to sew, tops have a fresh, updated look when you make them in knit velour. You'll find this plush fabric extra-simple to sew with these tips.

(Near Right) Easy-fitting sleeves and shawl collar work together nicely in a sportive pullover. The sleeves are sewn in quickly while the garment is still flat (A) (see page 164). The collar shapes up with fusible interfacing and topstitching.

(Middle) Stitch up snappy stripes, matched as you sew with the help of an even-feed foot (B). Or, if you don't have this attachment, try close pin-basting instead (page 100). Get to the point—of every V, that is—without a pucker. Just reinforce the neckline with small stitches, 18-20 per inch (2.5 cm), and attach the band as directed on page 98.

(Far Right) Here's a handsome top in a lush knit velour—a real pleasure to sew and wear. Seaming knits is easy, no matter what type of machine you have. If yours is a straight-stitch-only type, double-stitch seams (C), stretching them slightly as you sew (page 161). With a zigzag machine, you don't need to stretch the seams. Just check out the options on page 161 and follow your machine manual directions for stretch knit seams (D, E).

C

D

E

Jacket classics

What makes a knockout jacket? Crisp collars and edges and perfect patch pockets! To assure your jacket's fashion appeal, just latch onto these techniques.

(Left) The traditional blazer with lapels and patch pockets should be a staple in everyone's wardrobe. Interfacing helps shape the collar and front edges. Grading bulky seams (A) lets you press sharp edges (page 158).

(Far Left) A shirt-tail jacket pairs off well with lean pants. Cutting the undercollar (or facing) a bit smaller than the upper collar is the secret to keeping the under-collar *under!* (B) (see page 111).

(Right) Casual, yet refined, this man's blazer has soft shaping—from top to bottom! The collar can stand up, thanks to interfacing. And curves turn out smoothly when you notch the fullness from the seam allowances (see page 159); on pockets, first gather curved seam allowances before turning them under (C) (see page 153).

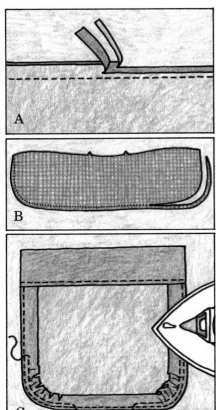

Outdoor gear

All-weather wear like this keeps you ready for whatever Mother Nature sends. Since the fabrics are what make these fashions special, all you really need to know is how to stitch them successfully.

(Top) A wet-look poncho takes to rain like a duck to water. To stitch ciré and other rainwear fabrics, use a size 11 or 14 universal needle and 10-12 stitches per inch (2.5 cm); hold the fabric taut as you stitch.

(Right) For a crisp spring or fall day, a classic double-breasted coat will keep the chills away. To stitch melton and similar coatings, first pin or hand-baste seams. Stitch with a size 16 needle and 8-10 stitches per inch (2.5 cm). Test-stitch to see whether tension and pressure need to be loosened.

(Far Right) Make your coat reversible and get two fashions in the time it takes to make one. Sewing a reversible garment like this one in corduroy and wool is similar to sewing melton, above. Just keep these points in mind: To reduce slippage and to get uniform stitches, do as much stitching as possible on the same fabric side. The nap on corduroy should run down; stitch in the direction of the nap — from the *top* of the garment *down*.

8 *press as you sew*

Since pressing influences the shape of your garment almost as much as the actual stitching, "press as you sew" is one of the most important sewing principles.

But you don't have to run to the iron every time you stitch a seam. Sew the seams or darts in several garment sections, then press them. Just don't cross a seam or a dart with stitching until <u>after</u> you have pressed it. The clothes you sew can look custom-made—all it takes is a little pressing know-how and the proper equipment.

A

equipment

Several helpful pressing tools are shown on page 48 in the Sewing Tools chapter. The most important ones are a steam iron, ironing board and press cloths. Set them up right near your sewing area, since you'll be using them often.

You can add extra moisture to very crease-resistant fabrics if your iron has a spray of steam pushbutton (A), or you can use a damp press cloth (B). You'll also need a press cloth or a soleplate cover (C) to protect some fabrics from "iron shine."

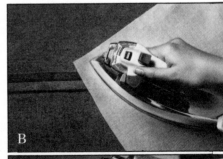

B

C

Pressing pointers

Heat, moisture and pressure are the variables to control when you are pressing. Test-press both sides of the fabric to see how much to use and whether or not you'll need a press cloth.

Always press with an *up-and-down* motion—not back and forth, as you do when ironing. You'll usually press on the wrong side of the fabric, but sometimes you must also press on the right side to get a smooth finish.

Heat: Most irons indicate the heat settings to use for certain fabrics. For example, the hottest setting usually works the best for linen, while the coolest one works best on acetate and silk.

Moisture: A steam iron provides enough moisture to press most fabrics. Crease-resistant or heavyweight fabrics may need more moisture than the iron can provide; or your fabric may require a heat setting that's too cool for the iron to make steam. For these fabrics, use a damp press cloth. To dampen the cloth, wet it and wring it to remove excess moisture.

You can also add extra moisture to a small area, such as a seam or dart, with a small damp sponge, brush or the steam-spray feature of most irons.

Pressure: As a rule, it's best to use light pressure, without resting the full weight of the iron on the fabric. Crease-resistant fabrics require slightly more pressure, while heavyweight coatings must be steamed and pounded with a pounding block (page 188).

To avoid flattening the texture of fabrics such as velvet and fur types, steam them. Hold the iron above the fabric and use your fingers to press seams, darts and edges. Or use a needle board.

The chart below is a guide for pressing today's common fibers and textures.

PRESS-AS-YOU-SEW GUIDE

Fiber	Pressure	Heat	Moisture	Special Instructions
Acetate	Light	Very low	Dry iron	Use press cloth on right side.
Acrylic		Moderate		
Cotton	Light to moderate	Moderate to high		Press with steam iron. For more moisture, dampen fabric and press with dry iron. To avoid shine on dark colors, press from wrong side or use press cloth on right side.
Linen	Light to heavy	High		
Nylon	Light			Little or no ironing required.
Polyester	Moderate			May need press cloth on right side; test first.
Rayon		Low to moderate	Dry or steam iron	Use press cloth to prevent shine and water spots.
Silk	Light			Press light to medium weights with dry iron. For heavyweights, use steam iron and dry press cloth to avoid water spots.
Wool	Light to moderate or pounding	Moderate		Press with steam iron. For more moisture, press with dry iron and slightly dampened press cloth. Use press cloth on right side to prevent shine. Press crepe with dry iron.
Blends	Press according to requirements of the more delicate fiber.			
Texture				
Crepe	Light	Low to moderate	Dry iron	Use press cloth on right side.
Deep Pile	Finger-press	Moderate	Steam iron	See Pressure, above, for finger pressing.
Glossy	Light	Low	Dry iron	Same as Crepe.
Nap, Pile	Light or finger-press	Low to moderate	Dry or steam iron	Press fabric over needleboard, using light pressure; or finger-press.

U sing the tools

In addition to the basics, there are many other pressing tools. Every one is designed to help you press specific areas easily for the most professional results. Since you may not want to buy *all* of the traditional tools, we've suggested some substitutes wherever possible.

paper and slip them under the edges of seam allowances, darts, hems and facings before pressing them on the inside (A). See also Seam Roll on page 189.

Needle Board

To avoid flattening the texture of napped or pile fabrics such as brushed flannel or velvet, you can place the fabric face down on a needle board and press seams or edges flat (C).

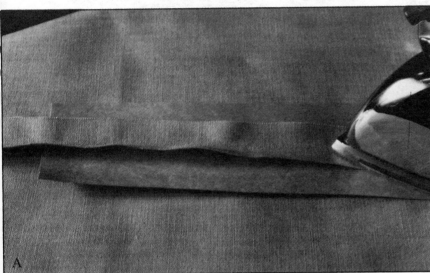

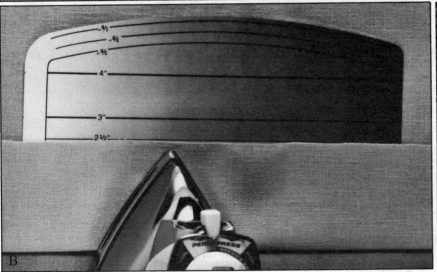

Paper Strips

To prevent imprinted lines from showing on the outside of fabrics that mar easily, such as crepe, satin and wool, cut strips of heavy

Substitutes: Instead of cutting paper strips, use *envelopes,* which don't need to be cut, or a *hem guide,* which allows you to measure the depth of a hem or cuff as you press (B).

Substitutes: Place napped or pile fabric face down on a fluffy *terry towel* or on the right side of a *scrap of your napped fabric* as you press from the wrong side. To press the right side, place the fabric scrap or terry towel face down on the garment section and press lightly (D).

Tailor's Ham

In order to mold their shape, press curved areas such as darts, princess seams and sleeve caps over a tailor's ham. Slip the garment over the ham so that the most curved part is over the narrow end of the ham (A). See also Seam Roll opposite.

Substitute: Press darts and sleeve caps over the *narrow, curved end of the ironing board* (B). Use the *side edge of the ironing board* for curved seams. Or, temporarily convert the *arm of an upholstered chair* into a ham by pinning fabric scraps to it.

Tailor's Mitt

Use a mitt the same way you would use a tailor's ham. It is smaller and slips over your hand or the end of a sleeve board. The mitt is especially good for pressing hard-to-reach areas (C).

Substitutes: See the substitutes for Tailor's Ham above.

Pounding Block

For tailoring heavyweight fabric, use a pounding block along with plenty of steam to coax a reluctant seam or edge into a sharp crease. Steam the fabric, then clap the block onto the fabric and hold it for a few seconds to force the steam out and flatten the edge (D). Be careful not to hold it down so hard that you imprint the fabric with the edge of the block.

Substitute: You can use any *flat piece of smooth wood* that fits your hand comfortably.

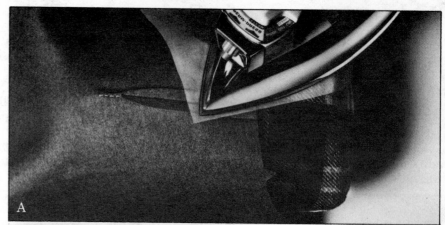

A

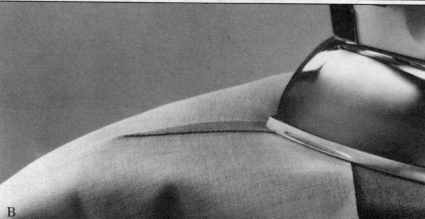

B

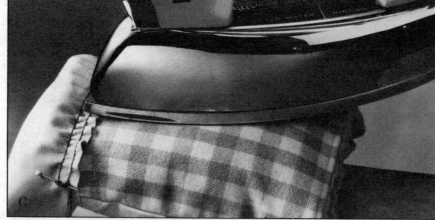

C

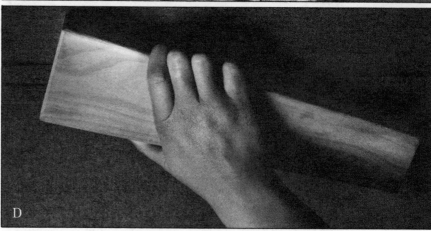

D

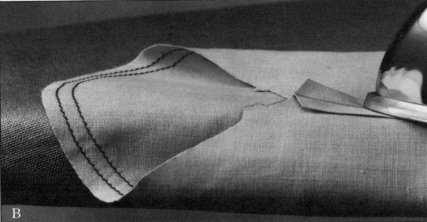

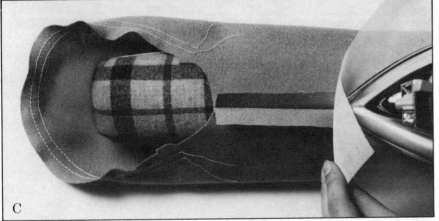

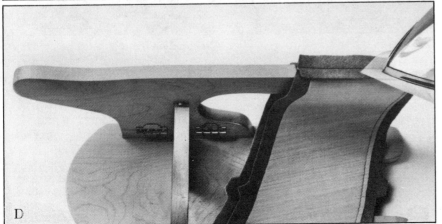

Sleeve Board

You can use the sleeve board, a small double ironing board, to conveniently press narrow garment sections, sleeves and pants legs that won't fit over the regular ironing board (A).

Substitutes: Place sleeve or leg seams along the *ironing board edges* with part of the sleeve or leg hanging off the board. This way you can press the seam open without forming unwanted creases in the sleeve or leg (B).

Seam Roll

Another option for pressing narrow garment sections is to use a seam, or sleeve, roll (C). The curved surface also allows you to press the seam open without the iron touching the edges of the seam allowances. This guarantees that there will be no imprints from seam allowance edges on the outside of the fabric. The end of a seam roll is also useful for pressing curved areas if you don't have a pressing mitt or tailor's ham.

Substitutes: See the substitutes for Sleeve Board above; or place *envelopes* or *paper strips* under the seam allowances to prevent imprints on the outside.

Point Presser

For pressing all types of straight and curved seams, darts and points, you'll find a point presser or tailor's board a great help. Just line up the garment section with the appropriate edge of the point presser and press with the tip of your iron. You can press the seams of collars, cuffs and facings open on a point presser before turning them right side out (D). This makes it much easier to press a sharp edge on the outside.

Substitutes: From the inside, press the facing seam allowance toward the facing to insure a sharply creased edge when the collar, cuff or facing is turned right side out (see page 194).

Construction pressing

The basic aims of pressing as you sew are to set the shape of sections that have just been stitched and to smooth the way for the next step. Because this is the only time many vital areas can be reached for pressing, you should never cross one line of stitching

After you have pressed a garment section, let it cool and dry completely before you move it. To store pressed pieces for the next sewing session, clip them to a multiple skirt hanger, hang them over a padded hanger or lay them flat to avoid unnecessary wrinkles and creases.

Straight seams can be pressed on the ironing board. If the garment section is too narrow to slip over the board, press the seam along the edge, on a sleeve board, or over a seam roll.

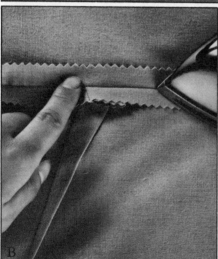

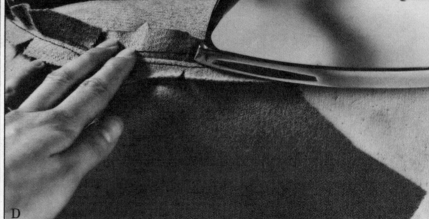

with another until the first one has been pressed.

Always press in the direction you stitched to keep the fabric from stretching or pulling off-grain.

To baste fabric layers before pressing, use a fine silk or cotton thread in a matching color. Remove pins or basting stitches as you press. Pressing over either one can make marks on your fabric, and pins will scratch the iron.

Seams

First press over the seam in the direction it was stitched (A). Next, press seam allowances open (B) or to one side, as your pattern directs. Remember to use paper strips or envelopes when necessary. Finally, press the seam from the right side, using a press cloth if needed for the fabric type (C).

Curved seams should be pressed over a ham, mitt, seam roll or the narrow end of the ironing board in order to set their shape (D). After pressing, little folds or tucks may form in one seam allowance, and may imprint on the right side. If that happens, cut notches in that seam allowance to eliminate bulk and press the garment underneath the seam allowance again.

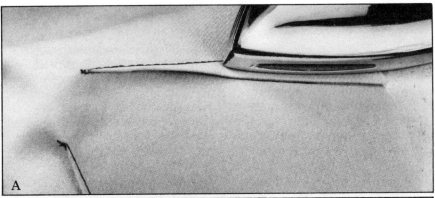

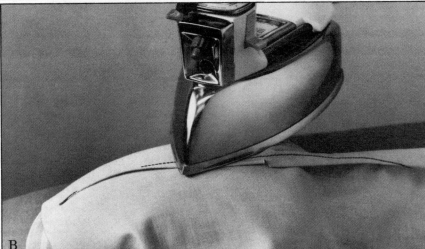

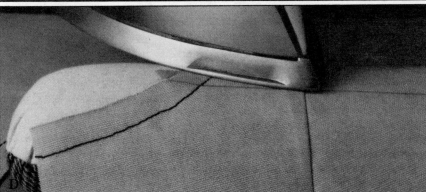

Darts

Begin by pressing the dart flat in the direction it was stitched. Next, press the dart on both the inside and outside of the garment, over a tailor's ham (A) or the end of the ironing board. If necessary, place paper strips or envelopes under the dart edge to prevent imprints. To prevent iron shine, use a press cloth on the fabrics that need it when you're pressing the outside. Never press beyond the dart point; this would make a tuck that would be hard to remove.

Bust darts and other horizontal darts should be pressed down toward the garment hem.

Contour darts, which are pointed on both ends, need to be clipped so they'll lie flat when pressed. Clip the widest part of the dart to within ⅛" (3 mm) of the stitching. Then press the dart toward the center front or back (B).

Darts in heavy fabric should be slashed along the fold to within ½" (1.3 cm) of the point. Press the slashed edges open (C); then press the uncut point as flat as possible.

Darts at hips and shoulders and other vertical darts, should be pressed toward the center front or back of the garment. After stitching the shoulder seam in a garment with a shoulder dart, press the shoulder seam flat, then press it open from the neckline to the armhole. Next, press the seam from the outside over a tailor's ham or seam roll (D). This will help shape the garment back to fit your shoulder contours.

If the back has ease instead of a dart, stitch the seam; then press it flat, perpendicular to the seamline, to smooth the fullness. Press the seam open from the inside, then from outside, the same as directed above for a shoulder dart.

Elbow darts should be pressed toward the sleeve hem. Then stitch the sleeve seam and press it open over a seam roll, sleeve board (A), or ironing board edge. On the outside, press the seam over a seam roll to set the curved shape. If there is ease instead of a dart, stitch the seam; then, press across the seam to flatten and smooth the fullness. Press the seam as described above.

Tucks

First press the tuck in the direction it was stitched. Then, follow your pattern instructions to find out whether to press the tuck to-

Pleats

Baste pleats before pressing, using fine cotton or silk thread. Then press, placing strips of paper, envelopes or a hem guide under the layers to prevent imprints. To press pleats on the outside, remove basting and use a strip of paper under the pleat to prevent an imprint (C). Use a press cloth if needed.

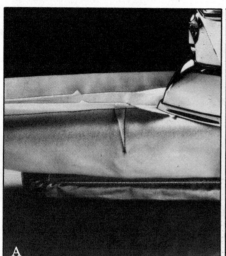

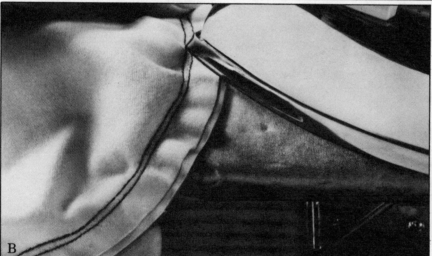

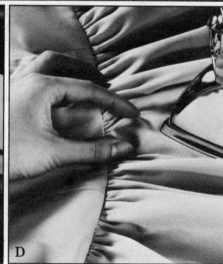

Sleeve cap

With the sleeve side up, place the upper portion of the armhole seam between the notches over the end of a sleeve board, tailor's ham or ironing board. With the point of the iron, press *only the seam allowances* to shrink out the eased fullness (B). No further pressing is needed; the seam allowances will naturally turn toward the sleeve.

ward the center or side, up or down. If necessary, use paper strips or envelopes under each tuck to prevent imprints, and use a press cloth when necessary for the outside of the fabric.

Gathers

Press gathers on the outside, spreading the fabric with your fingers to avoid creases. Press toward the seam, working the tip of the iron into, never across, the folds of the gathers (D).

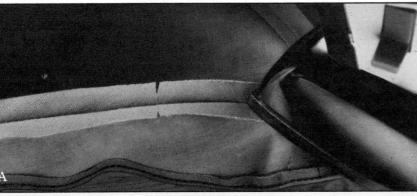

Faced edge

Before turning the facing to the inside, place the seam over a point presser or the end of the ironing board. Use the point of the iron to press the seam open, working on a small portion of the seam at a time (A). Then press the seam toward the facing and understitch (page 126). Now, turn the facing to the inside. Use your fingers to smooth and hold the faced edge, rolling the seam slightly to the inside of the garment as you press (B). Then press the outside of the garment, using a press cloth if needed for the fabric type.

Turned-under edge

Pattern instructions often call for a facing or hem edge to be pressed under and stitched. Before pressing, it's helpful to staystitch the edge for a guide. Then, turn under a small portion of the edge along the stitching and press. As you press, use your fingertips to hold the edge (C). Continue this way along the entire edge. Then stitch close to the pressed edge.

For an edge that is turned under twice, first staystitch the edge as your pattern directs. Then, turn the raw edge under so that it *meets* the line of stitching; press. Turn the pressed edge under *along* the stitching; press again (D). Stitch the pressed edge in place.

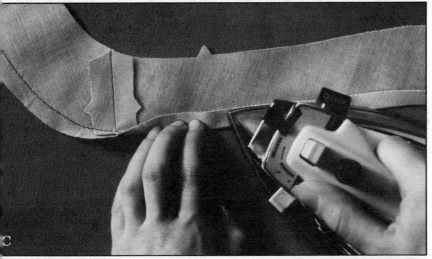

Collars

Before turning the collar right side out, press the seam open to insure a sharp edge. Use a point presser (page 189), or simply press the facing (or undercollar) seam allowance toward the collar (A).

After turning, use your fingers to roll the seam slightly to the underside and press, using a press cloth if needed.

final pressing

After the garment is completed, a touch-up pressing will remove those last-minute wrinkles. Follow the same guidelines you used during sewing: use a press cloth; place paper strips or envelopes under edges; use special aids for shaped areas; and press in the direction of the grain. Use light pressure to prevent impressions from seam allowances and other details from showing up on the

steam iron a couple of inches (centimeters) away from the fabric, allowing the steam to penetrate; brush. This method is particularly helpful when pressing a rolled collar or a lapel because the extra moisture permits the fabric to be manipulated into shape with your fingers.

• To remove creases or "iron shine" from areas that have been altered, apply white vinegar with a small paint brush. Then steam-

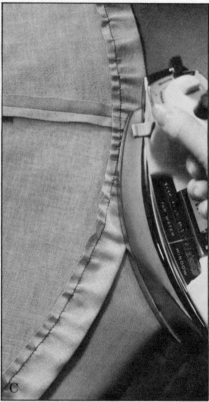

Hems

Place the garment wrong side out over the ironing board. Lay pants and sleeve hems on the narrow end of the board, rotating them as you press (B). Lift and lower the iron from one section of the hem to the next. Use paper strips or envelopes under the edge to prevent the hem edge from imprinting on the outside of fabrics that can be marred. Or, avoid resting the iron on the raw hem edge. Very curved hems must be ease-stitched first, then steamed lightly to shrink out fullness at the edge (C).

right side. If your garment is made of very thick or crease-resistant fabric, consider sending it to the dry cleaner or tailor for a final pressing.

Keeping a Well-pressed Look

Your garments can look well-pressed even after you've worn and washed them if you follow these tips:
• To help remove accidental "iron shine," raise the nap and eliminate an overpressed look, hold the

press the altered area. Pretest this method on a scrap or on an inconspicuous area of the garment.
• Press a laundered garment on the inside first to reopen seams, set darts, smooth the sleeve cap, etc.
• Minimize touchup pressing by hanging your garment properly. Choose a strong, contoured hanger to maintain the shape of the garment. Never hang a garment inside out. Fasten some of the buttons and close any zippers. Remove accessories (belt, scarves or jewelry) that might pull the garment out of shape.

9 *making your garment fit*

You're probably eager to see just how your creation looks before the sewing's finished. The try-on fittings explained in this chapter are just what you're looking for! But trying on a partly-sewn garment is more than a sneak preview—it has lots of practical benefits, too.

This is your first opportunity to judge how well the garment fits your figure. If you adjusted the pattern before cutting into the fabric, as shown in Chapter 5, you've already taken care of any major fitting changes. But some minor adjustments might still be needed.

Fitting problems are easiest to spot and correct during the early stages of sewing. To help you know what to look for when you try the garment on, the following pages describe standards for good fit. One quick look in a mirror will tell you what needs fixing—wrinkles, sagging seams or strain lines are some of the obvious alerts.

A try-on session is also a great time to fine-tune details such as the placement of patch pockets and trims, or the hang of pleats and gathers, so everything about your garment will be flattering.

Any fitting problems you encounter at this point won't take much time or fuss to solve. We show you how in this chapter.

195

What is good fit?

To check fit, start at the top—shoulders and neckline for dresses, shirts and jackets, waistline for skirts and pants—because fit there affects everything below.

Basically, good fit means clothes that feel good and make you look terrific. They should allow you to move freely as you perform normal activities, like sitting, walking or reaching, and should lie smooth when you're standing still.

Other key checkpoints are dart positions, armholes and seams. Horizontal seams should be parallel to the floor; vertical ones should hang straight, without swinging to the front or back.

The standards of good fit, illustrated here, will guide you when trying on and checking any garment. If you think *good fit* all the way, you'll be sure to achieve it, and look just great besides!

Fitting Standards

Shoulder seam, a straight line on top of shoulder, ends at top of arm—unless designed otherwise. Neckline is smooth, lies close to body without gaping.

Smooth fit over chest or bust, without wrinkles or strain. Darts point to fullest part of bust, ending ½" (1.3 cm) from apex. Lapels lie flat.

Underarm ½" (1.3 cm) below armpit for sleeveless styles, 1" (2.5 cm) below for set-in sleeves.

Sleeves hang smoothly, bend slightly when arm is relaxed, cover wrist when arm is slightly bent; elbow dart is at middle of elbow; for a man, ½" (1.3 cm) of shirt cuff shows.

Waistline seam or waistband at natural waist unless designed otherwise; waistband snug, but comfortable.

Gathers or pleats hang vertically over hips; darts point to the fullest part; jacket vent hangs straight.

No sign of strain across abdomen, no folds or bagging.

Smooth, comfortable fit over the seat—no bagging, pulling or wrinkles.

Hem even, parallel to floor and at a flattering height. Pants hem touches shoes in front, ends at top of heel in back.

Fitting methods

When to Fit

Take a moment for a try-on fitting as soon as the darts are stitched and the shoulder and side seams are pinned or basted (A). Try on a skirt or pants after you've pinned or basted the side seams and crotch seam (pants only) and basted the waistband in place.

What to Look For

Check the garment for overall comfort and appearance. Is it symmetrical? Are the seams and grainlines straight? Are there wrinkles that indicate too much fullness? Check specific areas against the standards on page 196.

After you've marked the necessary adjustments, you can final-

How to Fit

For more accurate fitting, try on the garment right side out—it's very easy to transfer changes to the wrong side for stitching later (see page 198).

When fitting, wear the undergarments and shoes you plan to wear with the finished garment.

A

B

Tops, Jackets, Shirts
Shoulder
Neckline
Bust or chest
Back
Armhole
Sleeve
Overall length
Pants or Skirts
Crotch depth
Crotch length
Waist
Hips
Abdomen and derrière
Crotch smile or droop
Overall length
Dresses and Jumpsuits
Above waist (see tops)
Below waist (see pants)
Waistline seam
Overall length

It's easy to make fitting changes at this stage—before zippers, sleeves and details are sewn.

If you're lining your garment, try it on with the lining pinned to the inside at the edges.

stitch and press the seams; then continue sewing as usual.

Have a final fitting session when the garment is ready for the hem, the buttonholes and other details to be finished. Take a good look!

Pin patch pockets, belts, tabs, flaps or trims in place to see where they look best. Then, mark their position with pins or tailor's chalk and mark the hem (B).

When you're satisfied with the fit of your garment and the added details, finish the garment.

Start at the top and work down, in the order listed above. Very often, a slight change in the fit of the shoulders or neckline can improve the fit of the whole garment.

Don't fit too closely for your figure. Usually, a trim fit is flattering to a slender figure, but a looser fit is kinder to a large one.

Changing seams: Watch the garment for wrinkles and folds; they're your clues to areas that need adjustment. Use pins to mark the new seamline.

If the garment is too loose, folds will form near the seams that need to be taken in (A).

If the folds fall vertically, smooth the excess fabric out to the side seams and pin in a deeper seam (A).

When horizontal folds or wrinkles fall near the waist, yoke or any horizontal seam, open the seam and smooth excess fabric into it (B).

If the garment is too tight, wrinkles or pulls will point to the area where there is stress. Open the seams to let them out, up to ⅜" (1 cm) for each seam allowance (C).

If you change one garment piece, you may have to change the piece that will be stitched to it.

Changing darts: You can easily change darts for better shaping. For a single pointed dart, first open the seam that crosses the dart. To make any dart wider or narrower, open the dart and re-pin it in the correct position (E). This may change the length of the seam, so adjust the length of the adjoining section if necessary.

Transferring changes to the inside: After pin-fitting your changes on the right side of the garment, turn it inside out and rub a chalk pencil over the pins to mark the new stitching line (F, H). Remove the pins, straighten the stitching line, if necessary, and repin it on the wrong side to sew the new seam (G, I). Or, machine-baste for another try-on fitting.

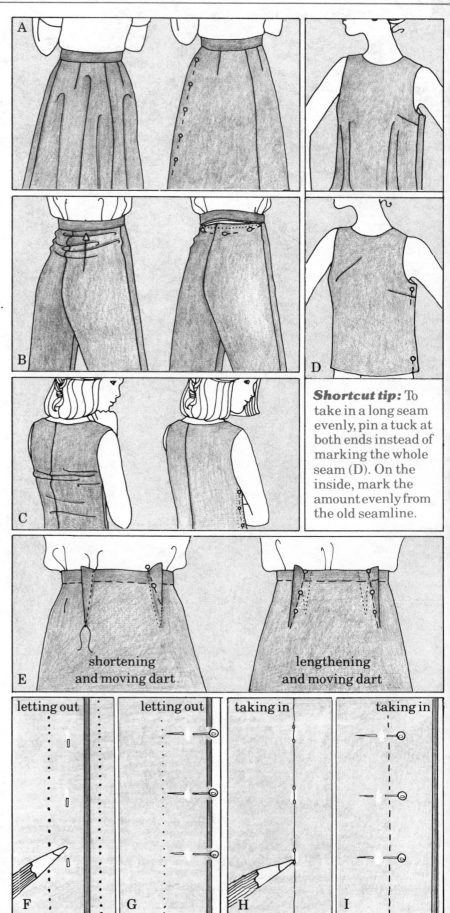

Shortcut tip: To take in a long seam evenly, pin a tuck at both ends instead of marking the whole seam (D). On the inside, mark the amount evenly from the old seamline.

shortening and moving dart

lengthening and moving dart

letting out — letting out — taking in — taking in

Fitting handbook

Shoulder Fitting Alerts

If you have broad shoulders, the shoulder area feels tight and has strain lines (A).
Solution: Pin-mark a new seamline, adding up to ⅜" (1 cm) and tapering back to the armhole notch (B).

If you have narrow shoulders, the seams fall off the ends of your shoulders (C).
Solution: Pin-mark a new armhole seamline to take out the excess width at the shoulder, and taper the new seamline back to the original one at the armhole notch (D).

If you have sloping shoulders, the garment will have diagonal wrinkles from the neck to the armhole front and back (E).
Solution: Pin out the excess at the shoulder seam near the armhole, tapering back to the original shoulder seamline at the neckline. Lower the armhole seam by the same amount (F).

If you have square shoulders, the garment pulls across the top from the end of the shoulder area (G).
Solution: Open the shoulder seams to add up to ⅜" (1 cm) at the end of the shoulder and taper to the original seamline at the neck edge. Raise the armhole the same amount (H).

Neckline Fitting Alerts

If the neckline is too tight, it feels too high or wrinkles at the neck base (I).
Solution: Carefully clip the neckline to the staystitching or past it, if necessary, to make the neckline lie flat. Pin-mark a new seamline (J).

If the neckline is too large, it doesn't lie smooth at the base of the neck, and exposes too much of your collarbone (K).
Solution: Mark a new neck seamline up to ⅜" (1 cm) above the old one (L).

If the neckline gaps, it doesn't lie flat and close to the body (M).
Solution: Pin out the excess from the front shoulder seam only until the neckline no longer gaps. Taper the change to original seamline at the armhole (N).

If your neckline is too low, it will be more revealing than you prefer and should be raised (O).
Solution: Pin-mark a new center front neckline edge up to ⅜" (1 cm) above the original one, and mark a new seamline to maintain the original shape (P).

Chest Fitting Alerts

If you have a hollow chest, horizontal folds form between the garment neckline and bust due to the excess length above the bust (A).
Solution: Beginning at the neck edge, take in the garment front seam allowance only, tapering to the original seamline at the armhole. Mark a new, lower neckline and a new shoulder seamline (B).

If you have a pigeon chest, the garment pulls, forming strain lines across the upper chest to the armhole due to lack of room above the bust (C).
Solution: Beginning at the neck edge, let out the garment front seam allowance only, tapering to the original seamline at the armhole. Mark a new, higher neckline and a new shoulder seamline (D).

Bust Fitting Alerts

If you have a low bustline, the bust dart or princess seam curve falls above your bust point (E).
Solution: Repin the dart, angling it downward to the bust point (F). Stitch the new dart. On princess styles, let out the seam up to ⅜″ (1 cm) at the fullest part of the bust and take it in above the bust.

If you have a high bustline, the bust dart or princess seam curve falls below your bust point (G).
Solution: Repin the dart, angling it upward to the bust point (H). Stitch a new dart. On princess styles, let out the seam up to ⅜″ (1 cm) at the fullest part of the bust and take it in below the bust.

If you have a large bust cup, C or D, clothes may pull across the front (perhaps the back, too) and ride up at the front waistline where more length is needed (I).
Solution: Let out the front seam allowances at the waist and sides up to ⅜″ (1 cm), and pin a deeper dart (J). If there is no waistline seam, let out the front shoulder seam allowance up to ⅜″ (1 cm).

If you have a small bust cup, an A or AA, clothes may form vertical folds in front and droop at the waistline from excess width and length (K).
Solution: Pin out the excess from the front seam allowances at waist and sides. Pin a narrower dart (L). If there is no waistline seam, take out some of the length at the shoulder seam, on the garment front seam allowance only.

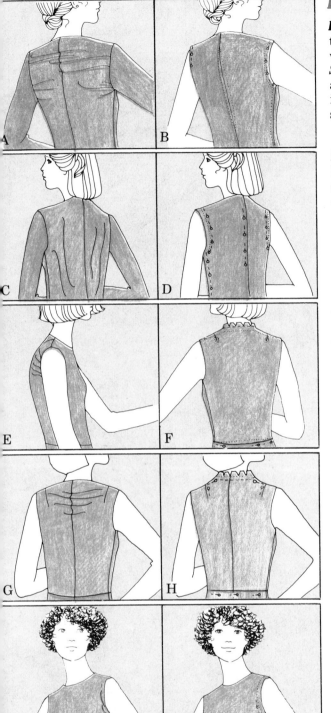

Back Fitting Alerts

If you have a broad back, there is pulling and tightness across the back because the garment isn't wide enough (A).
Solution: Let out the center back and back side seam allowances and armhole up to ⅜″ (1 cm) (B). If there is a center back zipper, let out only the back side seam allowances, up to ⅜″ (1 cm).

If you have a narrow back, vertical folds on the back of the garment will show that it's too wide (C).
Solution: Take in the back seam allowances and armhole to remove the excess width (D).

If you have a round back, your clothes will pull across the back and ride up at the back waistline (E).
Solution: Let out the back shoulder seam allowance up to ⅜″ (1 cm), tapering to the original seamline at the armhole. Also, let out the back neckline seam allowance up to ⅜″ (1 cm). If there is a waistline seam, lower it on the back bodice seam allowance. Reshape neckline or shoulder darts slightly for better fit over the curve (F).

If you have a very erect back, your clothes have horizontal wrinkles below the neck in back (G).
Solution: Pin out the excess length from the back shoulder seam allowances, tapering to the original seamline at the armhole. Lower the back neckline by marking a deeper seam allowance. If there is a waistline seam, raise it on the back bodice. Reshape neck or shoulder darts slightly for a better fit over the curve (H).

Armhole Fitting Alerts

If the armholes are too high or tight, you have trouble moving your arms (I).
Solution: Mark a deeper armhole by making the seam allowance deeper at the underarm. Taper the new seamline back to the original seamline at the notches (J). For more room, let out the shoulder seams as on page 199.

If the armholes gape, this may be caused by problems in other areas—shoulder, bust or garment back (K). See pages 199-201, or the solution below.
Solution: Mark a higher armhole by making the seam allowances up to ⅜″ (1 cm) narrower at the underarm; taper the new seamline back to the original seamline at the notches (L).

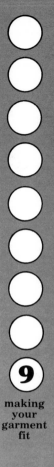

9

making
your
garment
fit

Sleeve Fitting Alerts

If your upper arm is large, sleeves are too tight when you stand normally, with your arms down (A). *Solution:* Open the upper part of the sleeve seam and the underarm part of the armhole seam. Let out the sleeve seam up to ⅜″ (1 cm), tapering back to the original seamline at the elbow or lower edge. Lower the bodice underarm seamline to correspond (B). Let out the side seam at the underarm if necessary.

If your upper arm is too thin, sleeves will have vertical folds when your arms are relaxed (C). *Solution:* Open the upper part of the sleeve seam and the underarm part of the armhole seam. Take in the sleeve seam up to ⅜″ (1 cm), tapering back to the original seamline at the elbow or lower edge. Raise the bodice underarm seamline to correspond (D). Take in the side seam at the underarm if needed.

If sleeve cap ease isn't evenly distributed, a set-in sleeve will have diagonal wrinkles at the front or back of the sleeve cap (E). *Solution:* Remove the upper sleeve between the notches and shift the fullness on the ease-stitching line so the wrinkles disappear (F).

If there's excess ease because your fabric resists steam-shrinking, the sleeve cap puckers (G). *Solution:* Remove the upper sleeve between the notches and make the cap seam allowance about ⅛″ (3 mm) deeper; don't change the depth of the garment seam allowance (H).

Hip Fitting Alerts

If your hipbones protrude, darts may not point to the hipbone on close-fitting garments (I). *Solution:* Open the waistband seam, front darts, and side seams above the hips. Repin wider darts, pointing to the hipbones; for a yoke, add a dart over each hipbone. Let out the front side seam allowances at the waist up to ⅜″ (1 cm) (J).

If you have one high hip, the hemline is higher on one side and the center front isn't vertical (K). *Solution:* Let out the waistline and hip seam allowances up to ⅜″ (1 cm) on the high side (L). If needed, mark a narrower hem allowance on that side; then trim allowance to an even depth before hemming.

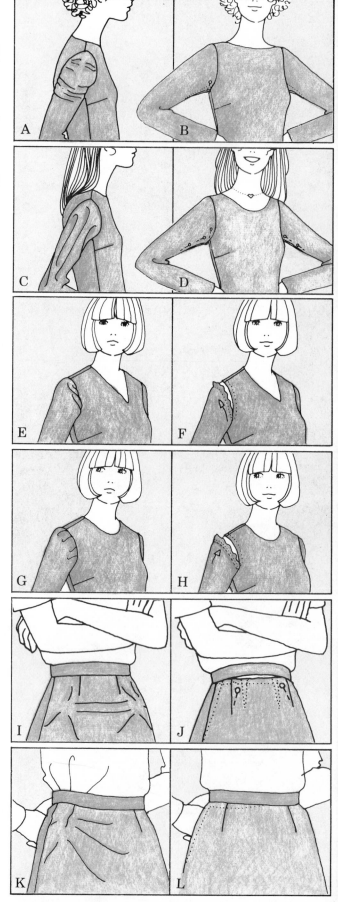

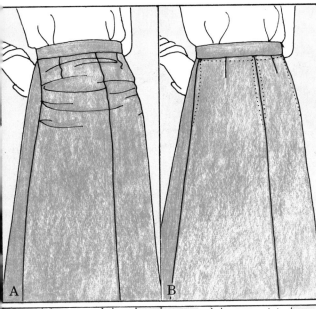

Abdomen Fitting Alert

If your abdomen is large, the garment pulls across the front below the waistline (A). The front waistline and hemline may ride up, and the side seams may pull toward the front.
Solution: Remove the waistband in front and open the side seams above the hipline. Let out the center front seam, if any, and the side front seam allowances above the hip, up to ⅜″ (1 cm) each, tapering to the original seamline at waistline and hipline.
Let out the front waist seam up to ⅜″ (1 cm) (B) or lengthen the front hemline .

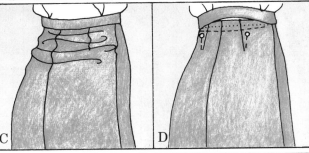

Derrière Fitting Alerts

If you have a swayback, wrinkles form below the waist in back (C).
Solution: Open the waistline seam or remove the waistband in back to make the back waist seam allowance deeper at the center back. Taper back to the original waist seamline at the sides. Widen darts to take out any width added to the waistline seam (D).

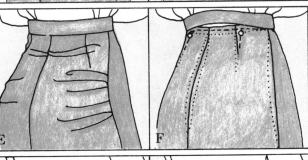

If your derrière is very round, clothes are too tight over the rear, the side seams pull toward the back (E), and the back waist and hemline may ride up.
Solution: Let out the center back and side seams at the back only, tapering back to the original seamline at the waist. If there's a zipper, let out only the back side seam allowances. Let out any back waist seams up to ⅜″ (1 cm) or lengthen the back hemline. Shorten darts to fit the curve (F).

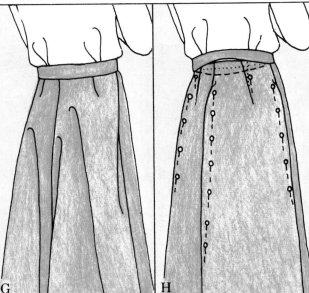

If your derrière is very flat, clothes may sag or bag because there's too much fullness (G).
Solution: Take in the center back and side seams at the back only, tapering to the original seamline at the waist. Take in the back waistline seam, if there is one, by making the seam allowance deeper. Lengthen any darts to fit the curve better (H). If the garment back is still too long, adjust the hemline as needed.

Pants Fitting Alerts

If the crotch is too tight, pants "smile" when you're standing, with wrinkles that point up from the crotch (A).
Solution: Lower the crotch seam to make a deeper curve and let out the center front and/or back seams up to ⅜" (1 cm), tapering to the original seamline just below the waist (B). If necessary, you can remove the waistband and let out the waistline seam up to ⅜" (1 cm).

If the crotch is too long, pants "frown," when you're standing, with wrinkles that point down from the crotch (C).
Solution: Raise the crotch seam up to ⅜" (1 cm), and take in the center front and/or back seams, tapering to the original seamline below the waist (D). If necessary, you can also remove the waistband and take in the waistline seam.

If your derrière is very round, your pants will be tight in the back and the side seams will pull toward the back (E).
Solution: Remove the waistband in back, open the side seams down to just below the hipline, and open the center back seam down to the notch. Then, let out the waistline seam, the back seam allowances at the side seams, and the center back seam up to ⅜" (1 cm). Shorten the darts, too, if necessary (F).

If your derrière is very flat, your pants will sag or bag in the back because there's too much fabric over the derrière (G).
Solution: Remove the waistband in back. Pin out any excess fullness on the back seam allowances at the side seams and at the center back. Then, make the waistline seam deeper at the center back. Lengthen the darts, too, if needed (H).

For rounded abdomen, swayback, protruding hipbone, and other fitting alerts, see pages 202-203.

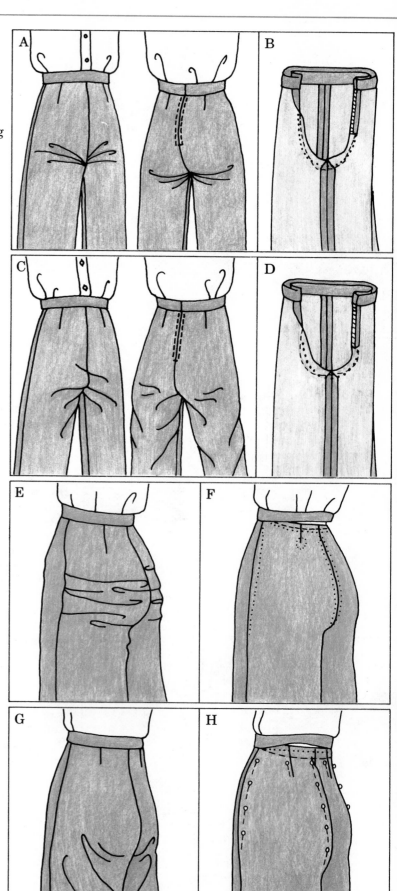

10 *special fabrics*

One sure way to make a sensational outfit is to choose an unusual fabric. It might be a slinky knit, a bold plaid, a filmy sheer, a fuzzy fur, or a sleek leather-like. Out-of-the-ordinary fabrics like these aren't hard to sew, but they do require a few special handling techniques.

general tips

Before you sew any fabric which seems new or unusual to you:

• Select a pattern style which recommends the fabric you've chosen. If the fabric is featured on the front of the pattern envelope and needs special handling, the pattern will include tips to help you with layout and sewing.

• Read the fabric labels to see if there are any special instructions for cutting, marking, stitching, etc.

• Experiment with fabric scraps to determine the best way to mark, handle seams, press, make buttonholes and finish raw edges.

• Make the seam tests on page 145 to determine the best needle size, thread, stitch length, tension and pressure for machine sewing on your special fabric.

To use border prints, large-scale prints and sheets creatively, see page 85 for layout ideas.

nits

Knits—so versatile and comfortable—are here to stay! Today, it's easier than ever to sew super knit fashions. In addition to a variety of knit fabrics, you'll find special patterns, notions and sewing techniques—all developed exclusively for knits.

Patterns

Throughout the Simplicity Catalog you'll find many patterns for knits. Chances are they'll be labeled with one or more of the following key phrases:

"Includes Time-Saver™ Stretch Knit methods." Patterns marked this way include easy-to-follow sewing techniques and an "All About Knits" sewing guide.

"See the Pick-a-Knit Rule®." Use the rule on the envelope to select a knit with the right amount of stretchability for your pattern.

"Sized for stretch knits only." For patterns with this label, use stretchable, unbonded knits for proper fit.

Check the fabrics suggested on the envelope back. Many regular patterns list knits—usually stable types—as suitable.

Knit Types

Knits can be just about anything—flowered prints, mock plaids, textured tweeds, dazzling metallics. The fibers can be naturals, synthetics or blends. Here are the most common knit constructions.

Single knits, also called plain knits or jerseys, can be recognized by a smooth right side with vertical ribs and a pebbly wrong side with horizontal ribs (A).

Double knits are made with two sets of yarns locked together for a firm knit with minimal stretch (B). Double knits can often be used interchangeably with woven fabrics of the same weight.

Rib knits have prominent vertical ribs on both sides (C), as well as good crosswise stretch and recovery.

Interlock knits are smooth-surfaced rib knits with identical sides and good crosswise stretchability (D). This knit can develop runs from one crosswise edge. Find out which edge runs by stretching the crosswise edges. Place the edge that runs at the hem, where there is the least stress.

Tricot knits are soft, drapable single knits with a flat, smooth appearance (E).

Raschel knits are textured novelty knits with an open, lacy look (F).

Jacquard knits are similar to double knits. They are made with two or more sets of yarns and needles for a patterned or textured appearance (G).

Bonded knits can be any type of knit that's fused to a backing (H), which provides stability and completely eliminates the stretch factor.

For more tips on selecting knits, see page 33.

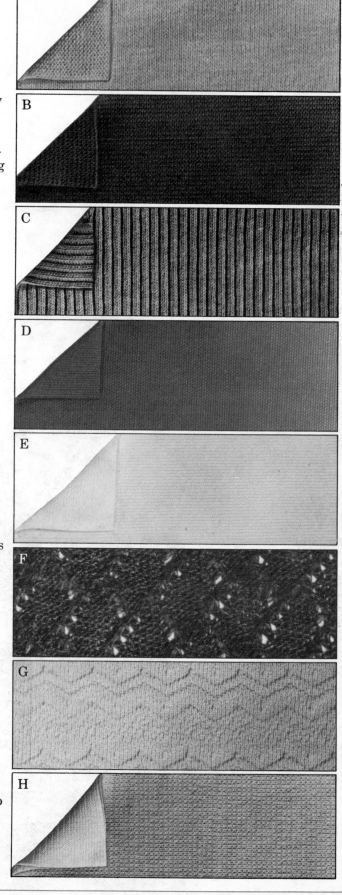

Notions

Many sewing aids have been developed for knits.

• *Polyester or cotton-wrapped polyester thread* stretches a bit to help keep seams from popping. For sewing very fine or synthetic knits, try fine, long-staple polyester thread.

• *Ball-point pins and needles* with rounded points won't snag or break yarns (A). For fine knits, use a size 9 or 11 needle; for medium to heavyweights, size 11 or 14. All-purpose needles also work well. Change needles frequently to avoid skipped stitches.

Layout

Before laying out your pattern, preshrink the fabric to prevent the garment from shrinking and to remove excess finish (sizing) which can cause skipped stitches.

The crease in the fabric as it comes off the bolt may or may not press out. If it doesn't, avoid placing pattern pieces on this crease when you lay out the pattern. Instead, refold the fabric along a vertical rib. Don't allow a knit fabric to hang off the edge of the cutting surface or it will stretch out of shape.

Cutting and Marking

Use sharp shears to cut knits. To mark symbols on seams that

Finishing

Edge finishes aren't usually needed since most knits don't ravel. If your knit does ravel or develop runs, double-stitched or overedged seams will help prevent both problems.

Stitch in the ditch to finish waistbands and to hold facings in place at seams. On the outside of the garment, stitch in the groove formed by the seam, catching the waistband edge or facing (B).

Hem a knit garment after it has hung for several hours. This will allow the fabric to relax into its permanent shape before you sew the hem. See pages 140-141 for hem types.

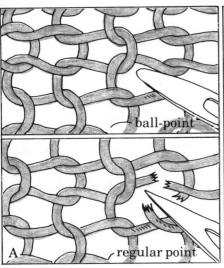

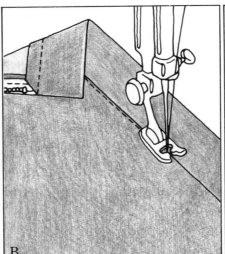

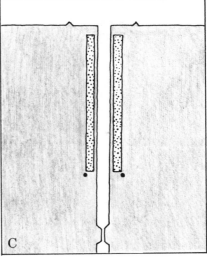

• *A snag-repair hook* comes in handy for fixing pulls on knits.
• *Serrated shears* provide snag-free cutting and stay sharp longer.
• *Lightweight zippers* with polyester or nylon coils and knitted tapes are extra flexible.
• *Non-roll elastic* is a must for pull-on pants and skirts.
• *Non-woven fusible webbing,* available in strips, helps you make invisible hems quickly.
• *Some interfacings,* either non-woven or knitted, are designed with one-way stretchability to be compatible with knits.

might be let out or that fall within the body of the garment, use pins or tailor's chalk. Tailor's tacks are best for bulky knits. Snip-mark notches, dots and ends of foldlines on seams that won't be altered.

Stitching

Seams in stretch knits must "give" so that stitches won't pop when the fabric stretches. To stabilize areas that shouldn't stretch—neck, shoulder and waistline seams—use twill tape or seam binding in the seam. Page 161 explains special knit seams that can be sewn on all types of sewing machines. Standard seam techniques are suitable for bonded or stable double knits.

Zipper openings in stretchy knits need to be stabilized so they won't become distorted when you apply the zipper. Baste seam binding to the seam allowances, or reinforce the zipper area with strips of fusible interfacing (C).

Fasteners

Machine-worked buttonholes are best for knits. If possible, make them in the direction that stretches least. First make a test buttonhole on a fabric scrap, using the same number of layers as the garment. Generally, buttonholes are not suitable for open-work or very bulky knits. For these fabrics, choose patterns without closures.

Knits for special fashions

Special-purpose knits for swim-wear, lingerie or active sports-wear often need extra attention. To sew these knits, follow the tips here and on pages 206-207.

Swimwear Knits

Knits for swimwear are extra stretchy. Most have two-way stretch and are suitable for any kind of close-fitting swimwear. A few have only one-way (cross-wise) stretch and should be used only for two-piece suits or men's swimwear. To buy a knit with the right type and amount of stretch, make sure your fabric measures up to the Pick-a-Knit® rule found on the back of Simplicity pattern envelopes for knits.

Stretch Terry and Velour

Sewing these plush knits is not difficult if you follow these tips.

• Terry and velour tend to curl at the edges. To minimize this tendency, stitch ¼" (6 mm) from all cut edges before seaming.
• If your presser foot has small toes that catch in the terry loops, wrap tape around the toes.
• When working with these thick, loopy fabrics, follow the methods for napped fabrics, page 211.
• Hems may be blindstitched, topstitched or fused in place.

the thread ends taut behind the presser foot to keep them from jamming in the machine.
• Don't backstitch; the tricot will pucker. Instead, knot the threads or, with the needle in the fabric, pivot and sew a few stitches over the first stitching at the ends.

Sweater Knits

These bulky, loosely-knit fabrics stretch freely in both directions and are fairly simple to sew when you use patterns designed specifi-cally for sweater knits.

• Before cutting, spread out your fabric and let it relax for a couple of hours. Then cut out the pattern.

Since most swimwear is designed to be skin-tight, seams must be *strong and stretchy* so they don't pop when you move; the best ones are those made with special stretch stitches or an overlock stitch (see page 161). Loosen the needle tension slightly; then test-stitch several seam types on scraps of your fabric. Stretch the seam to see if the stitches pop.

• Special stretch and overlock stitches are very hard to remove and may leave permanent marks in the fabric. If you have to alter seams, use a straight stitch.
• Special *swimwear* elastic keeps its elasticity even when wet; be sure to use only this type.

Lingerie Knits

Sometimes called tricot, these are usually very lightweight single knits, made of cotton or synthetic fibers such as nylon. To deter-mine the right and wrong side, pull the fabric crosswise; the edges will curl toward the right side. To minimize curling, stitch ¼" (6 mm) from the cut edges be-fore seams are sewn.

• For best stitching results, use a *new*, fine needle (size 9) and extra-fine nylon or special fine lingerie thread.
• Seams on lingerie should be double-stitched or overedged. When you start to stitch, hold

• On sweater knits that tend to ravel, stitch ¼" (6 mm) from edges before seaming. Be careful not to stretch the fabric.
• Overlocked or overedged seams are preferred for sweater knits. If your machine doesn't do these stitches, make double-stitched seams. Do not stretch as you sew.
• To feed openwork fabric smoothly through the machine, wrap the presser foot toes with tape, or use a roller foot.
• Press sweater knits over a towel to avoid flattening the texture.
• Styles without fastenings are best for sweater knits. If you must use closures, loops or machine buttonholes are both good choices.

Leather-like fabrics

These special sewing methods are meant for the synthetic suedes and leathers, including vinyls, which *do not ravel*. For woven suede-like fabrics which do ravel, follow the techniques for napped and pile fabrics on page 211.

Patterns

Simple styles with little easing and few darts are best unless your fabric is very soft and light-weight. Then you can choose a style with more fullness or detailing. Raglan or kimono sleeves are easiest to sew; with set-in sleeves, you must reduce the ease in the sleeve cap (see page 68) *unless* the pattern is specifically designed for leather-like fabrics.

Stitching

Instead of using pins, hold layers together for stitching with paper clips or double-faced basting tape. Place paper clips at right angles to the seamline and remove them as you stitch. Position tape within the seam allowance so you won't stitch through it; remove it after stitching. Stitch with sharp or wedge-pointed needles. Use 8 to 10 stitches per inch (2.5 cm) and strong thread—polyester, cotton-covered polyester, heavy mercerized cotton or silk.

Plain seams will work on most leather-likes. On heavyweights, don't press seam allowances open; keep them flat by gluing, fusing (except on vinyl), or topstitching.

Collars

Attach a collar as follows, using the Lapped Seam method.

With a back neck facing: Trim away the neck seam allowances on the garment, back neck facing and front facings; also trim the shoulder seam allowances on the front facings only. Lap the front facings over the back facing at the shoulders; stitch.

Trim the seam allowances from the outer edges of both collar sections. *Do not trim the collar neck edges.* If the collar neckline is curved, staystitch and clip it. Lap the neck facing over one collar neck edge to the seamline and

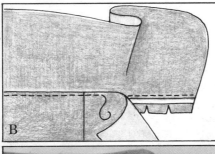

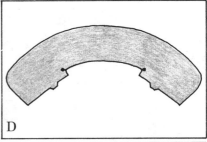

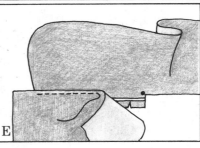

Layout

Make all adjustments on your pattern before you cut, since holes from let-out seams may leave permanent marks in the fabric. Use a "with nap" layout. Run the nap down to give the fabric a light shading effect or up for a darker one. Hold the pattern down with tape or weights, or pin in the seam allowances only. Cut one fabric layer at a time for accuracy.

Marking

On the wrong side of the fabric, mark with tailor's chalk or dressmaker's carbon and a smooth-edged tracing wheel.

Lapped seams give a flat, smooth, professional look. Trim away the seam allowance on the overlap section and tape-mark the seamline on the other section. Lap the trimmed piece over the un-trimmed one at the seamline. Fuse (A) (except vinyl), tape (page 158) or glue layers together. Then, stitch close to the overlapping edge and again ¼″ (6 mm) away.

Use this guide to determine which garment sections to overlap: lap front over the back at side seams, back over the front at shoulders, garment and neck facing over the collar, and small pieces (cuffs, yokes, pockets, waistbands) over the main garment pieces.

tape or glue them together (do not fuse); edgestitch (B). Repeat with the garment and the other collar neck edges. Glue the collars to-gether along the neck seam. Fuse, tape or glue the outer collar edges together; edgestitch and stitch again ¼″ (6 mm) away (C).

Without a back neck facing: Trim garment, front facing and collar sections as above. Trim one collar neck edge between the dots (D). Attach the garment to the collar piece with the untrimmed neck seam, as above. Lap the front facings over the untrimmed parts of the other collar neck edge; edgestitch (E). Complete as for With a Back Neck Facing.

Fasteners

Zippers may be inserted in plain seams in the usual ways (see pages 170-176). To insert a zipper in a lapped seam, use this method.

Trim ⅝″ (1.5 cm) from the overlap edge, cutting the strip to the length of the zipper opening. Glue or fuse the strip to the wrong side of the overlap; edgestitch. On the underlap, trim ½″ (1.3 cm) from the zipper area only. Place the underlap over the zipper tape, close to the coil, with the top stop 1″

Buttonholes may be machine-worked; or you can make an easy, slashed buttonhole as follows.

Mark buttonhole ends on the garment with pins. Stitch a rectangle twice, 2 to 3 stitches wide and the buttonhole length, using 12 to 15 stitches per inch (2.5 cm). Carefully slash the opening with a single-edged razor blade (C).

Creative edge treatments are easy when fabrics don't ravel.
• With pinking shears, trim away the seam allowance; then stitch ⅛-¼″ (3-6 mm) away from the pinked edge.
• Decorate by punching small holes to form a design (F). A rotary leather punch (available at craft and leather shops) will punch different-sized holes; or you can use an eyelet punch.
• Cut scallops or other designs along edges (F). Draw the curves with the help of a spool of thread; then cut.

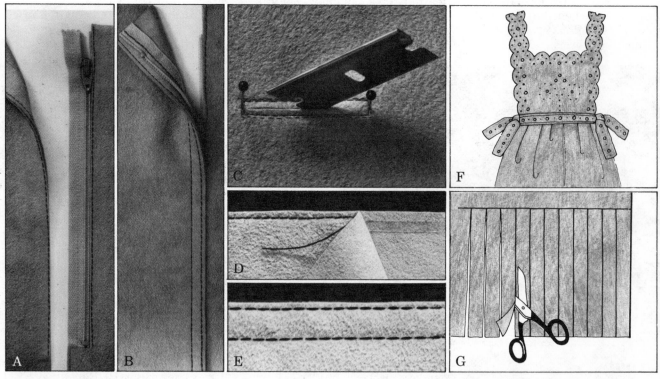

(2.5 cm) below the upper edge; hold it in place with basting tape. Using a zipper foot, edgestitch along the zipper opening (A).

Place the overlap edge over the zipper, with the raw edge along the underlap seamline; hold it in place with basting tape. Edgestitch the seam below the opening. Then, using a zipper foot, topstitch the entire seam ¼″ (6 mm) from the first stitching, catching the zipper (B).

Finishing

Faced edges, such as front openings and armholes, can be finished without facings if the fabric has enough body.
• If your fabric has a lot of body, trim away the garment seam allowance; then edgestitch and topstitch for a finished appearance.
• Where body is needed at the edge, trim away the seam allowance from the facing and garment. With wrong sides together, fuse, tape or glue facing to the garment. Edgestitch (D); then stitch ¼″ (6 mm) away (E).

• Fringe the edge (G). On the wrong side of your fabric, mark off the desired length of fringe at ¼″ (6 mm) intervals. Then cut on the marked lines.

Hems can be treated like faced edges, left, if the fabric has body. For soft fabrics, try one of these methods.
• Turn up the hem allowance and stitch it in place.
• Cut off the hem allowance and trim it to ⅝″ (1.5 cm). Use this strip to face the hem, holding it with glue or double-faced basting tape. Stitch close to the hem edge and ¼″ (6 mm) away.

Napped and pile fabrics

Napped fabrics (brushed suede cloth, mohair, melton, fleece) (A) have a plush, hairy or downy surface created by brushing, or otherwise raising, the surface of the fabric. In contrast, pile fabrics (fur types, velveteen, velvet, corduroy)(B) have an extra set of looped or clipped yarns on the right side. In pattern layouts, the term "with nap" refers to any fabric that is directional, either because of a shaded effect created by the surface texture, or a printed, one-way design (C). On

For cutting, fold short-pile and napped fabrics lengthwise, with the nap or pile side out, to prevent the layers from shifting as you cut. Never fold them crosswise because the nap or pile would not run the same way. Don't fold deep-pile fabrics; instead, cut them one layer at a time.

Stitching

Wherever possible, stitch in the direction of the nap. Work with a medium, balanced tension, 10-12 stitches per inch (2.5 cm) and a size 11 or 14 needle. Reduce the pressure on the presser foot slightly so that the fabric feeds smoothly and the nap doesn't become flattened. Since the top layer tends to "creep" during stitching, guide both fabric layers through the machine evenly by holding them together with generous pin or hand-basting. An even-feed foot is also helpful.

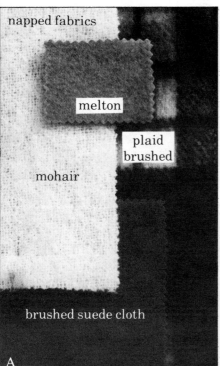

napped fabrics

melton

plaid brushed

mohair

brushed suede cloth

A

pile fabrics

velveteen

fur type

wide wale corduroy

pinwale corduroy

shearling

B

one-way fabric

C

all these fabrics, pattern pieces must be laid out with their tops facing in the same direction.

Layout, Cutting and Marking

See page 83 to determine nap or pile direction and its effect on color and wear, as well as how to use a "with nap" layout—a necessity for all napped, pile or one-way fabrics.

Note: To reduce bulk on very thick fabrics, you may prefer to cut facings from a lightweight fabric such as taffeta or tricot. To determine the amount of facing fabric to buy, lay out the facing pattern pieces on the fabric in the store before you buy it.

To mark fabrics with surface texture, use pins and chalk on the wrong side, make tailor's tacks or use snip and pin marking. Other methods either will not show or may damage the texture.

To sew deep-pile fabrics, see the extra tips on page 212, in addition to the general information above. To sew vinyl-backed shearling types, also see pages 209 and 210.

If your fabric tends to ravel the way velvet does, zigzag, pink or bind the edges (see Edge Finishes, page 123).

When pressing napped and pile fabrics, you should avoid flattening the surface texture. Directions for pressing these fabrics are on pages 186-187.

Extra Tips for Deep Pile or Fur-like Fabrics

• Choose patterns with few seams.
• For accurate cutting, trim away the pattern tissue margins (*not* the seam allowances).
• To eliminate straight seams on straight grain, such as a front facing seam, overlap the seamlines of the pattern pieces and cut them as one piece.
• Do not fold the fabric to make two layers. Instead, pin the pattern pieces to the backing side of a single fabric layer, with the nap running down. On vinyl-backed shearling types, pin only within

• Stitch fabrics that have knit backings with a ball-point needle.
• Overedged, narrow zigzagged or double-stitched seams (pages 160-161) are good choices because they are less bulky than regular seams. While stitching, keep deep pile away from the seamline with a large needle or the tips of small scissors (B). For vinyl-backed shearling types, stitch lapped seams as directed on page 209.

• Finger-press fur types by opening the seam with your thumbnail or fingers. Never steam-press these fabrics without testing a scrap first to be sure the heat won't harm them. Press from the wrong side over a needle board or self-fabric scrap; avoid heavy pressure on these fabrics.
• To flatten a plain seam, steam-press *lightly* from the wrong side *if possible*, or finger-press. On the right side, brush the seam to bring up the pile and to hide the seam. To flatten darts, slash them open almost to the point, trim the edges to ¼" (6 mm) and treat them as plain seams.

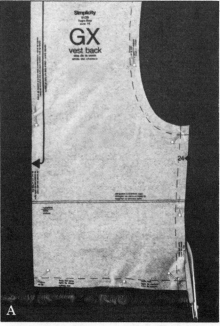

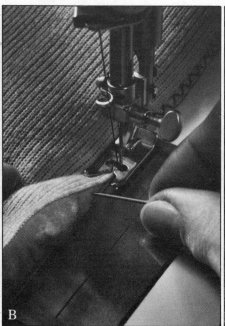

the seam allowances, because pins make permanent holes in vinyl; or tape the pattern in place. To cut a piece that's to be placed on a fold, follow the directions for diagonals on page 215. Also, be sure to reverse any pattern pieces that must be cut twice, such as a left and right sleeve.
• Cut fabric through the backing only, using the tips of shears to avoid cutting the pile (A).
• Mark the backing with tape, pencil or chalk pencil. Snip-mark symbols and notches at edges.

• To stitch a plain seam, first trim the pile from a ½" (1.3 cm) wide area of the seam allowances so the fabric layers won't be too bulky to fit under the presser foot. Then stitch the seam, using a zipper foot. After stitching, use a needle or pin to free any hairs caught in the seams (C).

• Stabilize shoulder seams with twill tape.
• To reduce bulk, make a faced hem (page 140).
• Blindstitch front facings to the inside of the garment front ½" (1.3 cm) from the front edges to hold them in place.
• It's best to avoid zippers and buttonholes as closures. It's easier to apply toggles (page 132), buttons and loops (page 133) or the large hooks and eyes intended for fur garments. When sewing on buttons, make extra-long thread shanks for thick pile.

Sheers and lightweight silky types

Working with sheers such as voile, organdy, chiffon, gauze or georgette, and featherweight silk and silk types like satin or crepe de chine (A) takes a little extra care. It isn't hard if you follow the information below. Also, see the chart on pages 124-125.

Notions

You'll need a few special notions for these fine fabrics.
• *Very sharp scissors* ensure easy and accurate cutting.

Layout, Cutting and Marking

To keep slippery fabrics from sliding around as you cut, pin or tape the fabric to a large cutting surface or to an old sheet. Slip scissors between the fabric and the sheet to cut. Transfer pattern symbols to fabric with pins, tailor's tacks or snip marking.

Stitching

• Use a small-hole throat plate (see page 43) to prevent the fabric from being pulled into the hole. Or, place pieces of tape on either side of the hole (B).
• Hold thread ends when you

enough for the buttons to go through. Work a blanket stitch over strands, with the needle eye toward the loop as shown (C). Small hooks and eyes are also fine. For a nice-looking finish, do the last step of zippers with hand-picking.

Sheers

• Seams and darts should be narrow and inconspicuous. For straight seams, use a French seam; on curves, a double-stitched seam. At collar and cuff edges, sew a nearly invisible *hairline seam*. Stitch the seam over a filler cord of pearl cotton or crochet thread, with a fine zigzag. Trim

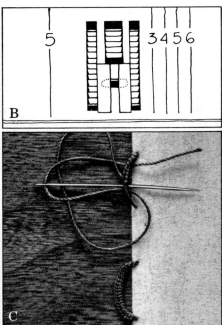

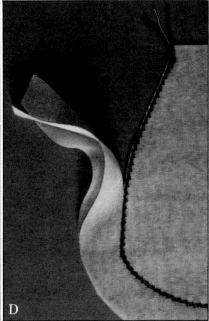

• For sewing, use *new machine needles,* size 9 or 11 all-purpose or ball-point, and *fine hand needles* such as sharps and darners.
• *Fine, smooth thread* — long-staple polyester, silk, or thread made especially for lightweight fabrics — will help prevent puckered seams.
• *Silk pins* are better than ordinary straight pins which may snag fabrics.
• *Lightweight zippers* are preferred for silky types.
• *Interfacing* should be lightweight and sheer. Use organdy, sheer non-wovens or self-fabric.

begin to stitch and avoid back-stitching to prevent jamming.
• To prevent puckers, don't stitch over pins, and edgestitch rather than topstitch, using a short stitch length and loosened tension. Also try tissue paper or tape under fabric as you stitch.

Fasteners

Closures should be as inconspicuous as possible. Use small hand- or machine-worked buttonholes, or tiny buttons and thread loops. To make loops, mark their location on the garment edge, opposite the button. Sew 2 or 3 strands of thread on the edge, long

to stitching (D); turn and press.
• Hems should be very deep or very narrow. A double hem 4-6" (10-15 cm) deep is attractive on a straight edge. Press half of the hem allowance to the wrong side and under again; slipstitch folded edge. On curved edges, use a hand-rolled or topstitched hem.

Silks and Silk Types

• Use a plain, French, or mock French seam. Clean-finish seam allowances of plain seams.
• Make a hand-rolled, narrow topstitched, or plain hem.
• In pressing, avoid water spotting or melting the fabric (see page 186).

Laces and openwork fabrics

Delicate laces and openwork fabrics, such as leno, mesh and lacy knits (A), lend a graceful feminine feeling to clothing. They're fairly transparent, so you can follow the information for sheers on page 213. In addition, laces and openwork fabrics have other qualities which call for special handling.

Patterns

With lace or openwork, the fabric is the first thing people notice. Play it up by choosing a simple

layout. If your lace has no selvage, align the pattern grainline with the lengthwise motifs. If your lace motifs are very large, match them so the design continues across seams (see page 83).

Because openwork fabrics and laces have holes, it's easier and faster to hold pattern pieces in place with weights, food cans, or books, rather than pins.

If a pattern symbol, such as a dot or notch, falls over one of the fabric holes, put a piece of transparent tape on the wrong side of the fabric and mark the symbol on the tape with a pencil (B).

Laces

• Take advantage of the lace motifs by using them as a decorative edge for a front opening or hem, as long as the lace does not ravel. This works best on heavier lace. Place the pattern piece *seamlines*, not the cutting lines, along the outer edges of the motifs; then lift up the pattern tissue and carefully cut around the motifs (C).
• Make French or double-stitched seams; double-stitch darts.
• For hems, use the types recommended for sheers on page 213.

A cluny lace leno lacy knit

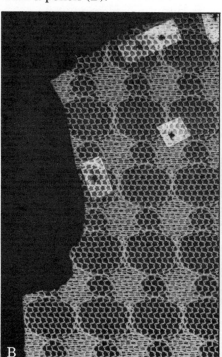

B

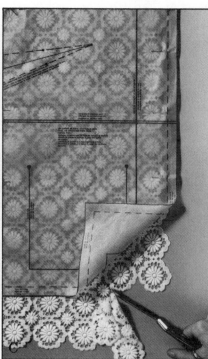

C

pattern with uncomplicated lines. If your style is shown in lace or openwork fabric on the pattern envelope, you'll know you've made a good choice for the fabric.

Layout, Cutting and Marking

Some lacy knits or meshes may be slightly stretchy, so it's a good idea to let the fabric relax on the cutting surface for a few hours before cutting. To prevent them from stretching, don't let these fabrics hang over the edge of the cutting surface as you work. Many lacy and open knits have a one-way design and will need a "with nap"

Stitching

If the presser foot toes get caught when you stitch, wrap the toes with tape or place tissue paper over the fabric as you stitch. To stabilize shoulder, neck and waist seams, include straight seam binding or twill tape in those seams (page 161); avoid facings and interfacing which might show.

Fasteners

Simple ties or small buttons and loops are the best fasteners for these fabrics. See pages 133 and 213 for how to make them.

• Lace with a distinct border eliminates the need for a hem. First make any necessary length adjustments on your pattern. Then place the pattern hemline along the lace border, omitting the hem allowance.

Openwork Fabrics

• French, overedged or double-stitched seams are fine for most openwork fabrics; for lacy knits, see the knit seams on page 161.
• If your fabric is stretchy, avoid letting it hang from the machine table as you stitch.
• The best hem is a narrow topstitched one (see page 141).

Plaids, stripes and diagonals

Some of the most dramatic, as well as classic, clothes are fashioned from plaid, striped or diagonal fabrics. *Plaids* and *stripes* may be *even* or *uneven* (A, B); page 84 explains the difference. Keep in mind that an even design is easier to work with. *Diagonals* are woven so the crosswise yarns form a diagonal line across the fabric. In fabrics such as denim (C), gabardine (D) and silk surah, the diagonal line is so fine you can barely see it; however, it produces a color-shading effect when the garment pieces are sewn together. For this type of fabric, use a "with nap" layout. Prominent diagonals, like the tweed shown here (E), require careful planning before they are cut so that the diagonal will create an attractive effect in the finished garment.

Choosing a Pattern

If the pattern envelope shows the garment in a plaid, stripe or diagonal, you can be sure the style is suitable. Otherwise, here are some clues to keep in mind: Look for styles with slim skirts, few seams, set-in sleeves and straight underarm darts (if any). *Avoid* patterns with bias seams, very wide A-line or multi-gored skirts, long kimono sleeves and V-necklines, as well as patterns marked "not suitable for plaids or stripes" or "not suitable for obvious diagonal fabrics."

Buying Fabric

Yardage will be given for a plaid, stripe or obvious diagonal if the pattern is shown in that fabric. If not, buy enough extra yardage to match the fabric lines at seams and position the fabric design attractively on the garment (see page 83). Small even plaids and stripes require about ¼-½ yard (.25 -.50 m) extra; large, even designs need another ½-1 yard (.50-.95 m).

Layouts

When using a plaid, striped or diagonal fabric, make all adjustments on your pattern before you lay it out. Otherwise, seams and designs will not match if you make changes after cutting.

Basic layouts for *plaids and stripes* are shown on page 84. Here's an additional tip: If the plaid or stripe is printed off-grain, follow the design, not the grainline, when you position pattern pieces. *Diagonals* should be laid out so that the design goes around the body (F), using a "with nap" layout. Work with a single fabric layer, right side up. First cut out each pattern piece with the printed side up; then turn it face down and cut it out again. For a pattern piece that would normally be laid out on a fabric fold, cut only along the cutting lines, *not along the foldline*. Make a tiny snip at each end of the foldline. Then turn the pattern face down so that the foldline aligns with the snip markings and cut out the second half of the garment (F).

To match up the lines of a prominent diagonal fabric at seams, or to match stripes or plaid lines, see the plaid matching tip on page 83, lower right.

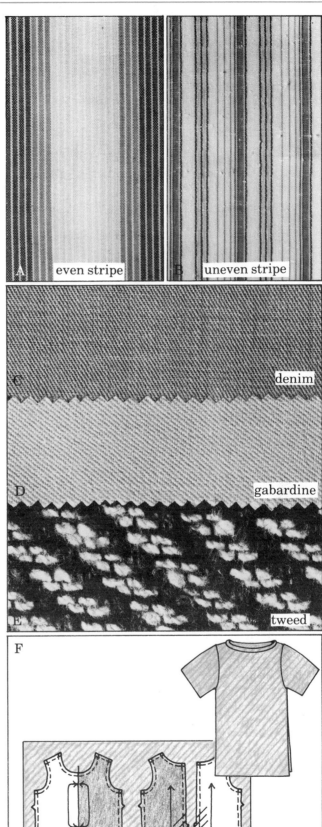

A even stripe

B uneven stripe

C denim

D gabardine

E tweed

F

10

special fabrics

215

Chevrons are the V's that form when plaids, stripes or diagonals are matched at an angle. For perfect chevrons, both seamlines to be matched must be on the same slant. (To match bars or stripes, see page 83.) Chevrons occur at center front, center back and side seams on bias skirts (A) and on flared skirts cut on a straight grain (B, C).

Use the plaid matching tip on page 83, lower right, to match the fabric design at seams during layout.

Even plaids or stripes form chevrons easily. Cut out the center front and back pattern pieces on a double fabric layer as shown (A). Be sure to align the fabric bars or stripes on both fabric layers before pinning the pattern in place (see page 84).

Uneven plaids and stripes must be laid out on a single fabric layer, using a mirror-image layout (see page 84). Cut out the front pattern piece with the printed side up; then reverse it and turn it face down to cut out the other side (B). Do the same for the back.

Diagonals, whether even or uneven, will form chevrons *only if the fabric is reversible*—that is, if it doesn't have an obvious right and wrong side. On a single fabric layer, cut out the front pattern piece twice, with the printed side up and facing the same direction (C). Cut out the back the same way. Use the right side of the fabric for half of the garment, and the wrong side for the other half.

Design details can be very effective fashion elements when you work with plaid, striped or diagonal fabrics. Experiment with the placement of collars, pockets, waistbands and yokes to see which way you want the design to run. Try cutting them on the bias, to contrast with a straight-cut body. If you use a diagonal, you might cut your collar on the bias grain, instead of the lengthwise grain. Cut it either along, or across, the rib, keeping in mind how the finished collar will appear. You can also mix large and small-scale plaids or stripes in one garment, using the small plaid for the details. Or, you might want to use plaid details on solid-color garments.

Stitching

After you've cut your fabric to match perfectly, you'll want to sew it that way, too. Most seams can be pin-basted to hold them in place. Or you can use an even-feed foot, an attachment that was developed to sew matched fabrics (see page 149). For extra-sure matching—on curves, angled seams or chevrons—try slip-basting (see page 100). A time-saving alternative to slip-basting is double-faced basting tape. Place tape on the right side of the seam allowance on one fabric section, next to the seamline. Press under the seam allowance on the other section and lap it over the taped one so that the raw edges are even and the bars or stripes match. With right sides together, stitch along the seamline; don't stitch through the tape. Remove the tape before pressing.

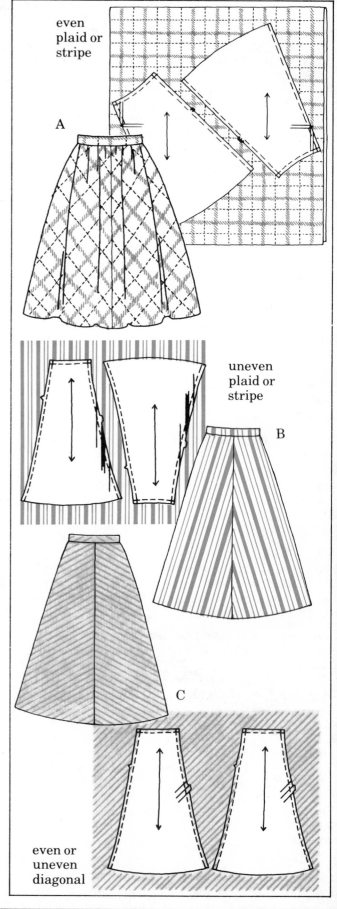

even plaid or stripe

A

uneven plaid or stripe

B

C

even or uneven diagonal

11

personal touches

One of the nicest things about sewing is the individual flair— that personal touch— you can give to all your creations.

Putting personality into your sewing projects can be as simple as just adding trim along edges, or as elaborate as working fancy stitchery. All it takes is a little creativity and a bit of know-how. Where, for example, will you find ideas for designs? How and where will you use them? And, most important, what method will you use for doing them?

This chapter has the answers to these questions for many of the creative touches you'll want to add: machine embroidery, hand embroidery, purchased trims, patchwork and appliqué. Some Simplicity patterns include these extras; or you can work up your own ideas for the fashions you sew. Simple-to-follow instructions are given on the next few pages.

(Left) Innovative appliqué... Scattered floral motifs cut from the skirt fabric make a pretty border on the soft challis stole. For instructions, see page 234.

Embroidery

Embroidery — by hand or machine — has a unique way of adding a personal touch to your sewing projects. Even when it's done in small amounts, with the simplest and quickest of techniques, it still adds that special plus, making a fashion distinctively yours. Before you begin, be sure that all materials are compatible in design and care requirements. Don't, for example, use wool yarn to embroider a dress you'll wash; or delicate thread and stitches on coarse, loosely woven fabric. If possible, do the stitchery before you sew the garment. That way, the work will be easier to manage.

Your machine may have built-in fancy stitches, but even ordinary straight or zigzag stitches can transform a garment from simple to super in practically no time. All it takes is a little know-how and your own bright ideas. See pages 226-227.

Even a novice can achieve dramatic effects with hand embroidery, from bold yarn painting to delicate cross-stitch. Although there are dozens of stitches to choose from, we've used the ones that are simple to do and cover a lot of territory quickly. See pages 228-229.

(Top Right) Machine embroidery is a colorful decorative accent on a shirt yoke. To see how it's done, turn to page 234.

(Right) Hand embroidery makes a handsome monogram on a man's robe. Charming hand-worked flowers give a fresh look to the bib of a crisp sundress or a child's dress.

Trims

Trims are big fashion news! Subtle or splashy, they spell out your personal fashion message beautifully.

Action — is that your image? Project it with trims. After all, racing stripes aren't only for cars. They're for all active sportswear, via contrast bands. Love frills and lace? Say so by adding pretty edgings, pre-gathered ruffles, ribbon or other feminine touches to your clothes. Are you the tailored type? If classic fabrics and simple lines are for you, you can tell your fashion story by using trims, too. Try quietly elegant foldover braid or piping to emphasize a well-turned collar or lapel, for example. Whatever your favorite fashion message, today's trims will get it across.

(Below and Right) Trims show their versatility in clothes for every lifestyle. Sleek braid jazzes up a jogging suit or skating outfit; lacy edging adds romance to a simple print dress; neat piping can finish off a sophisticated shirtdress. See pages 230-231 for more trim ideas.

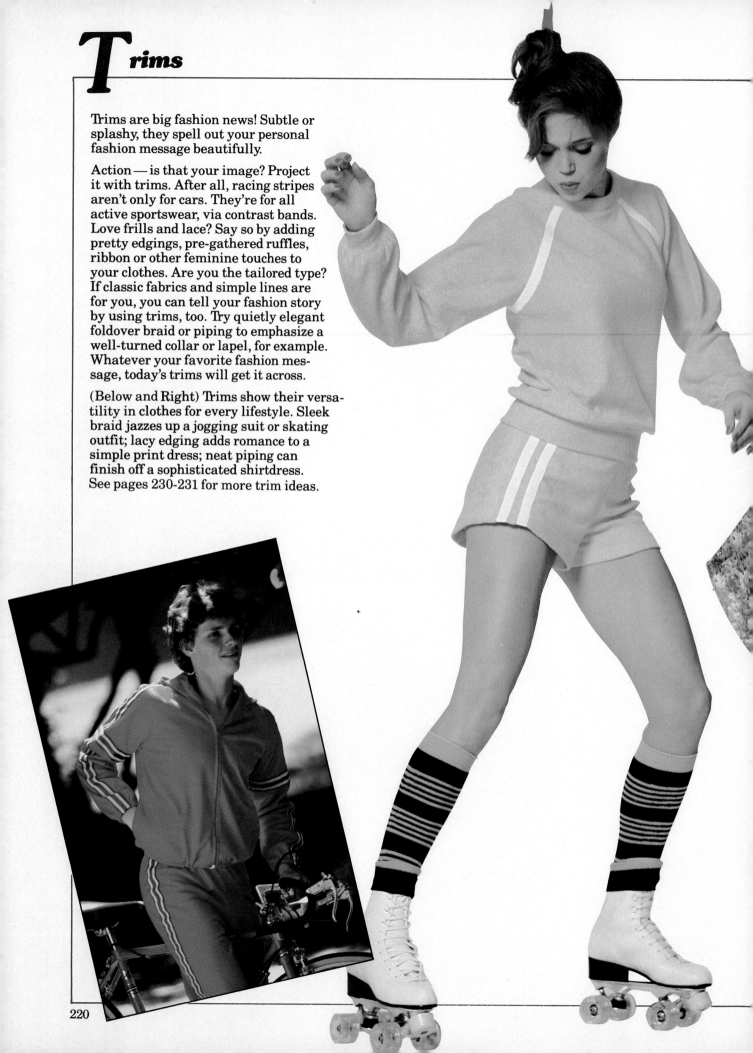

Patchwork and appliqué

With their newly important place in fashion, you'd never guess that patchwork and appliqué had their origins in Granny's homespun, old-time quilts!

Keep a bit of yesterday in your patchwork designs, or opt for the strictly contemporary. Whichever style you choose, you can whip up designs that will bring some freshness into your wardrobe. And, with today's shortcut stitching and fusing methods, just about all the *work* has been taken out of patchwork. See how on page 232.

Appliqué designs and techniques are up-to-the-minute as well. Two of the easiest methods are machine-stitching and fusing— they make the job go very fast! Of course, if you prefer, you can still do the traditional type of appliqué, using invisible hand sewing or some pretty hand embroidery stitches to hold the appliqué edges in place. See pages 228-229.

(Left) A romantic pairing of lace and embroidered linen appliqués (we used table linens) makes this drawstring skirt and T-shirt top a most fantastic dress-up ensemble. You can do it yourself! Instructions are on page 234. (Below) For his shirt yoke, modern machine patchwork mixes traditional calico prints. See how it's done on page 234.

11
personal touches

223

Design decisions

When it comes to sewing something special, the first step is choosing a design. Iron-on transfers are a handy source of designs. Whether you embroider, appliqué or work with purchased trims, Simplicity offers a selection of patterns with iron-on designs and instructions.

Color

You'll find that a few general color rules (see page 7) make the work of planning your design easier. Keep them in mind when selecting designs, supplies and fabrics.

When personalizing a garment, consider the color of the fabric as well as those colors which are flattering to you. For example, if the garment will be made in multi-colored fabric, choose one of the dominant colors for your decoration (A). On solid fabric, use a contrasting color (or colors), such

For the most appealing results, accent only one or two main features, such as an interesting yoke and pocket flaps.

Design Size

Having made most of the important design decisions, you must now find a suitable size for your design. If the design needs enlarging or reducing, there are several ways to do this. The easiest

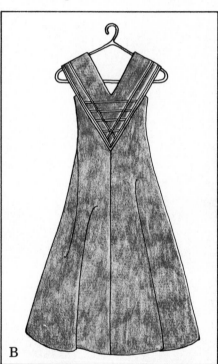

Don't stop with purchased transfers...create your own original design. Sources of inspiration are endless! Just look around you—you'll be amazed at what you can find. Here are just a few ideas:

- china patterns
- picture books
- fabrics
- scarves
- works of art
- lettering (monograms)
- seed packets
- greeting cards
- playing cards
- magazines
- souvenirs

as red on white, for design impact; or use a closely-related shade for a more subtle effect.

Design Placement

Now, you've got a great design idea. Where should it go on the garment? Certain garment areas —cuffs, collars, pockets, yokes, waistlines and hemlines—are all natural locations for adding special touches. If you're in doubt, use the strongest design lines as a guide and play them up. Shaped seams or an unusual neckline or closure are some of the features you may want to emphasize (B).

method is to take the design to a photostat house where it can be enlarged or reduced to the desired size for a few dollars. However, you can easily do the job yourself by using the folded paper method. Draw a square around the design and fold the paper horizontally and vertically to form a smaller square. Cut a second square piece of paper the size you want the design to be; fold it into the same number of squares as the design paper. Draw the design onto the second piece of paper, using a sharp pencil. Work square by square for accuracy (C).

Design transfer

To center a design on your fabric, fold the design paper and the fabric in half lengthwise, then crosswise. Crease the paper; mark the fabric folds with pins. Tape the paper to the fabric, centering the creases over the pin markings (A).

Transfer Methods

The following methods are suitable for transferring designs to fabric. Consider your fabric type and design choice to determine the best method to use.

perature or use a pencil to make the design lines more visible. Test removability of the motif by washing (if the fabric is washable) or with a cleaning fluid. If the design doesn't come off, be sure to cover the lines completely when you embroider or appliqué.

Transfer pencils: Trace a mirror image of the design onto the back of the design paper, using a transfer pencil. This is available at needlecraft and art supply stores. Then transfer the design to the fabric with a hot iron, following the instructions for iron-on transfers, below left.

Napped or pile fabric transfer: Trace the design onto the wrong side of the fabric; then hand-baste along the design lines to bring them to the right side. Or, if you're going to embroider, transfer the design onto organdy. Baste this to the napped side of the fabric and embroider through both layers. Clip the basting threads and cut away the organdy (D).

A

B

C

D

E

Iron-on transfers: Test the transfer for clarity of imprint. Pin or tape a scrap of your fabric, right side up, on an ironing board or tabletop which is protected by a bath towel. The transferred design usually will show more clearly if you place aluminum foil under the fabric while pressing. Cut out a trial motif, leaving a margin. Tape, pin or baste the motif, printed side down, on the fabric. Press straight down on the motif (B). Do not glide the iron; this will cause the design to smudge. If the iron is warm enough, the print should be clear. If it's not clear, try a higher tem-

Tracing designs: Tape the fabric, right side up, on a hard surface. Place the design, face up, on the fabric. Slip dressmaker's tracing paper, shiny side down, under the design and tape it in place. Transfer the design by going over all lines with a pencil or stylus (C). Press hard enough so that the lines transfer. This is a good way to transfer a dark blue iron-on design onto a dark fabric, or to preserve the transfer so that it can be used more than once.

Multiple transfer: To transfer the same design several times, trace it as described above, or cut a template or master pattern. Trace the design onto cardboard (or use sandpaper, which won't slip on the fabric) with tracing paper and a sharp pencil, adding seam allowances if appliqués will be machine-stitched or hand-sewn. Cut out the template with sharp scissors, a mat knife or a razor blade. Trace around the template to transfer the design to the fabric (E), repeating as often as necessary.

Machine embroidery

There are two types of machine embroidery. One is like regular sewing, with a variety of stitches and threads. The other is free-motion embroidery, done without a presser foot and the machine feed mechanism. Instead, your hands move the fabric as the machine stitches. With either kind of embroidery, you can use straight, zigzag or automatic decorative stitches.

Getting Started

Before you start any machine embroidery project, familiarize yourself with the technique. Use this practice period to find the best combination of thread, needle, tension and pressure for your fabric. These may vary, depending on your project and especially on your sewing machine. The following suggestions will help.
• Choose a firmly-woven, light to medium weight fabric or a stable knit.
• After transferring the design to the fabric, back it with a lightweight woven fabric or apply lightweight fusible interfacing to the wrong side to keep the fabric from stretching or puckering. You can also stabilize a lightweight fabric by spray-starching and pressing it, or by stitching with tissue paper underneath.
• Check your machine manual for information on using the special stitches, adjusting tension and lowering or covering the feed dog for free-motion embroidery.
• Be sure your machine is in top condition— clean and well-oiled. Use a new, sharp needle.

Regular Machine Embroidery

You can create many decorative effects with regular machine stitching. These include striped or checkered designs, areas filled in by stitching over yarn or cord, or outlines made by stitching around simple designs.

Different threads give new dimensions to stitches. You can use mercerized cotton or polyester thread, polyester buttonhole twist, pearl cotton, metallic or ombré thread or embroidery floss. You can even buy thread, available in many colors, that's especially meant for machine embroidery. Since pearl cotton and embroidery floss are too heavy to go through the needle, you must wind them onto the bobbin by hand and use regular thread in the needle. Then, stitch on the wrong side of the fabric so the heavier thread will be on the right side. Straight stitching is usually best for outlining but multiple rows make a pretty border design when done with heavy threads.

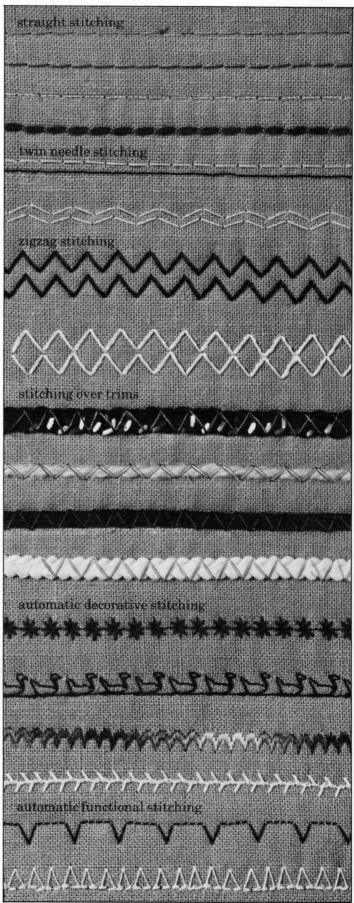

straight stitching

twin needle stitching

zigzag stitching

stitching over trims

automatic decorative stitching

automatic functional stitching

Zigzag stitches can be worked with the threads suggested for straight stitches. Align the rows so the points either interlock or meet to form diamonds (see left). To outline, space the stitches closely for a satin stitch; for filling, space them wider apart or close together, as desired.

You can use satin stitching and automatic decorative stitches to outline or fill in an area. Or, zigzag over trims such as narrow braid, yarn or satin cord (A). To apply sequin trim on a string, set the stitch width so that it just catches the outer edge of the sequins; stitch in the direction that the sequins overlap.

Free-motion Machine Embroidery

To add personal flair to your sewing projects, use free-motion embroidery as a substitute for hand embroidery. To prevent thread buildup on the wrong side of your work, some manufacturers make a special fine thread to be used only in the bobbin for machine embroidery. Experiment with dif-

Before you stitch, loosen the needle tension. Set the stitch length at 0 for either straight or zigzag stitching. Remove the presser foot and lower or cover the feed dog (see your machine manual). If you have one, a darning foot can be used for free-motion embroidery. It holds fabric taut under the needle while allowing the free movement of your fabric. To stitch, lower the presser bar. Hold the fabric down by keeping your fingers somewhat close to the needle. Move the hoop slowly as you stitch, following the design outline (B). Stitch in place a few times to lock the threads. Don't move abruptly or the thread—or

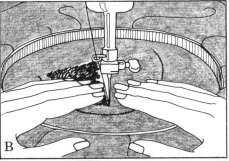

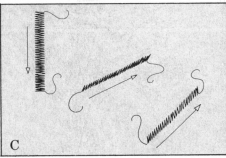

Automatic decorative stitches, which are available on some machines, can make designs such as stars, animals or scallops. In plain or ombré thread, these stitches can be used to outline or fill in an area. You can explore the decorative potential of stretch, blindstitch and other functional stitches, too (see left).

Twin needles double the impact of any stitch—straight, zigzag or fancy. Use the same or different colors of threads in the needles. Twin needle zigzag stitches are especially effective for filling in an area or creating outlines.

ferent threads to see what works best in your machine because stitching varies from one machine to another. Use a 6-8" (15-20.5 cm) embroidery hoop as follows: place the larger ring on the bed of the machine, position the fabric over it and snap in the smaller ring. You may have to remove the needle to do this on some machines. Keep the fabric very taut!

needle—may break. Always keep the design in line with the needle.

For zigzag stitching, move the fabric forward slightly, blending stitches as you go, then from side to side as needed to follow the design lines. When lines cross, make the first line of stitching less dense and the second more prominent. For parallel rows of zigzag stitches, keep the work straight; for thick and thin lines, change the angle of approach as you feed the fabric (C). Practice on scraps first. Don't limit yourself to filling in; as you become more adept, try swirls, flowers and initials (D).

11

Hand embroidery

For a hand-embroidered fashion, choose a plain weave fabric, such as cotton, linen or muslin. If the garment area to be embroidered will be too small to fit in an embroidery hoop, or if the design will come too close to the edge, work the embroidery before cutting out the garment section. Otherwise, you can cut out the fabric first and then do the embroidery.

Other supplies include an embroidery hoop to keep the fabric taut and smooth, a thimble and small, sharp, pointed scissors.

Stitches

Cross-stitch: Work in rows from left to right. Keeping the needle straight, insert the needle at equal intervals, forming slanted half-crosses (A). Then, working from right to left, complete the crosses by inserting the needle in

Backstitch: Work from right to left. Bring the thread up on the transferred design line and insert the needle a little to the right. Now bring the needle up again an equal distance to the left. Insert the needle again at the beginning of the last stitch (D). This stitch makes a sharp outline or solid background filling.

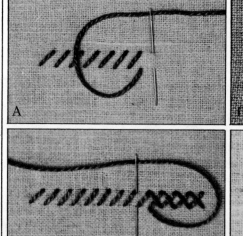

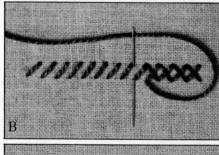

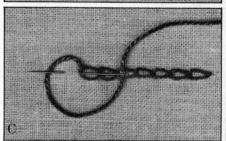

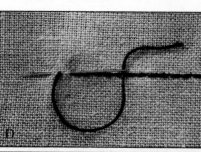

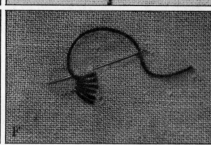

When the embroidery is finished, press it face down over a terry towel; press lightly to avoid flattening the stitches.

Equipment

Yarns and threads: Six-strand embroidery floss can be separated into strands. Pearl cotton has a slight sheen and comes in various weights. Heavier matte-finish cotton has no sheen.

Crewel or embroidery needles have sharp points and long eyes for easy threading. The higher the number, the finer and smaller the needle.

the same way as before (B). Cross-stitch is used for borders and for geometric, floral and folkloric designs.

Chain stitch: Bring the needle to the right side of the fabric on the transferred design line. Make a small loop with the thread and hold it in place with your left thumb. Insert the needle back where the thread first came up. Bring the needle out a little to the left, over the thread loop (C). Use this stitch for decorative outlines and flower stems or work it in close rows to fill in an area.

Running stitch: Working from right to left, weave the needle in and out of the fabric at regular intervals. Keep the stitches uniform in size (E). Use the running stitch for lines and outlines.

Straight stitch: Work in any direction. Bring the needle up through the fabric and insert it straight down to make a stitch of the desired length (F). Make a single straight stitch to create a detail such as a stem or a blade of grass, or a group of stitches close together to fill in an area. This stitch can also form flowers.

Blanket stitch: Work from left to right. Bring the needle up and hold a loop of thread down with your left thumb. Keeping the needle straight, insert it at equal intervals and bring it out over the loop of thread. Continue in this way, spacing stitches ⅛"-⅜" (3 mm-1 cm) apart (A). Use this stitch to outline or cover an edge. It can also be used at an edge to hold layers of fabric together.

pointing downward. Draw the needle through, over the thread loop. Alternate these two steps (C). Use this stitch for lines, borders, outlines and fern-like leaves.

Herringbone stitch: Work from left to right. Bring thread out at left end of lower guideline. Make a small stitch from right to left on upper guideline. Make a similar stitch from right to left on lower guideline (D). Repeat. This stitch is good for borders and wide lines.

French knot: Bring the needle up from the wrong side. Wrap the thread around the needle two or three times. Hold the thread taut and insert the needle into the fabric close to the starting point (G). Use your thumb to hold the knot in place as you draw the thread through to the wrong side. For a larger knot, wrap the thread around the needle four or five times. Make one or several French knots for flower centers.

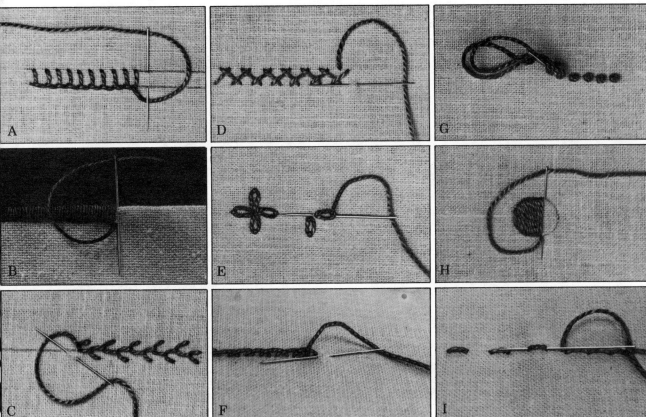

Overcast stitch: Work from left to right. Take straight stitches over the edge right next to each other (B), or space stitches widely to finish and decorate edges.

Feather stitch: Work from right to left. Bring the needle to the right side of the fabric slightly above the transferred design line. Hold the thread with your left thumb. Make an upward-slanting stitch below and a little to the left of where the thread emerged, with the needle passing over the thread loop. Carry the thread along the line, form a loop above the line and make a similar stitch above the line with the needle

Lazy-daisy stitch: Bring the thread up and hold it in a loop with the left thumb. Insert the needle back where the thread emerged. Then bring the needle out the length of the stitch desired and pull it through the loop. Make a small straight stitch to anchor the loop at its crown (E). This makes flowers, leaves or petals.

Outline stitch: Working from left to right, insert the needle a short distance to the right and bring it out a little to the left at a very slight angle. Keep the thread above the needle (F). Use it for outlines, stems and long lines.

Satin stitch: Bring the needle to the right side at one edge of the design to be filled in, insert it at the opposite edge and return to the starting edge by carrying it underneath the fabric. Keep the stitches parallel and close together (H) to cover the design area completely.

Holbein stitch: Make a running stitch at even intervals in one direction. Turn around and repeat, filling the spaces between the first stitches (I). Use this for lines and outlines.

Trims

Trims can make the difference between a satisfactory or a really spectacular fashion. Whether you prefer tailored or frilly clothes, there's a trim that's just perfect for your personality. Often, a simple trim is all that's needed to highlight a seam or detail and bring it into focus.

Trimming Hints

Here are some practical tips:
• To figure out how much trim to buy, measure the area to be trimmed. Add at least ½ yd. (.5 m)

• Stitch trims in place with a slightly loose thread tension.
• Miter corners of band trims (see page 150). To finish trim ends, catch them in a seam, or turn one end under and lap it over the other at a seam.
• When combining trims, such as bands and rickrack, stitch them together and apply as one.

Edgings

Trims with at least one decorative edge, such as fringe, piping and pre-gathered ruffles, can be applied two ways.

When you apply a pre-gathered trim, allow enough fullness to go around a corner by making tiny tucks in the trim at the corner. Taper the trim ends into the seam allowance, clearing the edge that will be stitched to the garment—for example, on a collar or cuff. Then pin and stitch in place (B).

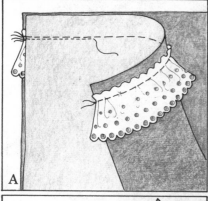

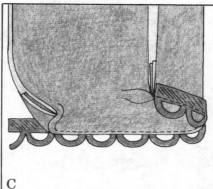

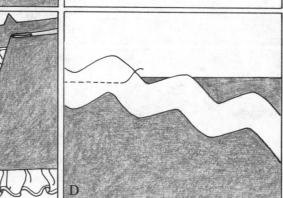

to join ends and go around corners and curves.
• Be sure the trim requires the same care as your fabric.
• For curves, choose a flexible trim such as rickrack, bias tape, foldover braid or knitted bands.
• When you pin the trim in place, allow extra fullness or ease in the trim to prevent the fabric from puckering after the trim is stitched to the garment.
• Hold the trim in place with pins, double-faced basting tape, strips of fusible web or fabric glue.

Inserted in a seam: Place the trim along the seamline on the right side of the fabric, with the decorative edge toward the garment and the raw edge inside the seamline, on the seam allowance. For pre-gathered ruffles, place the bound edge just over the seamline. Machine-baste along the straight edge of the trim (or the middle of rickrack), following the seamline. Use a zipper foot to stitch bulky trims such as piping or bound ruffles. Pin the garment sections together and stitch close to the basting (A). Trim the seam allowances and press to one side.

Topstitched along an edge: Lap the finished garment edge over the straight trim edge and topstitch it in place (C). Trims with two decorative edges, such as scalloped braid or rickrack, can be topstitched to the garment edge instead (D). You can also lap the garment edge over rickrack so that only one set of points shows. Use a zipper foot to apply piping; an edgestitcher foot helps guide stitching for other trims (E).

Borders or Top Trims

Bands or any other trim with two finished edges can be used for borders or top trims.

Wide trims: There are lots of imaginative ways to use wide trims. You can create multi-stripes with rows of banding; or place bands along a hem edge for an attractive border (A). Add new dimension to fabric by crisscrossing bias tape or ribbons on a bodice, yoke or cuff for a checkered or woven effect (A).

both edges, depending on the trim width. Hold the fabric taut while stitching and keep the trim slightly loose to ease it to the fabric. Some narrow trims can be turned at a corner without mitering, while others must be mitered like wide trims (see page 150). For very narrow braid or yarn, use a special braid foot. It has a groove that makes application easier (B).

For machine couching, zigzag-stitch over the braid or yarn. The zigzag stitches should be wide enough to pass over the braid without stitching through it (C).

For a see-through effect, cut fabric away from the wrong side to within ¼″ (6 mm) of the stitching. Press the seam allowances away from the trim. From the right side, stitch over the first stitching to hold seam allowances flat (D).

You can also join the trim to the fabric in one stitching. First, cut the fabric apart where you plan to put the insertion. Press the raw edges under half the width of the

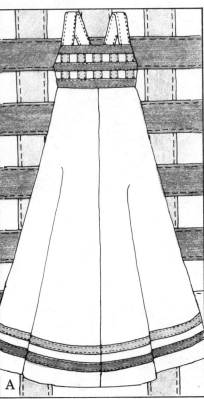

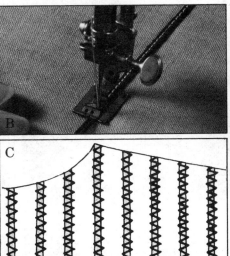

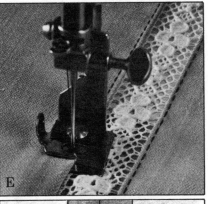

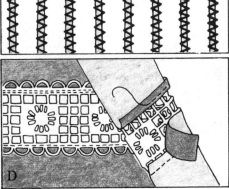

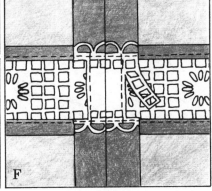

Apply a wide trim before stitching the garment sections together so that the trim ends will be caught in the garment seams. Topstitch along both trim edges; use a decorative stitch for extra appeal. To miter corners, see page 150.

Narrow trims: Narrow, flat braid or yarn is especially good for intricate, curved designs or machine couching. Stitch through the center of the trim or along

Insertions

See-through trims with two finished edges, such as lace or eyelet, are perfect for insertion on flat garment areas where there are no darts or curved seams. Apply insertions on garment sections before seaming so that ends of the trim can be included in the seam. Pin the trim in place and topstitch close to both edges. For scalloped edges, stitch just inside the points, leaving the decorative edges free. Miter the corners as described on page 150.

insertion, finishing them if necessary. Then, lap the garment edges over the trim and stitch; an edge-stitcher foot is handy for this (E).

At seams, pin carefully so the insertion edges match. Stitch a plain seam and press it open.

To make the seam allowances as inconspicuous as possible in the insertion area, stitch each one ¼″ (6 mm) from the seam; then trim the insertion close to the second stitching (F).

Patchwork

Patchwork is a multi-fabric design with patches of fabric sewn or fused together. Yokes, cuffs or borders in patchwork fabric are a delightful way to add Western or Americana flavor to a garment. Or, why not make an entire fashion from patchwork?

Fabric: You can mix fabrics with contrasting or coordinating colors, prints or textures. Just be sure the fabrics are similar in weight and have the same care requirements.

Traditional Patchwork

Make a cardboard template (cutting pattern) for the patch shape, adding ¼″ (6 mm) seam allowances. Use this to trace the shapes onto your fabric, placing all patches on the same grainline. Cut the patches, then stitch them together in ¼″ (6 mm) seams to form a block (B, C); press the

Super-quick Patchwork

Cut fabric patches and identical fusible web shapes, omitting seam allowances. Following the manufacturer's instructions, fuse the patches to lightweight background fabric. You can use the background as part of the design if you let it show between the patches. Zigzag over the edges to keep them from raveling (F).

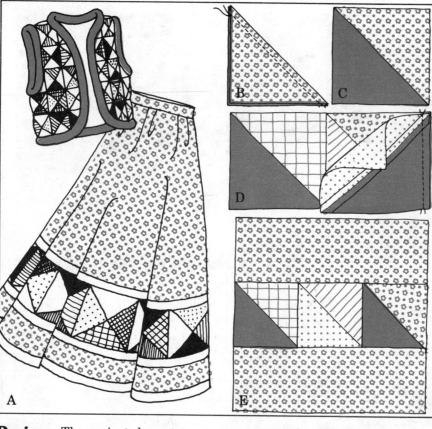

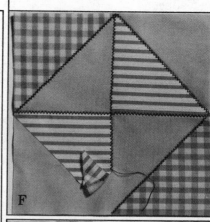

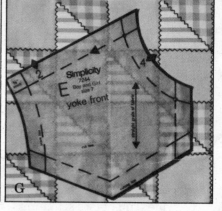

Designs: The easiest shape to work with is a square, but other geometrics—triangles, diamonds—are nice, too. Make a plan to combine these shapes in various designs, forming a square or rectangular block. Decide how many blocks you'll need to lay out your pattern pieces. Block size depends on the size of the area where the patchwork will be used. For example, 2″ (5 cm) blocks are fine for a yoke or vest, but larger blocks will be more attractive for a patchwork border on a skirt (A) or a long caftan.

seams open (for complicated shapes, such as hexagons, press the seams to one side). Sew the blocks together, forming strips (D). Then join the strips (E) until the patchwork fabric is large enough for you to lay out your pattern pieces.

Pattern Layout

Now that you've finished creating your patchwork fabric, you can use it to make beautiful garments or accessories. Lay out pattern pieces on the patchwork to get the desired effect (G). Pin and cut the pieces; then staystitch around all edges to keep the seams of the patchwork from coming apart.

 ppliqué

An appliqué is a fabric design that is stitched or fused to a base fabric. It's a fun add-on that you can make in any size and shape for fashions or accessories. Some patterns come with appliqué transfers. If not, buy ready-made appliqués or make your own designs. Attic treasures, such as lace handkerchiefs or doilies, also make charming appliqués. For more ideas, see page 224.

Hand-sewn: Before applying, machine-stitch ¼″ (6 mm) from the appliqué edge. Notch outward curves and clip inward curves; then press the raw edge under, rolling the stitching to the underside. Pin the appliqué to the base fabric; then baste it in place. Invisibly slipstitch the appliqué in place (A). Or use embroidery floss and a decorative embroidery stitch to secure the appliqué. Popular stitches include the blanket stitch, overcast stitch and feather stitch (see pages 228-229).

Machine-stitched: Pin the appliqué to the base fabric. Machine-baste ¼″ (6 mm) from the raw edges. Trim the excess fabric close to the stitching. Then satin-stitch all around, covering the basting stitches and the raw edges (C).

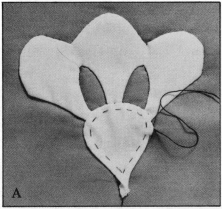

A

C

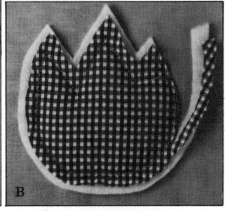

B

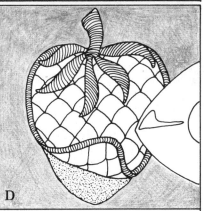

D

How to Apply

If you're making your own, transfer the design to your fabric, following the methods described on page 225. Include ¼″ (6 mm) seam allowances if the appliqués will be machine-stitched or hand-sewn; add ½″ (1.3 cm) seam allowances if they will be padded. Cut out the appliqués. To apply them, use one of the following methods.

Padded: Cut identical shapes of appliqué fabric and two layers of batting, including ½″ (1.3 cm) seam allowances. Sandwich the batting between the appliqué and the base fabric; pin in place. Then machine-baste ½″ (1.3 cm) from the edges. Trim the appliqué and batting close to the stitching (B). Satin-stitch over the edges, covering the basting.

Fused: Cut identical shapes of appliqué fabric and fusible web, omitting seam allowances. Fuse the appliqué to the base fabric, following the manufacturer's directions (D). If the appliqué fabric ravels, or the finished project will get hard wear, satin-stitch around the appliqué edges after fusing.

Project instructions

Appliquéd Stole
(Shown on page 217)

Buy floral fabric for appliqués and 1½ yds. (1.40 m) of 54″ (140 cm) wide solid-color fabric for stole. Cut the stole fabric in half along the crosswise grain. Join two short ends in a double-stitched seam, forming a long rectangle. To fringe the other short ends, stitch across the stole 2″ (5 cm) from the ends parallel to a thread; pull out threads parallel to the stitching. Narrow-hem the long stole edges. Cut appliqué shapes from the floral fabric and fusible web. Ar-

Trimmed Top and Skirt
(Shown on page 222)

To trim both top and skirt, you'll need the following: tablecloth or placemats with at least 5 embroidered or appliquéd motifs and embroidered edges, about 10½″ x 7″ (26.8 x 18 cm) each; 6 smaller corner motifs from napkins or bun warmers; stretch lace instead of braid or binding if your top pattern requires trim; four different 1¼″ (3.2 cm) wide lace trims— 3¼ yds. (3.0 m) A, 4 yds. (3.7 m) B, 3¼ yds. (3.0 m) C, 2 yds. (1.85 m) D; 2½ yds. (2.3 m) of ¾″ (2 cm) wide satin ribbon for drawstring.

an embroidered motif from the tablecloth about 7″ (18 cm) wide and the length of the sleeve. Press the edges under ¼″ (6 mm) and center the motif on the sleeve with the embroidered edge at the sleeve hem. Edgestitch the edges and cut away the fabric underneath. Follow the pattern instructions to finish the top.

Skirt: Choose a pattern with a drawstring casing. Cut out the skirt, omitting any pockets; stitch the center front and back seams and press them open. Using the diagram (B) as a guide, position and pin trims on each half of the

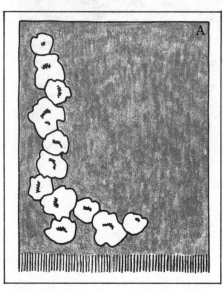

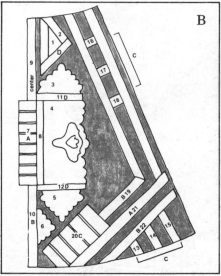

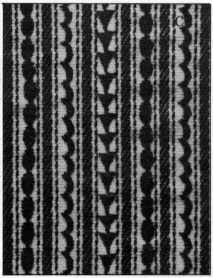

range them, slightly overlapping, at each end of the stole as shown (A). Fuse the appliqués in place and satin-stitch over the raw edges (see page 233).

Patchwork Shirt
(Shown on page 223)

Before assembling the shirt, use scraps of calico prints and fusible web to make Super-quick Patchwork as described on page 232. Fuse the patchwork to the right sides of the yoke and cuff sections; then cut away any excess that extends beyond the garment sections. Zigzag-stitch over the patchwork edges. Interface the collar; then fuse and zigzag-stitch a patch to each collar point. Assemble the shirt, using a decorative stitch and contrasting thread for all topstitching.

These descriptions and amounts are approximate; you can vary them according to availability and your preference.

Top: If your top pattern calls for braid or binding at the neck or shoulder edge, substitute stretch lace and apply as the pattern directs. Sew the top back and front together at shoulders and finish the neck edge as directed by your pattern. Cut a motif with an embroidered edge from the tablecloth, allowing extra fabric around it for turning the edges under (see page 233). Press the raw edges under ¼″ (6 mm). Center the motif on the top front, with the finished edge at the neckline. Edgestitch it in place; then cut away the fabric underneath. Hem the lower edges of the sleeves. Then, for each sleeve, cut

skirt front in numerical order, covering or turning under all raw edges. To make pieces 1 and 20, use plain areas of the tablecloth, stitching in tucks or adding lace. Edgestitch all trims in place. Then assemble the skirt and insert a ribbon drawstring.

Western Shirt
(Shown on page 218)

Choose a striped fabric with white or light-colored stripes. Before assembling the shirt, make rows of decorative stitching (page 226) on the white stripes of the yoke sections (C). Use three thread colors and a different stitch for each color, keeping the sequence symmetrical on both right and left yoke sections. Then, assemble the shirt, following your pattern.

12 tailoring

With the importance of the suit in fashion, tailoring takes on new interest. The perfectly shaped jacket is now a fashion must, and you'll certainly want one—or more—in your wardrobe. Fortunately, shaping and finishing methods have been updated, so tailoring needn't be as time-consuming as it once was. Choose the technique that suits you best, and turn out a beautifully tailored fashion that makes you look terrific.

tailoring methods

Nowadays, there's more than one way to tailor! The traditional methods involve quite a bit of hand sewing and will take a little time. On the other hand, there are shortcut tailoring techniques that focus on fast results—your sewing machine or fusible interfacing replace most of the hand sewing. These methods are so quick and easy, that even if you have little time, you can create a perfectly shaped coat or jacket.

In this chapter you'll find the traditional, as well as the faster, methods. For example, we show you how to attach interfacing to lapels by hand or by machine, and how to shape a coat or jacket by fusing instead of stitching.

How do you decide which method is best for you? If you enjoy hand sewing (many do!), you'll want to consider the traditional tailoring techniques. Or, if time is a factor, use the machine-stitching or fusing methods to shape your garment. A combination of all three is a possibility, too. Your approach to tailoring may change from garment to garment, or within a garment. You can create a well-tailored garment, no matter which method you choose.

Supplies

Fabric

Let yourself splurge a little when you pick out a fabric for your tailoring projects. Treat yourself well — choose a favorite color, a wonderful plaid, a beautiful print, a luxurious texture. After all, you'll spend more time making this garment and you're going to keep it longer, so why not love the fabric from the start?

Look for a good quality fabric. Buy one that's tightly constructed, either woven or knit, in

or elegant contrast collars, cuffs and lapels. Linen, denim, piqué, seersucker, heavy cotton, raw silk and some upholstery fabrics tailor nicely into suits or warm-weather coats and jackets.

Interfacing

In regular sewing, interfacing adds firmness to garment details. For tailoring, it plays an even more important role — molding fabric into shape. That's why entire sections of a tailored garment are sometimes interfaced. The traditional interfacing for tailoring is medium weight hair canvas, although available weights

Lining

For those items you've tailored so beautifully, you'll need a lining that lasts as long as the garment. See page 34 for information on lining fabrics. In addition, linings with napped or thermal backings add extra warmth to a heavy-weight outer fabric for cold-weather clothes. Deep-pile fabrics also make warm linings. If you use this type, line the sleeves with a smoother, less bulky fabric so the garment will be easy to slip on.

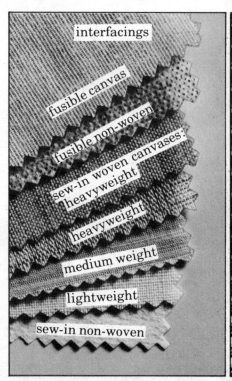

interfacings
fusible canvas
fusible non-woven
sew-in woven canvases:
heavyweight
heavyweight
medium weight
lightweight
sew-in non-woven

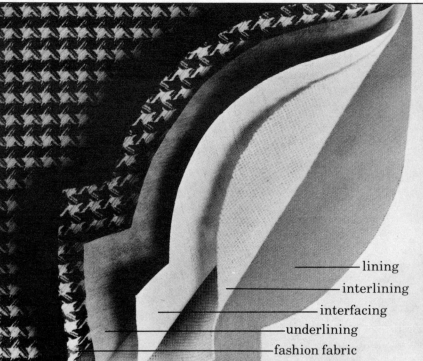

lining
interlining
interfacing
underlining
fashion fabric

a medium to heavy weight. These fabrics shape best. A very light-weight fabric lets construction techniques show through to the right side and can't hold its own. Also stay away from limp or loosely-woven synthetic fabrics; they can't be shaped properly.

Woolens and wool blends are perfect for tailoring because they're easily shaped and long-wearing. Melton, crepe, camel cloth, gabardine, tweed, double knit, and flannel are some of the popular woolens. Pile fabrics such as velvet, velveteen and corduroy make wonderful tailored blazers

range from light to heavy. There's a choice of sew-in or fusible canvas types; some canvases are even washable. For resilient knits, the best interfacing is often a fusible. Medium weight non-woven interfacings are suitable alternatives to hair canvas and come in sew-in or fusible versions, too. The interfacing should provide support without stiffness and have care requirements that match those of the garment fabric. See page 34 for additional selection advice.

Underlining and Interlining

You may want to add these optional special-purpose fabric layers in a tailored garment. An *underlining* adds body to the fashion fabric and serves as a "buffer layer" for hand stitches, preventing them from showing on the outside of the garment. On light-colored or lightweight fabrics, underlining also prevents the seam allowances from showing through. Any lightweight, sturdy fabric with the same care requirements as your outer fabric will do for an underlining. Choose one as close as possible in color to the outer fabric. Use the garment pattern pieces to cut out the underlining. Baste the underlining to the wrong side of the outer fabric sections before sewing the garment together; then handle the two layers as one.

An *interlining* is a layer of lamb's wool or nonwoven polyester fleece used to add warmth. You won't need this if your lining is a deep-pile fabric or has a napped or thermal backing. Cut the inter-

Check the back of your pattern envelope when you are at the store to see which notions you'll need for your fashion.

Twill tape is a very important tailoring item. When stitched next to seams or along the roll line of a collar or lapel, twill tape prevents stretching and helps preserve the tailored shape for the life of the garment. Use ¼″ (6 mm) wide tape, either cotton or polyester. Before using the tape, preshrink it by soaking the entire card of tape in hot water. Bend the card to let the tape dry.

Shoulder pads are a useful addition to tailored garments. They keep the shoulders square and protect the garment on the hanger. Shoulder pads also fill out the natural hollow just beneath your shoulder, giving a smooth shoulder line. Use shoulder pads to help disguise common figure faults, such as round shoulders, thin shoulders, one shoulder higher than the other, etc.

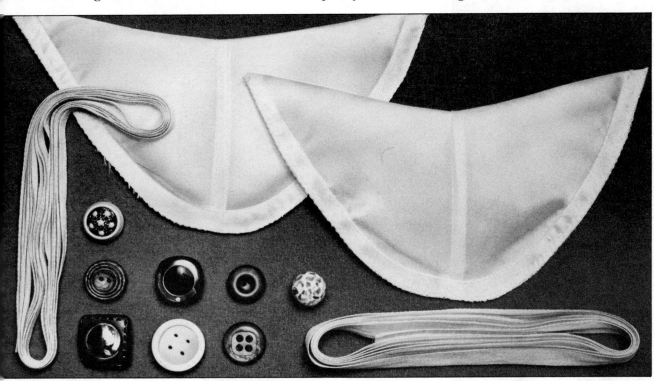

lining from the lining pattern, omitting the hem allowances. Baste it to the wrong side of the lining sections; trim the interlining close to the stitching. Handle the two layers as one when you sew the lining together.

Notions

Certain notions — thread that's compatible with your outer fabric, the proper size needles, very sharp scissors and plenty of pins — are basic to any sewing project. For tailoring, there are a few additions to this list: twill tape, buttons and shoulder pads.

Buttons on a tailored garment can be important design features. Since button types range from small jeweled or metallic styles to large plastic, leather or wooden ones, keep an eye on the suitability of the button for the fashion. Leather buttons with a sporty image, for example, look terrific on corduroy and velveteen. Jeweled buttons are set off by lush, solid-color velvets. Plain sew-through or shank buttons are low-key, blend into any design, and are the most versatile for daytime tailoring.

Many kinds of shoulder pads can be purchased, including washable styles. For today's tailored garments, select supple, lightweight pads. Shoulder pads come in various sizes and thicknesses. The size to buy depends on your shape and on the look you want—the larger the pads, the more pronounced your shoulders will appear. You can also make your own pads from polyester fleece as described on page 248.

Lapels

As the focal point of the front, the lapels are the most important part of a tailored garment. On a well-tailored garment, the lapels *roll* at the front edge instead of lying flat with a creased fold.

The instructions that follow show you how to create that rolled effect. After cutting out your fabric and interfacing, mold the lapel roll with padstitching and twill tape, using one of these methods:
• the *machine* method—for sewing convenience

Marking the roll: To reduce the extra bulk caused by the fabric layers in the seam at corners, first trim the lapel interfacing corner diagonally ¼″ (6 mm) inside the seamlines (A). Use a pencil to mark the end of the top buttonhole on the interfacing between the center front line and the front seamline. Make another mark on the front seamline, ½″ (1.3 cm) above the buttonhole.

Darts: If there are darts, stitch them separately in the interfacing and in the garment fabric. On the garment fabric, stitch the darts as usual; then slash and press them open. On the interfacing, cut out the darts on the stitching line (B). Bring the cut edges together and zigzag-stitch (C). For added strength, zigzag over a piece of seam binding, underlining or lining fabric.

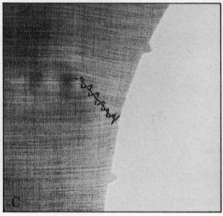

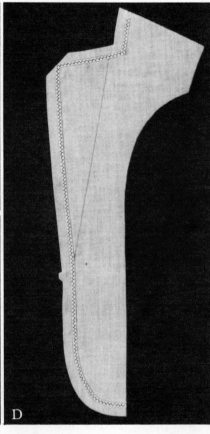

• the *fused* method—for the speediest way to a tailored look
• the *hand* method—for those who enjoy hand sewing

Machine Method

Padstitching and taping can be done entirely by machine. This is more convenient and less time-consuming than doing it all by hand, but still produces nicely rolled lapels. However, the rolled shape is only pressed in rather than hand-sewn and must be re-pressed after dry cleaning.

Next, position one end of the ruler ¾″ (2 cm) out from the point where the neck and shoulder seamlines meet; place the other end of the ruler at the mark above the buttonhole. Draw the roll line from the top of the lapel to the mark above the buttonhole (A).

Taping the edges: To prevent the lapel edges from stretching out of shape, tape the interfacing edges. Sew twill tape ⅝″ (1.5 cm) in from the neckline, lapel and front edges of the interfacing, using a very wide zigzag stitch. To avoid bulky seams, keep the tape from covering the seamlines. (Later on, you'll stitch the seam next to the edge of the tape.) Ease the tape around curves. Cut the tape and overlap it at corners (D).

Applying the interfacing:
Machine-baste the interfacing to the wrong side of the garment front ½″ (1.3 cm) from the raw edges of the armhole, shoulder, neckline, lapel and front. Do not stitch along the inner edge of the interfacing. Trim the interfacing close to the basting *except* at the armhole; leave the interfacing seam allowance untrimmed there to help shape the sleeve later (A).

Padstitching: To shape the lapel and hold the interfacing securely to it, machine-padstitch the interfacing in place. Using a pencil and ruler, draw stitching guidelines on the lapel interfacing as follows: Starting at the top of the roll line, draw parallel rows down to the seamline, spacing them ¼″-¾″ (6 mm-2 cm) apart (the closer the rows of stitching, the firmer the lapel will be). Space the rows closer together as you approach the point of the lapel.

Using a matching color thread and a straight stitch, start stitching at the roll line and proceed toward the seamline. Stitch continuously along the guidelines and pivot at the ends to reverse your direction. Don't padstitch over the twill tape (A).

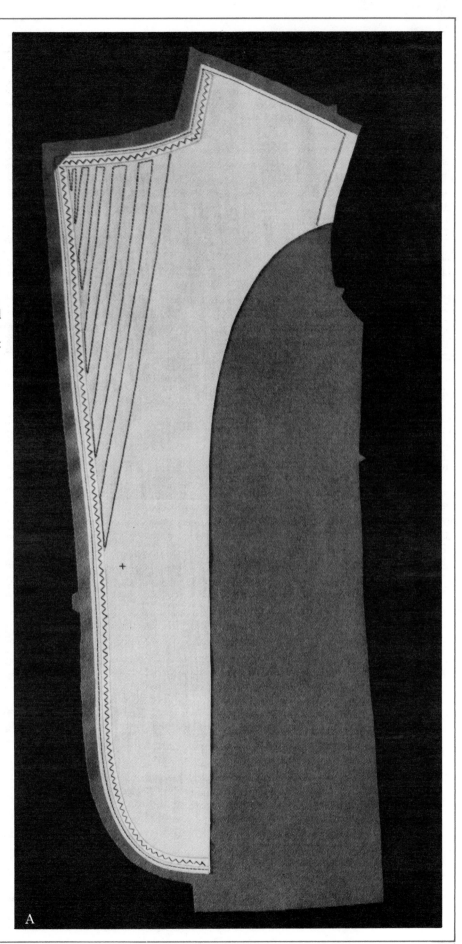

A

Lapels

Taping the roll line: Cut twill tape the length of the roll line minus 1" (2.5 cm). The tape is cut shorter than the roll line so you can ease the fabric to the tape; this will encourage the lapel to roll beautifully.

Position the tape on the garment just next to the roll line as shown (A). Pin the upper end of the tape at the top of the roll line; don't let the tape extend over the seam-line. Pin the lower tape end ½" (1.3 cm) up from the lower end of the roll line. In between, pin the tape in place, distributing the fabric evenly.

To ease the garment to the tape, hold the tape taut and stitch through all layers, using a wide zigzag stitch through the middle of the tape or a straight stitch along both tape edges (A). This stitching will be hidden by the finished lapel.

Steam-pressing: To shape the lapel, place it over a seam roll or a tightly rolled towel, with the roll line along the length of the seam roll. Steam it (B), shaping the roll with your fingers. Let the fabric dry completely before handling it again.

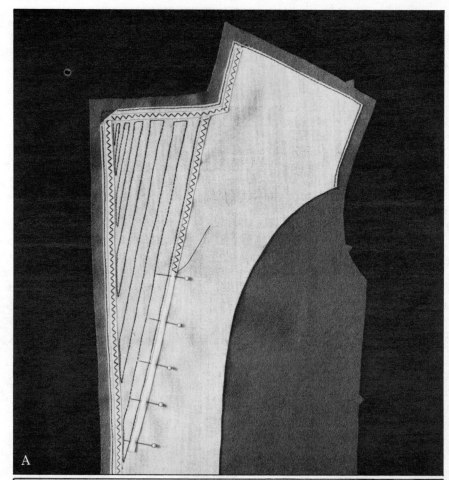

A

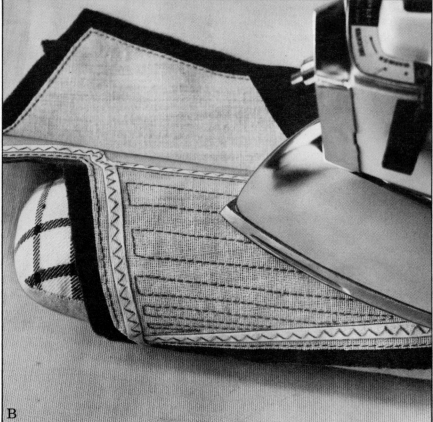

B

Fusible Method

Fusing layers of interfacing to a lapel is a quick alternative to padstitching. With this method, you can get the look of custom tailoring, even when you're in a hurry.

Before cutting out the interfacing, test a scrap of it on your fabric to see if a ridge shows on the right side of the fabric where the interfacing edge ends. If it does, cut the interfacing from the entire front pattern piece.

Begin by stitching twill tape to the neck, lapel and front edges of the interfacing as described for the Machine Method, page 238.

Darts: If there are darts, reduce bulk at the dart seams by trimming the interfacing ⅛″ (3 mm) inside the dart stitching lines before fusing (A).

Applying the interfacing: Before fusing, trim ½″ (1.3 cm) from all interfacing seam allowances, except at the armhole; this seam allowance will help support the shoulder and sleeve later. Then fuse the interfacing to the wrong side of the garment section (B).

Padstitching substitute: Weight and firm up the lapel point with an additional layer of fusible interfacing. Cut a triangle of interfacing for the lapel point only, shaping it to fit inside the tape. Fuse the triangle to the lapel on top of the front interfacing, next to the taped edges (C).

Tape the lapel roll line on the garment front and press the lapel as described opposite.

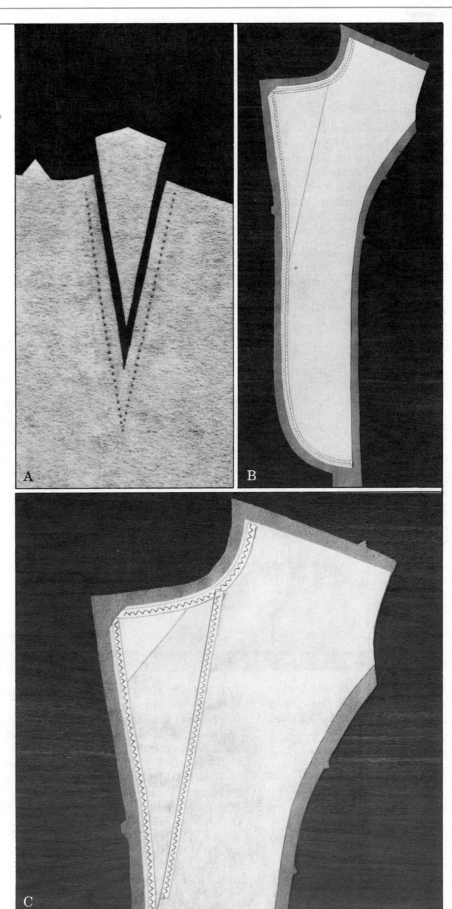

A

B

C

Hand Method

Traditional hand padstitching allows you to control the degree of lapel roll because the curve forms as you sew. First, draw the roll line on the interfacing and stitch twill tape to the neckline, lapel area and front edge of the interfacing as described for the

Padstitching: The hand padstitch is a small, slanted basting stitch, worked in rows through both the interfacing and the garment fabric. It molds the lapels into their permanent shape. When you padstitch, roll the lapel over your hand, with the rest of the garment away from you (A). Continue rolling the lapel as you work from row to row.

As you near the point of the lapel, make the padstitches shorter and the rows closer together (B). This makes the point firmer and helps it roll toward the garment.

Finishing: There's no need to baste the interfacing to the garment in the lapel area, since the

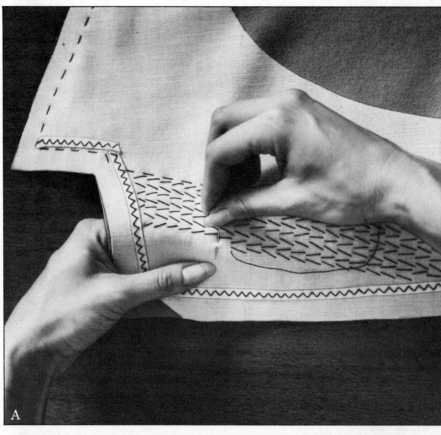

A

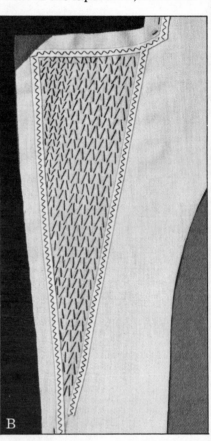

B

Machine Method on page 238. If there are darts, treat them as described for the Machine Method on page 238.

Applying the interfacing:

Hand - or machine-baste the interfacing to the garment front section at the armhole, shoulder, neckline and front edge below the first buttonhole; leave the lapel area unbasted.

To padstitch, use thread which matches the garment. Start the first row at the top of the roll line, securing the thread with a few backstitches, and work toward the front edge. Work the next rows back and forth. With the needle pointing toward the front edge, take a tiny straight stitch through all fabric layers, catching only a thread or two of the garment fabric. Repeat ¼″–½″ (6 mm–1.3 cm) away from the first stitch. Make rows of padstitches ¼″–½″ (6 mm–1.3 cm) apart, parallel to the roll line (A).

padstitching holds it in place. Tape the lapel roll line (B) and press the lapel as described for the Machine Method on page 240. On the shoulder, neck and front edges, trim the interfacing seam allowances close to the basting; trim them close to the twill tape on the lapel edges. Don't trim the interfacing at the armhole edge, because it will help shape the sleeve later on.

Undercollar

Stitch the garment shoulder seams, stabilizing them with twill tape (see page 161). Also, stitch the side and any princess seams. Press the seams open. Now, you're ready to shape the undercollar with padstitching or fusing. The upper collar will take the shape you've tailored into the undercollar when sewn and pressed.

Machine Method

This is a quick contemporary approach to shaping the undercollar and setting the roll line.

Applying the interfacing:

First, stitch the center back undercollar seam and press it open. Then, trim the interfacing diagonally at the outer corners to ¼″ (6 mm) inside the corner seamlines. Lap the center back edges of the interfacing, matching seamlines. Stitch along the seamline and trim close to the stitching. Machine-baste the interfacing to the wrong side of the undercollar ½″ (1.3 cm) from the raw edges. Trim the interfacing close to the stitching (A).

Marking the roll line: To find the roll line, baste the undercollar to the garment, lapping the neck seams. Try the garment on; have a friend help you arrange the undercollar so it frames your neck evenly and so the outer collar *seamline* covers the neck seam. If there are lapels, the undercollar and lapel roll lines should form a continuous line around the neck and down the front. Have your friend pin-mark the location of the undercollar roll line (B).

Remove the undercollar. Mark the roll line with machine basting, following the pin markers. Then, machine-padstitch as follows.

Padstitching: With matching thread, stitch the first row on the roll line. Make parallel rows of stitching between the roll line and the neck edge, ¼″ (6 mm) apart (C). On the other side of the roll line, start at the center back and stitch diagonally, following the grainline. Stitch parallel lines ½-¾″ (1.3-2 cm) apart, pivoting at ends of rows (C).

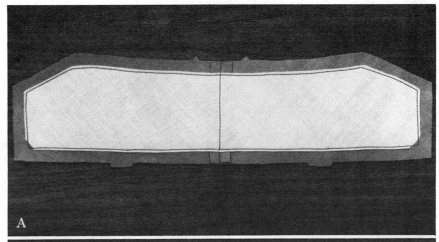

A

B

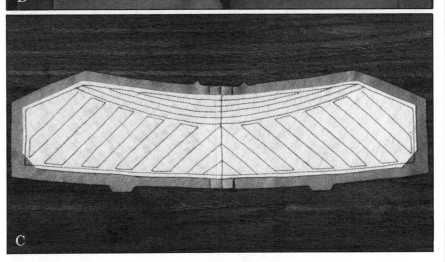

C

Undercollar

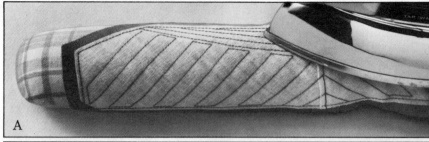

A

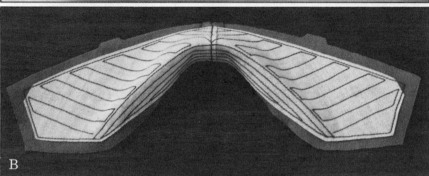

B

Steam-pressing: To mold the shape of the undercollar, place it interfaced side up over a seam roll or tightly rolled towel. Steam-press the collar (A), using your hand to make it conform to the curve of the seam roll. Remove the collar from the seam roll and arrange it into the curved shape of the finished collar (B); let it dry completely.

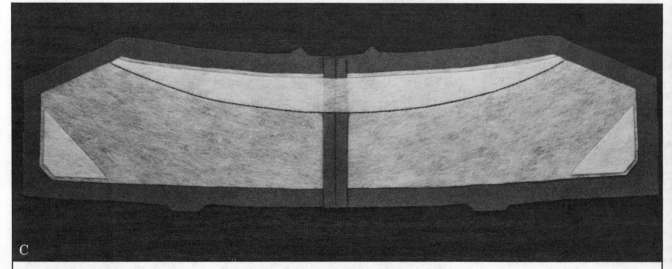

C

Fusible Method

In this shortcut method, a second layer of interfacing is used as a substitute for padstitching.

Applying the interfacing: At the outer collar corners, trim the interfacing diagonally to ¼″ (6 mm) inside the corner seamlines. Also, trim off ½″ (1.3 cm) from all the interfacing seam allowances.

Fuse the interfacing to the undercollar sections according to the manufacturer's directions.

Stitch the center back seam of the undercollar and press the seam open. Trim the seam allowances to ¼″ (6 mm). Mark the roll line of the undercollar with basting as described for the Machine Method on page 243.

Padstitching substitute: To give the neck area of the collar a firm shape, cut a second layer of interfacing that fits the undercollar from the roll line to the neck seamline. Omit the center back seam on this interfacing layer by folding the interfacing (fold woven interfacing on the true bias grain) and placing the center back seamline of the undercollar pattern on this fold.

Trim ¾″ (2 cm) from the neck and side edges of this strip. Then, fuse it to the undercollar with one edge along the roll line and the other edges ⅛″ (3 mm) in from the first interfacing (C).

Firm up the outer collar points by cutting two triangular pieces of interfacing to fit the collar points between the seamlines. Trim the points diagonally. Fuse these triangles to the collar points ⅛″ (3 mm) in from the first interfacing edges (C).

Steam-press and shape the collar as directed above.